PR

Everyday Adventure

In a world that tells us we need to go somewhere else to be adventurous, *Everyday Adventure* shows us that our true meaning is found in the lives we are already living. Stephen Glasser helps us open our eyes to how God is moving all around us, inviting us into the greatest adventure available: saying 'yes' to Jesus every day.

Zach Windahl, Author and Content Creator

Stephen is so positive and so present in every moment. You can see it in his relationship with his wife, his kids, and all of his professional undertakings. I think it's a real gift that he's sharing the lessons and insights that brought him to this point. Scientifically speaking, Stephen is a ninja turtle of great vibes, and in this book, he shares the ooze that made him this way. I give it 4/4 cowabungas.

Anthony Russo, Creator of *The Bible is Funny* and *The Bible is Funny* Card Game

Everyone needs a friend who lives their lives through eyes of wonder, who sparks our own sense of anticipation for adventure, and who kindles our own curiosity around the creativity of our Creator. Stephen Glasser is that kind of friend – With the heart of a pastor and the pen of a pal, Glasser invites us to open our eyes to the beauty all around, reminding each one of us of the adventure awaiting our everyday lives.

Craig Allen Cooper, Bestselling Author of *Glad You're Here* with Walker Hayes

I've had the privilege of knowing Stephen since he was a young man growing up in the church I pastored, and it's been a joy to watch him become a passionate husband, father, and pastor with a heart fully alive to God's purpose. In *Everyday Adventure*, Stephen brings that same contagious passion to the page—inviting readers to rediscover the wonder and purpose woven into ordinary life. His stories, authenticity, and pastoral insight remind us that following Jesus is the greatest adventure of all.

Doug Graham, Former President of North Central University

With the heart of a pastor and the voice of a friend, Stephen Glasser helps you find purpose in the mundane and adventure in the ordinary. A must-read for anyone longing to live fully.

Micah McDonald, Evangelist; Author of *Death to Life*

Everyday Adventure is a fresh reminder that meaning isn't only found on mountaintops, but also in the moments right in front of us. Stephen Glasser invites us to trade distraction for presence, complacency for curiosity, and fear for faith. With warmth and wisdom, he shows us that following Jesus is about learning to see the extraordinary in the everyday. This book will help you to pause, reflect and discern what to carry and what to let go as you pursue a life of true adventure.

Jason VanRuler, Therapist; Author of *Get Past Your Past*

Everyday Adventure reframes what it means to live a life of purpose. Stephen Glasser reminds us that adventure isn't about seeking constant adrenaline or waiting for the 'next big thing'—it's about choosing boldness in the ordinary. What if our daily tasks weren't chores, but opportunities? Opportunities to connect, to grow, to see the people in front of us, to live fully awake. This book invites you to embrace the season you're in and discover the depth, joy, and fulfillment available right here, right now. I truly believe the world would look different if we all lived the way Stephen writes about.

Olivia Haman, Co-Founder of The Invitation

Adventure is different for everyone. But one thing is the same and that is adventure invites us to step from what we know into something that we don't. It invites us from something that is more comfortable, into something less comfortable. In this book, Steven invites us to consider the possibilities of movement, from where we are to something different, something better, if we dare. I have watched him do this in his life, and now he's inviting us to join in this great journey.

Paul Hurckman, Executive Director of Venture

Over the past two decades, I've had the privilege of watching Stephen grow from a young student in my youth ministry into an extraordinary leader who embodies the very message of this book. In *Everyday Adventure*, he captures the sacred beauty of finding God's purpose in the ordinary moments of life. With warmth, authenticity, and pastoral wisdom, Stephen reminds us that true adventure is not reserved for the spectacular, but discovered in daily faithfulness to Jesus. This book will inspire readers to awaken to the wonder woven into every day.

Dr. Terry Parkman, DMin; Founder, Next Generation Leader; Global Co-Chair, Empowered 21 NextGen; Global Ambassador, OneHope

Stephen has a zest for life, and his love for God is infectious—and it spills out on every page.

Laurie Polich Short, Author of *Tracking God in Your Life* and *Faith, Doubt, and God's Mysterious Timing*

Everyday Adventure is a timely and hope-filled invitation to wake up to the meaning woven into the life you're already living. Stephen writes with the heart of a pastor and the honesty of a friend, reminding us that purpose isn't found in epic moments but in the ordinary ones we often overlook. This book helps you slow down, pay attention, and discover the joy and intentionality God has been offering you all along.

Jordan Smucker, Lead Pastor, Ethos Church

Stephen's genuine approach and authenticity hit right in your soul. Impact comes in many ways, shapes, and sizes. Stephen's impact on our program and myself directly, cannot be measured! Keep it simple, master the mundane, own the ordinary… Might not be the exciting things you want to hear, but it's the TRUTH you need to hear!

Dave Richman, Men's Basketball Coach, North Dakota State University

The adventure you long for is closer than you think—it's right where you are in your life because the Lord Jesus is there with you. That's Stephen Glasser's message in his inspiring book *Everyday Adventure*. We don't have to fear mundane activities. We don't have to live for a future mountaintop experience. Instead we can learn to live with childlike wonder—enjoying moments, learning new lessons, and appreciating people. It's a new way of living that's for the 1,440 minutes that make up each day. It's the life God created you for. It starts with being curious enough to read this book.

Dr's Bill & Kristi Gaultiere, Founders of Soul Shepherding; Authors of *Journey of the Soul* and *Deeply Loved*

Through the many years of friendship and ministry together, I've had the privilege of watching Stephen live out the very truths he shares in *Everyday Adventure*. His life consistently reflects what it means to maximize the mundane and embrace the ordinary with purpose and joy. In these pages, he invites readers to see their daily rhythms as sacred opportunities for growth, learning, and intentional living. This book isn't theory—it's a reflection of his life well-lived and a guide for anyone who longs to find meaning and adventure in the everyday moments that shape us most.

Dave Leedahl, Lead Pastor, Northview Church

Everyday Adventure offers the inspiration and tools to the turn the seemingly mundane into something extraordinary. It's an excellent book to wake up from everyday complacency and step into a life full of purpose and adventure.

Hannah Schermerhorn, Author of *A Single Life to Live*

Stephen Glasser is the perfect person to take us on an Everyday Adventure. He knows how to mine treasure from every moment. He could tell of a night spent in a rest stop in a spring break blizzard. Maybe the bachelor party camping trip with no place to camp the first night. He is a dear friend and I am so thankful for the adventures we have shared together.

Brad Lewis, Author of *Small Group University*,
Chi Alpha State Director, North Dakota

After almost 2 decades of friendship with Stephen, I can confidently say that he lives out what he writes in this book. From random fun shenanigans to intentionally stepping into divine moments and opportunities, Stephen is a modern-day adventurer on all fronts. As you read this book, your walk with Jesus is sure to be challenged as you learn how to say "yes" to the next adventure with Him. Have fun!

Steven Pavek, Missionary; Vice President of
Alaska Student Partnership

I've known Stephen Glasser for almost twenty years, and everything I love about him—his uncontainable joy, his contagious laughter, his genuine love for people, and his passion for Jesus—leaps off every page of Everyday Adventure. With refreshing honesty, humor, and pastoral wisdom, Stephen dismantles the lie that the ordinary is boring and shows how Jesus invites us to live wide-awake, purpose-filled lives right where we are—diapers, deadlines, and all. If you're tired of waiting for "someday" to start really living, this book will open your eyes to the adventure God has placed in your today. Read it. You'll laugh, you'll be challenged, and you'll never see an ordinary Tuesday the same way again.

Kirk Graham, Executive Pastor, River Valley Church

Many of us feel like we're missing out, waiting for "epic" moments to feel fulfilled, seeing our routines as obstacles to a meaningful life. In Everyday Adventure: How to Live Your Ordinary Life to the Fullest, author Stephen Glasser challenges that thinking. He knows what it's like to feel the "minutiae of the mundane" dragging him down, and in this inspiring guide he shares his discovery: life to the fullest is possible today. This isn't about escaping your life; it's about engaging with it. It's packed with wisdom, heart, and humor, and it will stir your soul.

Winston Titus, Former District Superintendent,
North Dakota Ministry Network (Assemblies of God)

Everyday Adventure

HOW TO LIVE YOUR ORDINARY LIFE TO THE FULLEST

STEPHEN GLASSER

Everyday Adventure

StephenGlasser.com
Copyright © 2026 by Stephen Glasser
Published by JourneyWay, LLC

ISBN: 979-8-9943984-0-1 (softcover)
ISBN: 979-8-9943984-1-8 (ebook)
ISBN: 979-8-9943984-2-5 (audio)

All Scripture quotations, unless otherwise indicated, are taken from The Holy Bible, New International Version®, NIV®. Copyright © 1973, 1978, 1984, 2011 by Biblica, Inc. Used with permission of Zondervan. All rights reserved worldwide. (www.zondervan.com)

Scripture quotations marked (NLT) are taken from the Holy Bible, New Living Translation, copyright ©1996, 2004, 2015 by Tyndale House Foundation. Used by permission of Tyndale House Publishers, Carol Stream, Illinois 60188. All rights reserved.

Scripture quotations marked MSG are taken from The Message, copyright © 1993, 2002, 2018 by Eugene H. Peterson. Used by permission of NavPress. All rights reserved. Represented by Tyndale House Publishers.

Scripture quotations are from The ESV® Bible (The Holy Bible, English Standard Version®), © 2001 by Crossway, a publishing ministry of Good News Publishers. Used by permission. All rights reserved.

Italics in Scripture quotations reflect the author's added emphasis.

Details in some anecdotes and stories have been changed to protect the identities of the persons involved.

This book is not intended as medical, psychological, or professional counseling advice and should not be used as a substitute for professional care or guidance.

All rights reserved. No part of this publication may be reproduced, stored in a retrieval system, or transmitted in any form or by any means—electronic, mechanical, photocopy, recording, or any other—except for brief quotations in printed reviews, without the prior permission of the publisher.

Additional resources connected to this book are also available at everydayadventurebook.com.

Cover design: Ryan Ham
Interior design: Ashley Ham

*This book is dedicated to my wife, Taylor,
and our three kids, Kinsley, Summit, and Rowan.*

*You are and will forever be my greatest adventure.
Let's follow Jesus together!*

CONTENTS

Foreword by Carson Wentz   1
Introduction   3
Chapter 1   Embrace Today   13

PART 1: PURSUE INTENTIONALITY
Chapter 2   Place Your Pins   33
Chapter 3   Maximize the Mundane   47
Chapter 4   Slow Down   65

PART 2: RESIST COMPLACENCY
Chapter 5   Cultivate Curiosity   91
Chapter 6   Become a Lifelong Learner   107
Chapter 7   Ditch Your Comfort Zone   123

PART 3: DEVELOP RESILIENCE
Chapter 8   Lighten Your Load   149
Chapter 9   Fix Your Focus   165
Chapter 10   Refuse to Quit   183

Conclusion: Let the Adventure Begin   199

Additional Resources   210
Acknowledgments   211
Notes   215
About the Author   223

FOREWORD
by Carson Wentz

Getting to this point in my life and career has been full of highs, lows, and a whole lot of moments where I've had to lean fully on Jesus. Looking back, I can see how God has placed certain people in my life at exactly the right time—and one of those people is Stephen Glasser.

Stephen and I actually grew up across town from each other in North Dakota. We went to rival high schools and even played baseball against each other. We knew of each other, but it wasn't until college—when I was a student-athlete at NDSU and he was serving as a college pastor—that our paths really crossed in a meaningful way.

Our friendship began when a teammate and I went over to his house for dinner one night. From that evening on, God started weaving our stories together in ways neither of us expected.

We spent our first couple years of friendship shooting pool and talking about faith, life, purpose, and what it really means to follow Jesus. Those conversations laid a foundation that would carry us into some very meaningful seasons together.

When God put it on my heart to launch an outdoor camp through my AO1 Foundation, Stephen was one of the first people I wanted involved. The camp was in North Dakota, and he stepped in right away; co-directing the first summer in 2018 and serving as our camp pastor, just a couple weeks after his first child was born. The next year, he and his family took a huge step of faith and moved to Philadelphia to serve full-time with us. That's when our families plus a few others, became what we called the "Philly Fam." In that season, we shared holidays, birthdays, late nights talking about life, and even the births of our kids. God brought us together in a really pivotal season, and over time Stephen became more than a friend—he became a brother. Someone who showed up for me and my family in every season, and someone I'll always show up for too.

I've walked through mountaintop moments—national championships, being drafted number 2 overall, once-in-a-lifetime opportunities, and even winning a Super Bowl. But I've also walked through injuries, disappointment, criticism, and seasons of real discouragement. There were stretches where things didn't go the way I hoped or planned, and I had to trust that God was writing a better story than the one I would've written for myself. Every valley pushed me to fix my focus back on Jesus and reminded me that His purpose always stands.

And through all of that, one of the biggest lessons God has taught me is this: the greatest adventures aren't the ones the world celebrates. I've lifted some pretty incredible things in my life—even hoisted a Lombardi Trophy with my teammates—but nothing compares to lifting my four girls into the air and hearing them laugh. Nothing compares to being a husband, being a father, and learning to love and lead my family the way Jesus calls me to. Those are the moments that last. Those are the adventures that matter most.

That's why I'm grateful for the message of this book.

Everyday Adventure is about living with purpose right where you are—in the ordinary, unseen, and surrendered moments that shape who you're becoming. It's about choosing faithfulness over fame, presence over pressure, and identity in Christ over anything the world can offer. I've lived enough life to know that money, fame, and success won't satisfy. They fade and are a facade. They can't hold you when life hits hard. Jesus can. And He will.

Stephen understands that, and he's lived it. This book comes from a place of real experience, real faith, and real obedience. My prayer is that as you read these pages, you begin to see your life the way God sees it—full of meaning, full of purpose, and full of opportunities to trust Him.

If you seek Him and give Him your whole heart, you'll find Him. And when you do, you'll realize that the greatest adventure isn't out there somewhere—it's found in following Jesus every single day.

Carson Wentz, NFL QB & Founder of the AO1 Foundation

INTRODUCTION

*"The thief comes only to steal and kill and destroy;
I have come that they may have life, and have it to the full."*[1]
John 10:10

As a boy, I was fascinated with adventure. I was so small and the world was so big, leaving much to be explored. I may have grown up in the middle of nowhere; but to young Stephen, it could lead to anywhere and everywhere. My friends and I would leap and bound through our neighborhood as if we had just discovered a new planet.

We would dart through the trees trying to avoid the villains who aimed to foil our expeditions, warding them off with our wooden guns as we weaved through our neighbors' yards. We would hide treasure just so we could come back to find it a few minutes later. We would hunker down in the treehouse my grandpa built in our backyard as if it were an impenetrable fortress. We told stories of danger and heroism and we refused to eat our vegetables—like true adventurers. This was our life.

As we journeyed through life, something happened. The backyard shenanigans ceased. Sticks became sticks, and sidewalks, once littered with invisible villains, were just sidewalks. Growing up seemingly brought our days of adventure to a halt.

However, deep down, I believe that each one of us is as adventurous as when we were kids. At the heart of adventure is a longing for more. At its core, adventure is about seeking out and exploring the spectacular around us. The unfortunate reality is that we have a propensity to seek it out in all the wrong places.

We sip on the watered-down Kool-Aid the world is pouring out, trying to find fulfillment in dim-lit bars, fleeting romantic flings, lengthy Netflix marathons, and one more scroll session before bed. Saint Thomas Aquinas put it this way: "Man cannot live without joy; therefore when he is deprived of the true spiritual joys, it is necessary that he become addicted to carnal pleasures."[2] In our pursuit of fulfillment, we end up empty, chasing all the wrong things. As Proverbs reminds us, "You're addicted to thrills? What an empty life! The pursuit of pleasure is never satisfied."[3] The world's version of adventure leaves us longing for something deeper, something real.

This longing for more can be witnessed in subtle ways every day. You don't have to go to the base of Mount Everest to find people infected by the adventure bug. It can be overheard in a conversation at the coffee shop, in the break room at work, or at the dinner table at home. It often sounds like, *"Is it Friday yet? I can't wait for the weekend!"*

Many of us have been trained to think that life truly begins on the weekend. We see our everyday lives—our work, school, chores, and to-do lists—as necessary evils keeping us from truly living. We formulate the belief in our hearts and our minds that certain aspects of life are better than others. We go to school in order to get a job, we get a job in order to make money, and once we work long enough and make enough money, we retire. Age 65 is the perfect age to truly start living, right?

If we are honest with ourselves, many of us think like this. We are living for the weekend, vacation, or retirement. In our minds, we think that true living will begin when we reach some distant day in the future. We daydream and long for what is next, hoping it will make us happier and make life more fulfilling.

As a boy sitting in a classroom, I would look out the window and think, *"Is it the weekend yet?"* Now, as I have entered a stage of parenting that includes chasing three kids under seven, I have caught myself in the middle of a Saturday, exhausted, thinking, *"Is it Monday yet?"* The gravitational pull to long for a future day, or any but the one you are in now, will track you down in whatever season or situation you find yourself in.

WAKING UP TO LIFE

This mindset of delayed living—always waiting for the "real" adventure to begin later—shows up clearly on university campuses. Lecture halls and auditoriums are filled with students who have adopted the, *"I'm here because I have to be"* mindset. Many young people view college as the stepping stone that leads to bigger and better things. They spend their days complaining about the amount of homework their professors give them and daydreaming about the next weekend adventure or summer vacation.

As a college student, that was me. While I was in class, I was either plotting my weekend plans with friends or daydreaming about a girl I would never get the courage to ask out. The last thing on my mind was whatever was supposed to be on my mind. I was living for the weekend and my next adventure.

It was in one of those daydream sessions that the idea for this book was born. I had recently returned from a trip with friends and while I was sitting in class, I started planning out my next adventure. It was in that moment that a more profound thought invaded my pre-frontal cortex, *"What if instead of living for the next big adventure, you treated everyday like an adventure?"*

This question captured my attention for weeks. I began noticing how seemingly everyone around me was living for a future season. Every day I would hear someone say things like *"Once I graduate, then I will _____"* or *"Once I get a job, then I will _____."* I noticed it in myself too. I was living for the next weekend and the next season instead of the one I was in.

I knew there had to be more to life than that. I began to see adventure in my everyday life. Instead of briskly walking to class with my head down, I slowed down and began noticing the people I once hustled past. Instead of ordering my coffee and disappearing into my own little world, I got to know the people making my coffee. Instead of rushing home between classes, I lingered on campus, making friends with people I previously didn't know existed.

My eyes were slowly being opened to the beauty of each and every day. I started to hear God's quiet voice on a regular basis and I was consistently experiencing joy in my life. I wasn't caught up in dreaming of some future season or adventure. I was simply living. Every day was an adventure.

Instead of seeing everyday life as a roadblock holding us back from "real living," an everyday adventurer sees everyday life as "real living." Nothing is holding us back from "real living" but ourselves.

There are no wasted days and no wasted seasons. To live a lifestyle of adventure, you don't have to travel across the world, climb a mountain, or jump out of a plane; you simply have to open your front door. Every day provides an opportunity for adventure.

AN INVITATION TO MORE AND BETTER LIFE

I pray this book serves as a key that unlocks your own everyday adventure. My goal in writing it is to equip and inspire you to live fully and to embrace each day as a divine and beautiful opportunity.

I didn't write *Everyday Adventure* for you to simply read it. I wrote this book for you to live it. My hope is that this book gets dirty, creased, and warped by the sun. That means it is well-traveled and that you have pulled it out again and again when everyday life seems monotonous and mundane.

> **TO LIVE A LIFESTYLE OF ADVENTURE, YOU DON'T HAVE TO TRAVEL ACROSS THE WORLD, CLIMB A MOUNTAIN, OR JUMP OUT OF A PLANE; YOU SIMPLY HAVE TO OPEN YOUR FRONT DOOR.**

We're all tempted to live for some future season or adventure instead of embracing the one we're in. This is for the young parent who is overwhelmed by dirty laundry, dirty dishes, and dirty butts. It's for the college student who feels like they're simply waiting for life to begin. It's for the professional who has believed the lie that five days at work are just to earn the other two.

In my journey, I have discovered that the greatest adventure is found in following Jesus. Since fully surrendering my life to him, my everyday life has been filled with purpose and divine opportunities. As Jesus makes clear in John 10:10, he didn't just come to offer eternal life; he came to amplify the life we get to live on earth.

The *New Living Translation* says that Jesus' purpose is to give us a *rich and satisfying life*.[4] Eugene Peterson puts it this way in *The Message:* "I came so they can have real and eternal life, *more and better life* than they ever dreamed of."[5] I like the sound of that. Here's my question for you: *Do you want a rich and satisfying life? Do you want MORE life? Do you want a BETTER life?*

Discovering the rich and satisfying life Jesus offers is like digging our shovel into the ground in search of an ounce of gold, only to uncover an entire golden city. It's better than we could ever dream or imagine! When we live each day for the one who created it, the adventure takes on a whole new depth. The full life Jesus promises isn't just an upgrade—it's the adventure our hearts were made for.

I challenge you to open your heart before you open this book. Living every day to the fullest isn't always easy, but it is always worth it. Allow God to soften your heart and renew your mind in a way that allows you to truly see your everyday life as an everyday adventure.

I'm proud of this book—not because it is perfect, but because it exists. I'm proud of this book—not because I have perfected its message in my own life, but because it continues to invite me into more and better life. For well over a decade, I have wrestled with the idea of everyday adventure. Again and again, I have returned to it when I feel stuck or disengaged from my everyday life. I have done my best to practice what I preach, and over the course of the past several years, I have done my best to put nearly fifteen years of wrestling into words that I hope will inspire you to engage life as the adventure it truly is and to live life to the very fullest. As much as this book has been a gift to me, I pray that it is also a gift to you.

EVERYDAY ADVENTURE BASECAMP

You may be coming to this book looking for step by step directions on how to live a full and meaningful life. If you are waiting to be handed a map outlining how to get from where you are to where you want to go, this book is going to come pitifully short. I could never write that book. For starters, I'm not you and I've never walked the path you are on. Your adventure is as unique as you are. My goal is to give you the tools you need to start marking your own map and encouragement to take your next step.

I desire to be a guide alongside you on your journey. I'm going to warn you about some dead ends I have come up against and some pitfalls that have tripped me up that I hope you can prepare for and even avoid. The first obstacle you must overcome is the lie that your life can't have meaning and purpose. When caught up in the current of the mundane and ordinary, it's easy to believe you're bound to a dull and inferior life, one where you simply make money to pay bills, cover taxes, and retire. Lifeless living is the reality for many people, but it doesn't have to be yours.

The goal of this book is not to trick you into believing everything you do is exciting, and it's definitely not to encourage you to radically abandon everything mundane and ordinary in your life to chase wild endeavors. The goal of this book is to help you understand that true living is not reserved for out-of-the ordinary experiences that are few and far between. It is to invite you into a new way of living that reframes true adventure and opens your eyes to the beautiful opportunities all around you. You may never summit the world's tallest mountains or traverse the deepest valleys, but you can be a great adventurer.

Before a mountaineering expedition takes place, the adventurers set up basecamp. A basecamp serves as a launch pad, a starting point, from which every great adventure gains its legs. A basecamp is used to gather gear, chart a course, and serve as figurative starting blocks. This book is broken into three parts that all play a key role in stepping into a life of everyday adventure.

1. **Pursue Intentionality**
2. **Resist Complacency**
3. **Develop Resilience**

The difference between life and life to the fullest is ***intentionality.*** We are all given the same 24 hours. What makes the difference is how we make the most of every second, minute, hour, and day we are given on this earth. *How can I discover meaning in the midst of the mundane? How can my seemingly insignificant and ordinary life become extraordinary? How do I slow down my life to become more aware of the adventure all around me?* We each have everyday opportunities to pursue intentionality on our way to pursuing life to the fullest.

One of the greatest threats to a meaningful and abundant life is **complacency.** Complacency stops adventure in its tracks and will always keep us from uncovering the life God has designed for us. As we progress through life and stack up more responsibilities, complacency is a vacuum that sucks the life right out of us and pulls us into mediocrity. *How can I regain a sense of childlike curiosity and wonder? How can I pursue growth in order to prevent stagnation? What does it take to boldly leave my comfort zone in the dust for good?* In our battle against the suction of stagnation, we must become the aggressor, resisting complacency every opportunity we get.

What separates an adventure from a *life* of everyday adventure? **Resilience.** The goal is not a season of adventure, but a life of adventure. Family and career are not adventure killers but propellers, unlocking new portals to meaning and fulfillment. However, we'll never experience life to the fullest if we don't persevere and grow our grit. *Am I carrying anything that is tripping me up and holding me back from where God is calling me? How can I keep going when it seems that I'm up against obstacle after obstacle? Why do I always give up and retreat when times get tough?* If you don't want to permanently live your life at basecamp, always on the verge of a great adventure, you must develop resilience to keep going.

A life of everyday adventure is not an easy pursuit, but it is worthwhile. The path that lies ahead is not always smooth and I can't tell you what is coming around the corner. I can tell you this—*you are not alone.* We are in this together and I am right there alongside you, doing my best to live a life of everyday adventure. And the best news: we have a guide who knows the way. He is inviting us to follow him as he leads us into a spacious place—into a full and meaningful life.

My life has been an adventure, not because I have filled my days with

> **FAMILY AND CAREER ARE NOT ADVENTURE KILLERS BUT PROPELLERS, UNLOCKING NEW PORTALS TO MEANING AND FULFILLMENT.**

dangerous endeavors, but because I have redefined adventure forever. If you want a life of adventure, you don't need to travel across the world, just open your front door. The adventure of a lifetime begins *today.*

TRAIL MARKERS

TRUE NORTH TAKEAWAY
Adventure isn't something you find "out there" someday—it's something you wake up to right where you are. The life Jesus offers is full, present, purposeful, and available today.

REFLECTION STOPS
1. Where in your life have you been "living for the weekend," retirement, or some future season instead of embracing the day you're in right now?
2. When you picture a full, meaningful, adventurous life, what do you imagine? Where do you feel God stirring hunger for "more and better life" right now?
3. Think back to your childhood. When did ordinary moments feel magical or adventurous? What might it look like to reclaim a bit of that wonder today?

EVERYDAY ADVENTURE CHALLENGE: THE BASECAMP BUDDY
Choose one person to journey through this book with you. Share one thing from the Introduction that stirred your heart and invite them to join you—whether that means reading alongside you, checking in weekly, praying for each other, or simply swapping takeaways as you go.

This is the perfect moment to begin your adventure with someone who will challenge, encourage, and sharpen you along the way.

If you're ready for more practical steps like this, check out the Everyday Adventure Challenge—a simple weekly challenge designed to help you practice intentionality and embrace the adventure in your everyday life. You can learn more at **everydayadventurebook.com**.

ONE
Embrace Today

> *"The decisions you make today will determine the stories you tell tomorrow."*[1]
> Craig Groeschel

What's in a day? A day consists of 24 hours. That is 1,440 minutes and exactly 86,400 seconds. Mathematically speaking, that's what is in a day. *But what else is in a day?*

Every day is filled with moments, decisions, and opportunities that will deeply impact your life and your future. In the beautifully articulated words of author Annie Dillard, "How we spend our days is how we spend our lives."[2] Our days—those hours, minutes, and seconds—add up and become our life. They become our story and legacy. Today plays a part in shaping your story and your life. What you do with every day you are given matters. This truth is encapsulated in a psalm I have prayed almost every morning of my adult life:

> "This is the day that the Lord has made;
> let us rejoice and be glad in it."[3]

This is the day—and it's the only day we're guaranteed. If you want to unlock a life of everyday adventure, you must recognize the worth and beauty of each moment. Every day is a unique gift, enticing us to open and enjoy it. Dare I say... *the present.*

Yesterday is in the past and so are all the days before it. The past cannot be changed, undone, or altered. When it comes to the past, there are no do-overs. Life isn't golf and if your day ends up at the bottom of the lake like many of my golf balls, there are no mulligans. You might as well make the most of it and do a cannonball when you go to get it out.

Tomorrow is not here yet and it is never guaranteed. It may be wise to plan for the future, but it is foolish to live there. Stress and anxiety about the future have overwhelmed many of our hearts and taken over our lives. In fact, over 40 million adults in the United States over the age of 18 struggle with various anxiety disorders[4]. Many of us struggle with what the Anxiety and Depression Association of America refers to as *everyday anxiety*.[5] These are the everyday worries and fears over paying the bills, a breakup, a big test, or a realistic danger. They are all projections of the *what ifs* of life.

For most of us, it's a combination of what took place in the past, what might happen in the future, and our inability to embrace today that holds us back from an adventurous life and ultimately experiencing all God has for us. We are called to replace tomorrow's worries with today's worship. We are invited into a unique adventure that can only be discovered today. Jesus is inviting us to lift our heads from the path in front of us and to look to him. When our eyes and our hearts are glued to the worries on the path in front of us, we will never recognize the adventure God is calling us into.

Embrace today and let God lead you. That's the beauty of adventure. We don't always know what's around the corner, but we are following a loving God who does. This is the day *that God has made.* It's crafted by the Creator of the heavens and the earth and everything in it. To top it all off, he made you and me too. Knowing who made something gives it greater value and significance. That macaroni necklace isn't wasted lunch; it's your child's art. It's a gift.

You are invited into the adventure, but you have a choice. *Will you choose to follow the script God is writing?* We are often tempted to carve our own path, thinking it will lead us to the full life we desire. It rarely does, but there is good news. God is still writing. Today may be hard and filled with challenges, setbacks, and discouragement; but God hasn't set the pen down yet. Just as God waves his figurative paintbrush across the sky to create a beautiful sunrise, he's waving it over this day and your life.

To recognize the grandiose possibility of today, we must learn how to embrace a life of gratitude. Gratitude is a key to a life of everyday adventure. When we start our day with gratitude, we remind ourselves of what we have. The fact that there is breath in my lungs is enough to add some pep to my step.

What is it that you are grateful for today?

What gives you reason to rejoice?

Voice it out and tell God a few things that you are thankful for. Take a moment to let the breath flow from your lungs and out your nose. Take advantage of the still moment to recognize the blessing that the new day brings. Make a habit out of it and keep a gratitude journal, taking time each day to jot down five to ten things you are grateful for.

Today is the only day you are guaranteed. There has never been and never will be another day like this one. *The Message* paraphrases this call beautifully, "Give your entire attention to what God is doing right now, and don't get worked up about what may or may not happen tomorrow."[6] Does today have your full attention? Are you awake and alert to your current moment? What will you make of today? Will you choose to embrace today as a gift from God and use it to bring glory to him in everything you do? *This is the day that the Lord has made, let us rejoice and be glad in it.*[7]

> **WE DON'T ALWAYS KNOW WHAT'S AROUND THE CORNER, BUT WE ARE FOLLOWING A LOVING GOD WHO DOES.**

I have a challenge for you. For the next week, I encourage you to speak Psalm 118:24 over your day before you open your phone and even get out of bed. Make it your daily declaration. Allow it to align your heart with God and join him in what he is already doing around you. Today has everything it needs for some everyday adventure.

THIS CHANGES EVERYTHING

Back in my day... we didn't have cell phones. What we lacked in personal technology, we gained in straight-up courage. If we wanted to ask a friend to play, we had to cold call their house like a telemarketer, not knowing who was going to pick up on the other end. If you were really bold, you would just roll up to their house, get off your bike, walk up to the front door and knock; and if they were home, you would ask them to *"come outside and play."*

Those were the days. Looking back, it seems as if we didn't have a care in the world. We probably did. We probably cared about which bush we were going to hide behind when we played hide and seek. We were likely concerned about whether the baseball cards in our bike spokes were firm enough to make it sound like we were riding a motorcycle. We were probably consumed by what *"be home by sundown"* actually meant.

When I was fourteen years old, I was having one of those carefree nights with my friends. I was in the middle of an intense game of driveway basketball at my friend Shane's house when my mom called and asked me to come home. I was annoyed because there was still plenty of sunlight left in the sky. "That's not fair, Mom! We are in the middle of a basketball game, and all my friends get to stay out later."

After putting up a fight, I angrily rode my bike home. Two minutes later, I was home. I flung my bike into the garage and walked into the house, slamming the door behind me. I wanted to be sure my parents knew how upset I was. To my surprise, I wasn't reprimanded for being a complete brat. Instead, my mom greeted me at the front door with a somber hug.

As I stepped back, I could see that she had been crying. I knew something was wrong and that's when she said the words that changed everything, "Stephen, your cousin Joshua passed away."

That night, my cousin Josh went to a local restaurant to eat dinner with some friends. While he was eating, he collapsed in the booth he was sitting. A nurse was sitting nearby and hurried to his aid and conducted emergency CPR until the paramedics arrived and rushed him to the hospital. Doctors frantically tried to save his life, but there was nothing they could do. His heart skipped a beat and never came back. He was just 24 years old.

Josh was my hero. He was ten years older than me, but we were close.

We shared many of the same interests and hobbies, including our love for the Minnesota Twins. In fact, he would give me his Twins hand-me-downs. It was awesome. During family get-togethers, we would often sneak away to play catch or a video game. A few weeks prior to his passing, he picked me up to play tennis. That afternoon, Josh brought me back to my house and we said goodbye. Little did I know that was the last time I would ever see him.

Josh's sudden passing changed everything for me. Up until that point, my life felt like a car cruising down the highway; but the news of his passing brought the car to an abrupt stop on the side of the road and smoke was billowing from under the hood. I had experienced the passing of two grandparents, but this was different. When my grandparents passed away, I was sad; but this time, I was angry and confused. *"How could this happen to Josh?" "Why would God let this happen?"*

I wrestled with these questions for months. In one moment, I would find great comfort in knowing Josh was in Heaven and in the next, I would grow irate thinking about how unfair it was that he died so young. For the first time, I was personally confronted with the reality of how fragile life truly is.

In my anger and pain, I cried out to God and began to feel his presence like never before. Many of my questions remained unanswered, but Josh's passing set me on a journey of discovering the reality of who God is for myself. Looking back two decades later, his passing serves as a landmark in my faith journey. It marks the beginning of a deeper longing for God.

LIFE IS A MIST

In a moment, the brevity of life became a reality, and I began to live my everyday life with a greater understanding that tomorrow isn't guaranteed—that *life is a mist.*

> "Come now, you who say, 'Today or tomorrow we will go into such and such a town and spend a year there and trade and make a profit'—yet you do not know what tomorrow will bring. What is your life? For you are a mist that appears for a little time and

then vanishes."⁸

This was written to encourage the early church to live their earthly lives in light of eternity. Life was not easy as they faced trials and difficulties of many kinds. It would have been easy to let their minds drift to some future season or place where life was more comfortable, safe, and secure. They were so caught up in their plans for the future that they failed to embrace the day they were given.

Like a mist, our earthly life is anything but solid or certain. We can eat healthy food, exercise, and plan for our future financially; but even wise practices can't *guarantee* a longer life or predict the years we will be on this earth. This isn't a free pass to go on a cookie and ice cream binge; and I'm not suggesting we throw in the towel, neglect our well-being, or lazily put off all our responsibilities. This is simply a reminder of the brevity and unpredictability of our lives in light of eternity. Or as *The Message* puts it, "You're nothing but a wisp of fog, catching a brief bit of sun before disappearing."⁹

SOAKING UP THE SUN

Famous inventor Thomas Edison invented the electric lightbulb in 1879. Edison's discovery, aided by the work of many other skilled inventors, was a game-changer in human history. Prior to Edison's invention and the mass utilization of his lightbulb, the sun's light was one of the most valuable resources to human life.

Take a moment to think of everything you do with the aid of a lightbulb. Your life is lit up by thousands of lightbulbs every day, both in obvious places like your home and in less obvious places, like in your smartphone. Some lightbulbs are activated by a switch, others with a gentle tug of the refrigerator handle, some with a clap, and still others by summoning a mysterious woman named Alexa.

Just a century ago, in many parts of our country, the only light after sundown came from kerosene lamps, candles, or other open flames. For many families, sundown marked the end of chores, work, and other household activities. During winter, when darkness outweighed daylight, working hours were shortened. In summer, longer daylight meant extended work hours and more time for chores.

Those who grew up prior to the utilization of electricity and the lightbulb had a greater appreciation for the sunlight. In those days, the hours of sunlight created a sense of urgency. There was only so much time to get work done before the sun would set on your to-do list. It was vital to take advantage of one's time in the sun.

We're in the sun for only so long. Our time in the light will eventually come to an end. George Bernard Shaw, an Irish-born playwright and critic, is often credited as saying, "The statistics on death are quite impressive. One out of one people die."[10] Death is a fate that each one of us will encounter.

In 1997, Billy Graham, one of the greatest evangelists of all time, spoke at Palm Beach Atlantic College in West Palm Beach, Florida. He said, "A student asked me some time ago, 'What is the greatest surprise of your life?' I said, 'The greatest surprise in my life is the brevity of life.' I never dreamed life was going to be so short. It seemed life yesterday I was in school."[11] One day, the morning fog that is my life will too disappear after a brief bit of sun. The burning question becomes, *"What will I do with my time in the sun?"*

God doesn't want us to become a bunch of morbid weirdos, obsessed with death. On the contrary, he's inviting us to be captivated by life—life to the fullest. The awareness of life's fragility and brevity should inspire us to see its true value. In her book, *Liturgy of the Ordinary,* author Tish Harrison Warren writes, "But in facing the reality of death, we learn how to live rightly. We learn how to live in light of our limits and the brevity of our lives. And we learn to live in the hope of the resurrection."[12] Embracing the reality of death isn't about dwelling in fear but allowing it to deepen our appreciation for the life we've been given.

We can continue to live our lives using our own hearts and passions as our compass, or we can let God's will be the compass that guides our lives. I believe that many of our plans and desires are made with the best of intentions, but until those plans and desires are submitted and surrendered to the will of God, they are only manmade plans.

We are a *Bucket List* generation and we have grown up with the world literally at our fingertips. Being lured in by the *American Dream,* many of us have been trained to crave a version of life that is marked by possessions, comfort, and self-seeking experiences. It's almost impossible not to get swept into the vortex of planning and building our lives through this lens. But there is a better way.

> "Many are the plans in a person's heart,
> but it is the Lord's purpose that prevails."[13]

God's purpose must always prevail over our plans. God's purpose for your life is far greater than whatever it is you could conjure up on your best day. His purpose and his will may be far different than your plans, but I can guarantee it is far greater. You may miss out on some experiences and your bucket list might have some unchecked boxes, but your life will be full of eternal purpose and value. A life surrendered to the will of God leads to kingdom-level joy and fulfillment.

The sun will soon set on all our lives, and even those who live well into old age will still be surprised by the brevity of life. Nothing in this life is guaranteed. We are called to live our lives with an eternal perspective while storing up treasures for the life to come.[14] To do that, we must live this earthly life with full recognition that it will soon come to an end.

We are called to take full advantage of the sunlight. The answer isn't to find the nearest skydiving company, as fun as that may be. Life to the fullest is far more than just making memories and enjoying the moment. True adventure begins when we surrender our lives to God's will.

LIVING WITH THE END IN MIND

If you've ever crumpled up a piece of paper and thrown it in the trash, you probably said, "Kobe!" NBA legend Kobe Bryant's skill on the basketball court inspired a generation. His relentless work ethic, known as *Mamba Mentality*, became a model for pursuing dreams. Yet his sudden death shocked the world.

On January 26, 2020, Kobe Bryant, his thirteen-year-old daughter Gianna, and seven others tragically died in a helicopter crash in Calabasas, California.[15] The news sent shockwaves through the sports world as athletes and celebrities expressed their disbelief and grief.

Just two days after the accident, NBA legend Shaquille O'Neal spoke openly on national television about losing his former teammate. Fighting back tears, Shaq admitted he hadn't spoken to Kobe since his final NBA game nearly four years earlier. Reflecting on the tragedy, he said, "I just really have to now just take time and just call and say, 'I love you.' I'm going to try and do a better job of just reaching out... rather than always procrastinating, because you never know. Life is too short. I never—I could never imagine nothing like this." He ended with a sobering reminder, "I just wish I could be able to say one last thing to the people we lost. Because once you're gone, you're gone forever. We should never take stuff like this for granted."[16]

> TRUE ADVENTURE BEGINS WHEN WE SURRENDER OUR LIVES TO GOD'S WILL.

Shaq's words hit home because they reflect a truth we often forget: *Why does it take tragedy to remind us of life's fragility?*

Loss causes us to take inventory of our life and our relationships. For some people, the shockwave of a tragedy is enough to jumpstart relationships and create a sense of urgency in our lives. Yet, for most people, we quickly fade back into the hustle and bustle of everyday life, and the promises we make in light of a tragedy are forgotten. And the cycle continues. Another celebrity or loved one will die young and we will have the same reflection with very little lasting change.

To stop the cycle of regret and guilt, we must begin to live with the end in mind. Instead of needing another tragedy or death to jumpstart you into truly living your life with intentionality and urgency, begin to live your life with eternity in mind.

Here are a few questions you can ask yourself:

1. What *really* matters in my life?
2. What is most important to me?
3. If everything was stripped away from my life and I was tasked to rebuild it with only a few of the most important things, what would they be?

Living your life with the end in mind isn't about just living as if today is your last day on earth. I hate to break it to you, but you probably can't afford to quit your job and neglect all the other mundane activities in your life. Living with the end in mind requires deep reflection. It requires you to look beyond the problems, stresses, and deadlines of today and look to the very end of your life. It isn't about planning for your future, it is about looking to the future and determining who it is God wants you to be today.

In his book, *Practicing the Way*, author John Mark Comer writes, "To 'remind yourself that you are going to die' is to remind yourself to live for your eulogy, not your résumé."[17]

What kind of spouse do you want to be?

What kind of parent do you want to be?

What kind of friend do you want to be?

What legacy do you want to leave in your career or your community?

When we're clear on the life we want to have lived, we gain clarity on how to live today.

Here is an activity for you. *Write your eulogy.* I know that sounds a little creepy but stay with me. Take a pen and a notebook and begin to write out what you hope is said about your life at your funeral. Write from multiple points of view. How do you want to be remembered by your spouse, children, friends, coworkers, neighbors, and your community? Imagine each one of them standing up at your funeral to share about you. What do you hope they will say? Be sure to write it from their perspective and couple this activity with prayer—*God, who are you calling me to become? What kind of parent, spouse, friend, coworker, neighbor, and person do you want me to be?*

Writing your eulogy gives you a vision for the kind of impact you want to have on the people who matter most. It offers a glimpse of the person God is forming you to become. With this picture in mind, you can begin taking action steps to become that person and to live the type of life you described in your eulogy. It won't happen overnight, but your *someday* can start today.

One day, your body will be placed in a box at the front of a room filled with your friends and family. People will take the stage to share nice words and stories about your life. Now picture the ones sitting in the front row—your family and closest loved ones. They will either be thinking, *"I wish I had known this incredible person everyone is talking about!"* or *"It's too bad these people never saw the best parts of him."* The difference lies in how you choose to live today. You can start building a better eulogy right now.

Living with the end in mind doesn't mean ditching your responsibilities to chase thrills. It means embracing every moment with the awareness that life is a mist: fleeting and never guaranteed. In the midst of your everyday tasks, you can still live your best life—one marked by purpose, meaning, vision, and passion. It's not about waiting for *someday*; it's about living fully today.

LANDON'S LIGHT

Throughout my professional journey, I've worn many hats: pastor, missionary, mentor, event planner, writer, podcast host, video editor, administrative guru, graphic designer, fundraiser, internship director, counselor, teacher, preacher—and yes, even cotton-candy aficionado. But one of the roles I'm most proud of is camp pastor.

In 2018, I was asked to lead the AO1 Foundation's inaugural Camp Conquerors,[18] and I have had the privilege of serving as camp pastor ever since. Camp Conquerors is a week-long summer camp for children aged 11-18 who have experienced life-threatening illnesses or other severe physical challenges. The kids get to do physical activities that challenge them and encourage them to push beyond their comfort zones. For many of the kids (and for me) it's the highlight of the summer.

The campers come from diverse backgrounds, and most don't know each other before arriving. Yet, they quickly find common ground through shared experiences of having their "normal kid life" interrupted by illness or trauma. Some have survived traumatic accidents, while others are battling cancer or other serious medical conditions.

For a week, camp is a non-stop celebration where our team works tirelessly to make every camper feel loved, valued, and seen. We aim to create an unforgettable experience that lifts their spirits and builds lasting connections. At the end of camp, we honor each camper with a personalized award, recognizing the unique strengths and characteristics their counselor has seen throughout the week.

One of the campers who has left a lasting impact on me is Landon Solberg. In December 2017, at just ten years old, Landon was diagnosed with an inoperable rare malignant brain tumor. Before his diagnosis, Landon was like any other kid: playing sports, excelling in school, and hanging out with friends. But in an instant, his life changed. Instead of running around with his peers, he spent months in hospitals, courageously fighting for his life.

When Landon first arrived at Camp Conquerors, his presence was instantly felt. Always dressed in style with his hair perfectly pushed to the side, he carried himself with quiet confidence. But it wasn't just his appearance that stood out—it was his kindness and generosity. Landon had a unique way of making everyone feel valued and loved, effortlessly connecting with those around him.

In 2019, Landon returned for his second year of camp. This time, he was noticeably weaker, struggling with activities that once came easily. Yet, his resilience shone brighter than ever. I'll never forget watching him scale the climbing tower, inch by inch, his face a mix of exhaustion and determination. When he finally reached the top, he raised his arms triumphantly as campers and staff erupted in cheers. I stood to the side, tears streaming down my face, moved by his unwavering spirit and the incredible strength it took to conquer that moment.

Just two months after camp, on September 17, 2019, Landon passed away at the age of twelve. Throughout his battle with cancer, Landon became a beacon of light for his entire community. His story was shared on local news, and support for "Landon's Light" was everywhere—on shirts, signs, and in the hearts of those who knew him. Landon's life and spirit left a lasting impact that couldn't be dimmed, even by tragedy.

> **THE MEASURE OF LIVING ISN'T IN THE NUMBER OF YEARS BUT IN THE WAY WE CHOOSE TO SPEND THE TIME WE'RE GIVEN**

A few days after Landon's passing, his father asked me to read Scripture and share a few thoughts at his funeral. I was deeply honored and immediately booked my flight back to Fargo from Philadelphia. In the days leading up to the service, I couldn't help but reflect on all Landon had taught me. His faith in Jesus was unshakable, and he lived each day with an acute awareness of life's preciousness. No twelve-year-old should have to endure what he did, yet he faced it with grace, courage, and unwavering hope.

As Landon's body weakened, his faith, hope, and joy only grew stronger; and those attributes became his legacy. In a video recorded just before his death, Landon said, "It makes me happy inside just to know that I have someone there already watching me from above. He (God) wants us all to live a happy life and just be grateful and cherish all the moments we have on this earth."[19] Landon's light shone because his joy was rooted in Jesus and his heart was anchored in eternity.

His perspective on life was beautifully simple: "Part of the reason I'm so positive is that I know God has something planned for me, and that it might not be what I want; but even after I die, I'll have eternal life in Heaven."

Landon lived only twelve years on this earth, but he outlived many of us in how he embraced life. The measure of living isn't in the number of years but in the way we choose to spend the time we're given. Inspired by Landon's legacy, I choose to live—to truly live—not counting down the days, but making every day count. Like it says in Ephesians, "Make the most of every opportunity."[20]

Life is truly a mist. Don't wait for tomorrow to start living; embrace today because it's all that's guaranteed.

TRAIL MARKERS

TRUE NORTH TAKEAWAY
Life is a mist and today is the only day you're guaranteed, so live this God-given moment with gratitude, eternal perspective, and surrendered intentionality.

REFLECTION STOPS
1. When you hear that life is "a mist," what stirs in you—fear, urgency, apathy, gratitude, or something else? Why?
2. Where do you tend to live most often—regretting yesterday, fearing tomorrow, or fully present in today? How is that shaping the story of your life?
3. If you truly believed "this is the day the Lord has made," how would it change the way you approach your schedule, your interruptions, and the people in front of you today?

EVERYDAY ADVENTURE CHALLENGE: WRITE YOUR EULOGY
Grab a notebook and begin writing your eulogy. Start with one perspective (your spouse or future spouse, a child, close friend, coworker, or neighbor) and write what you hope they'll say about your life, character, and the way you used your days.

If you're up for it, add a few more voices over time—imagine what different people in your life might share. As you write, underline one phrase or sentence that stands out and ask: What is one small way I can live more like this today?

If you're ready for more practical steps like this, check out the Everyday Adventure Challenge—a simple weekly challenge designed to help you practice intentionality and embrace the adventure in your everyday life. You can learn more at **everydayadventurebook.com**.

PURSUE INTENTIONALITY
Part One

PURSUE INTENTIONALITY
Part One

I want to introduce you to my friend Cal Thompson. Cal was a youth pastor at the church I've been a part of since college. For over 30 years, he poured into students and genuinely loved everyone in his path.

Cal had a rare ability to light up a room: not by being loud or flashy, but by making you feel like the most important person in the world. He had this intentional way of locking in, of seeing people. I don't mean a glance and nod—I mean *really* seeing you.

Cal passed away suddenly on July 2, 2022. His death shocked our church and community, but the legacy he left behind was unmistakable.

At his memorial service the night before his funeral, one person after another stood up and shared a story or talked about how Cal impacted their life. Nearly every story started with the same line: *"I was Cal's favorite."* The funny thing? They meant it. And in a way, they were right. Cal made people feel seen, known, and loved.

He was intentional with his time, his conversations, and his presence. I'd walk into Starbucks and Cal would already be there, not quietly working at a corner table, but standing at the counter cheerfully talking to the baristas. He knew their names, their stories, and their favorite drinks. Eventually, Cal even started working at Starbucks; and at his funeral, over 25 Starbucks employees showed up in their green aprons to pay tribute to the man who made every Tuesday feel like a holy encounter.

In *Everybody Always*, Bob Goff says, "We don't need to call everything we do 'ministry' anymore either. Just call it Tuesday."[1] That's the heartbeat of this section. We're not talking about grand gestures. We're talking about being fully alive on a random Tuesday—present, grounded, intentional.

We often live like life happens somewhere else—down the road, on the next vacation, after the next promotion, once the kids sleep through the night. Author John Ortberg puts it this way:

> "Life counts—all of it. Every moment is potentially an opportunity to be guided by God into His way of living. Every moment is a chance to learn from Jesus how to live in the kingdom of God."[2]

Every moment. Not just the milestones. Not just the mountaintops.

The secret is presence in the moment. That's where joy is found. But to live with that kind of presence? It takes *intentionality*. We don't drift into meaning. We don't stumble into growth. If we want to live lives that matter, we need to be where our feet are and live like the ordinary moments matter. Because they do.

So many of us live with a quiet fear of missing out—on adventure, opportunity, the good life. But what if we've been missing out not because we've missed our chance, but because we've missed *the moment*?

> IF WE WANT TO LIVE LIVES THAT MATTER, WE NEED TO BE WHERE OUR FEET ARE AND LIVE LIKE THE ORDINARY MOMENTS MATTER. BECAUSE THEY DO.

What if our real FOMO should be about Tuesday afternoons, bedtime routines, awkward but meaningful conversations, or the joy of slow mornings? *Everyday FOMO*. A fear of missing out on the best parts because we're not paying attention. Because we're not intentional.

In this section, we're going to talk about three key ways to pursue intentionality in your everyday life:

1. **Place Your Pins**
   You can't get where you want to go if you don't know where you're starting from. This chapter will help you name where you are, clarify where you're headed, and map out a plan to get there.

2. **Maximize the Mundane**
   Life is mostly ordinary—and that's not a bad thing. This chapter explores how to stop resenting the ordinary and start embracing it, finding meaning in dishes, diapers, desk jobs, and Tuesday traffic.

3. **Slow Down**
   In a culture obsessed with hustle and speed, the most radical thing you can do is slow down. We'll talk about embracing rest, noticing beauty, and creating margin for what matters most.

This part of the book is about choosing to live on purpose, even when life feels painfully normal. It's about waking up to what God is doing right here, right now. So take a breath. Be present. And let's pursue intentionality—*one Tuesday at a time.*

TWO
Place Your Pins

"Your word is a lamp to guide my feet and a light for my path."[1]
Psalm 119:105

If you survived middle school, congratulations. You've already endured one of life's greatest adventures. A building full of hormonally charged teenagers awkwardly stumbling into their identities and their bodies? It's chaos disguised as education.

Walking those halls is a five-senses experience you'll never forget. Your ears hear squeaky voices and out-of-tune tubas. Your eyes catch motivational posters and enough TikTok dances to make your head spin. If you're lucky enough to score a lunch invite, your taste buds will reunite with their long-lost friend, the legendary nacho boat. Beneath your feet? An unidentified stickiness. And the smells... oh, the smells. A lethal combination of body odor and Axe body spray.

Most of my middle school years are a blur, but a few things still stand out. I remember struggling to remember my class schedule well into the year. I remember having a good basketball game, thinking I became an overnight legend, only to realize no one cared about the eleven points I scored in front of a bunch of parents. I remember putting notes in the lockers of girls I liked (and avoiding those same girls like the plague when

I saw them in person). I remember discovering a way to get changed for gym while exposing the least amount of my scrawny pre-pubescent body as humanly possible. I remember running for student council with *"Don't be a dweeb, vote for Steve"* as my campaign slogan. I even made pins.

I also remember a particular assignment given to us by our geography teacher. We were instructed to create a world, based on things we loved. We then had to create a map of this new world. My world was "Vikings Island." It included Moss Toss Mountain, Culpepper Canyon, Burleson Butte, The Hovan Hills, and Touchdown Town. Let's just say it was a lot more valleys than peaks…

My map of Vikings Island, although fun and colorful, ultimately didn't give any meaningful direction, unless you're looking for directions to disappointment and heartbreak (Vikings fans know). The entire purpose of a map is to provide geographical information and to help you find your way from point A to point B. A map is used to gather information about where you've been, where you are, and where you're headed next.

When I was a kid, my family would often take summer road trips. Back then, we didn't have GPS, so we traveled old school. My parents had a stack of maps in the glove compartment of their car and it was mom's job to "Lewis and Clark" our way to wherever we were going. I don't know about you and your family, but this didn't always go perfectly in our car. But as a tool of survival, we kids learned the basics of reading a map.

Although reading a map is difficult and I am beyond grateful for the map apps on my phone, I discovered that there are three basic keys to reading a map:

1. **Orient your map so that it is facing north**
2. **Identify where you are on the map**
3. **Identify where you are going next**

Every great adventurer knows how to navigate a map and if you desire to live a life of everyday adventure, you need to as well. Life is full of pitfalls and obstacles; and having a bird's eye view whenever you can will help you navigate some of life's challenges. Many of us lose track of where we are and end up heading back in the direction we came from, only to stumble over the same obstacles. In the adventure of life, it is easy to become disoriented, making it difficult for us to navigate which way is up and which way is down. We can even find ourselves wandering aimlessly, never able to figure out where we are, let alone point our feet in the direction we are called to go.

Like a map of a nearby hiking trail, not every danger along the path will be identified. A map doesn't give us step-by-step directions. We're still the ones walking. We're still the ones keeping our eyes out for branches we could trip over and cliffs we could stumble down. A map's purpose is to keep us headed in the right direction and to show us how far we've come.

It's time to pull the map out of the glove box and figure out which way is north. It's time to become reoriented to where you are at and where you're going. For a map to have much use, you need to place two pins: where you are and where you're headed.

It's time to place your pins.

SETTING THE MAP

The first key to being able to read a map is to orient it so that it's facing north. For centuries, people have used a variety of tools and methods to help them find true north. A compass is one of the most common tools used to know which direction you are facing. By holding the compass flat, a person can identify north, based on what direction the compass's needle is facing.

Before the invention of the compass, explorers used a variety of methods to identify north. Since the beginning of time, stars have been a natural tool used to find north. By locating the Big Dipper, you can draw an imaginary line through the two stars at the end of it, following it upward, leading you to the North Star.[2] Another method used for centuries is to cut into a tree's stump to observe the tree's rings. There tends to be more growth on the north side of the tree.[3]

> A MAP'S PURPOSE IS TO KEEP US HEADED IN THE RIGHT DIRECTION AND TO SHOW US HOW FAR WE'VE COME.

Here's my point: A map is useless if you are holding it upside down. If you've ever been on a hike and have gone the wrong direction, you know. If you hold the map upside down and think you're going an hour north, when in fact you go an hour south, you will now be two hours away from where you're headed. Not ideal.

We do this in life all the time. We become disoriented and disillusioned and end up holding our map upside down. We think being successful or popular will get us the fulfillment that we are seeking, ending up less fulfilled and emptier than when we started. We get confused, adopting the world's values as our own, allowing the world to define true north for us. We set our map by the world's definitions of success, happiness, and fulfillment and call it true north. We hustle for promotions and bigger paychecks. We buy bigger homes, enroll our kids in endless activities, chase picture-perfect vacations, and fill our calendars to the brim. All the while, we hope the next milestone will finally make us feel fulfilled.

When my friend Brian was a teenager, he went to church and youth group regularly. But somewhere along the way, he got swept up with a different crowd and started chasing sex, alcohol, drugs, and money. He was living fast, partying hard, building successful businesses, and had more girls than he could count on speed dial. From the outside, it looked like he was living the dream. But on the inside, he was drifting—and quietly unraveling.

What most people didn't see was the anxiety. The pressure to keep up appearances. The constant restlessness. The nights when his mind wouldn't shut off and the weight of it all settled in his chest. What started as excitement slowly gave way to panic, and the life he had built to feel free began to feel suffocating.

A series of events brought him face-to-face with the truth: He had everything he thought he wanted—success, popularity, pleasure—and yet, he felt completely empty. The anxiety only intensified, exposing what the noise and distractions had been masking all along. He thought he was headed toward true north, only to realize he had been walking in the wrong direction for years.

In the months that followed, at the end of himself and desperate for peace, Brian encountered the love of God in a way he never had before. He embraced God's forgiveness and committed his life to following Jesus.

It wasn't easy. Reorienting his life meant recalibrating his values, letting go of toxic habits, and unloading baggage that had no place in the life God was calling him into.

Brian began to see that the things he once chased weren't fulfillment, they were the very things keeping him from the full life found in Jesus. He had discovered what Jesus meant when He said:

> "If you try to hang on to your life, you will lose it. But if you give up your life for my sake, you will save it. And what do you benefit if you gain the whole world but lose your own soul? Is anything worth more than your soul?"[4]

What Brian gained by following his upside-down map came at a steep cost: *his soul.* His story hits closer to home than most of us would like to admit. Many of us have followed a path we thought would lead to fullness, only to arrive feeling just as empty as when we started. We aimed for "north," but something got flipped. This isn't a new problem; it's the oldest temptation in the book.

> "They traded the truth about God for a lie.
> So they worshiped and served the things God created instead of the Creator himself…"[5]

To experience the hope God offers us through Jesus, we first must confess: *I've believed the lie.* We've all, at some point, worshiped the created instead of the Creator. We've chased moments, achievements, and experiences, hoping they would fill us; but they can't. They were never meant to.

True fulfillment is found in Jesus alone, not just in believing in him but in walking with him. When we follow his path, we don't just find direction; we find life. We don't just need a better map. We need a new compass. One that always points us back to the heart of God.

The good news is that we have a compass that never fails: *the Word of God.* The Bible doesn't shift with culture or emotion; it consistently points us back to true north. It doesn't just give us direction for our feet; it realigns our hearts. It's the ultimate compass for a life of purpose, meaning, and adventure.

Maybe you've opened the Bible before, looking for direction, and walked away discouraged or confused. I get it because I've been there too. Unlike any other book, the Bible's power comes from its author. God didn't just inspire the words on the page; he authored life itself—the world, your story, and the path you're walking.

On this journey called life, God doesn't hand out step-by-step instructions like Google Maps. That's not how adventure works. The real adventure is found in following him—trusting not just where he leads, but who he is. God isn't interested in micromanaging your every move. He offers something better: *himself*.

YOU ARE HERE

Shopping malls and airports have more in common than we think: food courts, endless walking, overpriced snacks, and people who have clearly lost track of time. Aside from the small detail of stepping onto a giant metal tube that launches you thousands of miles through the air, they're practically the same experience. Honestly, malls could benefit from a few TSA agents to keep the unchaperoned teens in check, and airports could learn from malls by adding gumball machines near every gate.

One thing I appreciate about both places is the giant map. Whether you're looking to kill some time before a flight or on the hunt for a hot pretzel, a good map is a lifesaver. And the best part? That little label that says, *"You are Here."* Before I can figure out where I'm going, I need to know where I am. That simple marker grounds me and it's more important than we often realize.

Without identifying where you are, it's difficult to get where you're trying to go. Sadly, life doesn't always come with a *"You are Here"* label. It takes work and intentionality to figure out exactly where you are. I'm not talking about geographically, but emotionally, spiritually, and relationally. Until you identify your current location, it's nearly impossible to know if you're headed the right way.

For some reason, many of us struggle to come to grips with where we are. In an effort to fit in and find acceptance, we try to be someone we're not. We start believing the untrue story about ourselves we tell other people in order for them to embrace us. To be loved, we are convinced that we can't be the person God designed us to be. So we mask our weaknesses, paint over our defects, and cover our flaws. In the process, we forget who we are. We forget where we are. We get caught up in the web of our own lies, losing track of where we are, making it nearly impossible to try to navigate our way to where we need to go.

When I was in middle school, I would do anything to fit in and find acceptance. All the popular guys had *wings*. Every single one of them. Their hair was curly in all the right places and their hair flipped over their ears in a way that I swore would help them fly. It seemed that girls were clearly attracted to boys with a higher potential for spontaneous aviation. I wanted wings. I needed wings. The only problem was that I had spaghetti-straight hair and my oversized ears made it difficult for my hair to find the correct wing pitch. But that didn't stop me from trying.

I discovered that if I rubbed the hair on the side of my head enough, it would produce some curls. So I rubbed and swirled all the way through English and Geometry until the side of head was so curly, I made Bob Ross want to paint more happy little trees to cope with the jealousy. It was clearly working because I was bombarded with people noticing my new look, *"Whoa, nice wings!"* I had arrived, or more accurately, I was ready for departure.

That is until I got into my dad's truck and pulled off my hat, unveiling my new hairstyle. I tried to act surprised, playing it off like it was my natural hair all along. The rest of my head, and the fact that he dropped me off with straight hair, gave me away. My wings were not FAA (Federal Aviation Administration) approved, or at least they were not DAD approved.

He laughed and said, "Stephen, those wings aren't you. You don't have to be someone you're not." I was not cleared for takeoff. In hindsight, he may have saved me from crash landing pretty hard.

My dad was able to see past my ploy. He was attempting to remind me of my original design, not to point out my defects, but to help me understand that where I was at was a good place to be.

We all need that reminder. We don't need to strain, convincing ourselves we are somewhere else. Look at the map of your life and place your first pin. Come to grips with where you are today. That's the perfect place to start.

Embrace your weaknesses and own your flaws. If you are heartbroken from a recent breakup, own it. If you are unsatisfied with your work, admit it. If you are mad at God or questioning your faith, say it. Until you come to grips with the reality of where you are, you will never get to where you need to go.

At times, the place you find yourself won't be where you want to be. You may discover that you are discouraged, damaged, or depressed. Your *"You are Here"* pin may be placed in the lowest valley on your map, or even in a pit. That's okay. Before you can move forward, you must identify your starting point and place your pin. By continuing to act as if you are somewhere you are not, you will continue to use an inaccurate set of directions. If you tell yourself you're on even ground, you will continue to trip over the rocks in the path. By admitting you are stuck in a hole, you can look up and see the way out. Here are some questions you can ask yourself:

1. Where are you?
2. What are you feeling?
3. Do you feel stuck?
4. Do you feel like you're missing out?
5. Are you feeling hopeful about the future?
6. Are you satisfied with your current relationships?
7. Do you look forward to going to work?
8. What do you feel when you pull into your driveway at the end of the day?

You may be a college student who is realizing that you are three years into a degree you don't want. You may be a young parent who finds themselves dreading the weekend because of how exhausting it is to be fully present to the needs of a young family. You may be in a marriage that has become a bond between two roommates, not soulmates. You may be a son or daughter who is filled with anger and bitterness toward a parent. Just because *you are here*, doesn't mean you're destined to stay there. It's time to move out.

But first, you must place your pin. It's time to be honest with yourself about where you are. By identifying your starting point and establishing your bearings, you will be able to move forward to where God calls you. Part of the adventure is knowing where you're starting from. *You are here.*

TAKE AIM

I was actively engaged in campus ministry as a student, so Welcome Week was a huge opportunity. Campus was buzzing as students returned and a new semester began. That one week would set the tone for the whole semester. We would set up tables in student hubs, inviting students to our ministry. We hosted pizza parties and game nights, encouraging students to bring their friends. We even offered free campus tours, helping freshmen find their classes.

> UNTIL YOU COME TO GRIPS WITH THE REALITY OF WHERE YOU ARE, YOU WILL NEVER GET TO WHERE YOU NEED TO GO.

As an upperclassman, I felt that I knew campus inside and out. However, one day, as I was guiding a group of students around campus, I couldn't seem to find one of their buildings. After confidently weaving them from building to building, I reluctantly admitted defeat, stopping at one of the giant campus maps near a parking lot. We quickly found the building we were looking for. It was located at the downtown campus, several blocks away. Our wandering ceased because we determined where we were trying to go.

Have you ever felt that way in your life? Hoping to eventually end up at your destination, you aimlessly wander. You go from place to place and season to season, hoping the next door you open will be the *right* one. I think if we're being honest, many of us have felt that way before. Some of us have wandered in our relationships, hoping that the next relationship is the one that brings us wholeness. Hoping the next job brings us career satisfaction and fulfillment. Hoping the next paycheck brings us security.

It's time to pull out the map and identify where we are trying to go. Wandering may feel like an adventure, but it's not the type of adventure God is calling us to. The adventure he calls us to has a destination—and that destination is found in him.

The wholeness we search for in relationships is found in relationship with him. The fulfillment and satisfaction we look for in our jobs is discovered in walking in his purpose for our lives. The security we seek is under his shadow and in his care.

In one of his letters, Peter puts it this way:

> "By his divine power, God has given us *everything we need for living a godly life*. We have received all of this *by coming to know him*, the one who called us to himself by means of his marvelous glory and excellence."[6]

We already have what we need for the life we're longing for, but we miss it when we keep aiming at the wrong targets. We pin our hopes on promotions, possessions, and achievements, believing they will deliver meaning and joy. But what if we've been aiming at the wrong thing all along?

> **IF YOU'RE LOCKED IN ON THE WRONG TARGET, YOU'LL NEVER ARRIVE AT THE RIGHT DESTINATION.**

In the 2004 Olympics, American rifleman Matthew Emmons had a commanding lead in the 50-meter competition with just one shot to go. A lifetime of training had prepared him for this moment, and he was poised to win gold. He steadied his breath, lined up his sights, and pulled the trigger.

Bullseye.

Confident he had just sealed his Olympic victory, Emmons looked up at the scoreboard, but nothing registered. Confused, he checked again. To his shock, and the crowd's disbelief, he had nailed a perfect shot… on the *wrong target*. What should have been gold turned into eighth place—all because he aimed at the wrong thing.

What if we come to the end of our journey, only to realize that we too took aim at the wrong target?

What if we reach the destination we expected to bring us fulfillment, meaning, and joy, but still feel empty and unfulfilled?

What we aim at matters. So let me ask you—what are you aiming at? If you're locked in on the wrong target, you'll never arrive at the right destination. That's why gaining clarity about where we're going and what we're truly seeking is so critical. Without it, we end up like a pirate desperately digging up sand under every palm tree, hoping to find gold without ever marking an *X* on the map. We need to define the treasure and align our direction accordingly.

So what are *you* seeking?

While teaching a crowd of eager listeners, Jesus offered a game-changing invitation. He said:

> "Seek the Kingdom of God above all else, and live righteously, and he will give you everything you need."[7]

This is more than a comforting promise; it's a call to reorient our lives. Jesus doesn't tell us to stop seeking; he simply tells us to aim higher. Seek *his Kingdom* and allow his rule, his ways, and his priorities to guide you first. Let your life revolve around him. When we do that, God promises to take care of the rest. The pressure comes off, and purpose comes in.

Throughout my life, I've aimed at a lot of different targets. Popularity. Performance. Relationships. Career success. Ministry growth. I thought each would finally satisfy me. But time and time again, I realized I was aiming at the wrong prize.

I've come to believe that the truest expression of everything our hearts are longing for is found in Jesus. When we seek *his* kingdom above all else, we discover that he not only provides what we need—he often gives us what we didn't even know we were missing.

So pull out your map and reevaluate your target. Be honest with yourself. What's been motivating you to get out of bed in the morning? Try finishing this sentence: **"I will be satisfied when _____."**

Your answer will reveal the direction your life is currently heading and whether it's time to adjust your aim.

A GUIDE FOR THE JOURNEY

If you're like me, you probably haven't used a map in years. Perhaps you are a younger reader and this whole chapter has completely confused you because you've *never* had to use a map. And no, Google Maps doesn't count. There is a big difference.

Google Maps is amazing, but it's not accurate to what the adventure of life is like. Life doesn't come with step-by-step directions and a voice saying, "recalculating," every time you take a wrong turn. Google Maps does us a solid by notifying us of speed traps and avoiding traffic jams and road construction. Sadly, we won't always know when a road we thought was going to lead us to our destination has a dead end and we are forced to reroute. The goal of Google Maps is to get you to your destination as quickly as possible, identifying the fastest route. If your life is like mine, the fastest route isn't always the best route.

I would never compare life to an adventure if it were easy. I find it comical when someone posts photos from their "hiking trip" and I can see a paved path in the background. I'm not trying to knock anyone, but true adventure will never be found on a concrete walking path with directional arrows pointing you where to go next. True adventure, the adventure that God has called us on, is found in trusting and following him.

True adventure isn't necessarily confined to the path containing the most difficult obstacles and challenges, but it certainly isn't a straight path. True adventure isn't the result of an unnecessarily risky lifestyle, one categorized by jumping from airplanes and hanging over cliffs without ropes. True adventure is found when we take a bold step forward, not knowing with certainty what lies ahead. We point our feet in the direction of our next pin and start walking.

When we start out on our journey, our map may have limited markings, but the longer we travel through life, our map becomes increasingly valuable. We add pitfalls and other dangerous obstacles to our maps to ensure we don't go back that way. We learn from the adventures of other people, noting how certain paths lead toward disaster and wreckage.

Next time you watch a pirate movie, pay attention to their maps. They're always wrinkled, torn, and worn; and for some reason, the edges are almost always singed. Apparently, those unruly pirates haven't learned to keep their maps away from open flames. Unlike the crisp, glossy road maps we used to snag at gas stations, these maps look like they've been through battle—because they have. They've been used again and again, marked with scribbles, warnings, and notes from the journey. They tell a story. Every crease, burn mark, and smudge is evidence of a life lived in pursuit of something worth finding.

When I was younger, I wished someone would just hand me a map that would clearly outline how to get from point A to point B. I wanted someone to tell me how to be successful and how to live a meaningful life. I desired someone to show me the easy path, the one that avoided pain, heartbreak, and danger. I have had trustworthy peers and mentors who have given me solid advice and who have pointed me in the right direction, even helping me clarify true north time and time again, but I've had to put one foot in front of the other.

As much as I want to be the person who tells you everything you need to know and perfectly outlines the path ahead of you, I can't do that. What I can do is help direct you toward true north for you to regain your bearings and get your map facing the right direction. I hope to help you identify where you are at in order to place your first pin and I hope to help you clarify where it is you're trying to go—and ultimately where you are called to go.

My greatest desire is to introduce you to the ultimate guide. If you invite God into your adventure, he promises to be with you every step of the way. Not only will God direct you through his Word, but the Holy Spirit will be your *guide*. Following God doesn't guarantee a life without pain and difficulty, but it does guarantee you will never be alone. He will use every obstacle to propel you forward into the full and abundant life he has designed for you.

His path may not always be the widest, but it will always lead you in the right direction. His way will not always seem to be the quickest, but it will always be the best way. Jesus said of himself, "I am the way and the truth and the life. No one comes to the Father except through me."[8] The path into life to the fullest is a *person*. He is the way and he is worth following.

TRAIL MARKERS

TRUE NORTH TAKEAWAY
True clarity begins when you let God set true north, honestly admit where you are, and take aim at the life He's calling you toward.

REFLECTION STOPS
1. Where have you been letting the world define "true north" for you—success, image, comfort, experiences—rather than letting God and his Word set your direction?
2. If your life were a map, where would the "You are here" pin honestly land right now—spiritually, emotionally, relationally, and vocationally? What words or phrases describe that spot?
3. Finish this sentence in your journal: "I will be satisfied when _____." What does your answer reveal about the target you've been aiming at?

EVERYDAY ADVENTURE CHALLENGE: ORIENT YOUR MAP
1. Pick one passage of Scripture to be your "true north" for this week (Psalm 119:105, Matthew 6:33, or another verse that resonates).

2. Write it out by hand.

3. Put it somewhere you'll see it every day (lock screen, mirror, journal).

4. Each morning, ask: "If this verse is my compass, how does it change the way I walk today?"

If you're ready for more practical steps like this, check out the Everyday Adventure Challenge—a simple weekly challenge designed to help you practice intentionality and embrace the adventure in your everyday life. You can learn more at **everydayadventurebook.com**.

THREE
Maximize the Mundane

"We are restful when ordinary is enough."[1]
Ronald Rolheiser

This morning, I awoke before dawn, greeted by the faint glow creeping through the blinds. My heart pounded with purpose. Today, destiny awaited.

I approached the porcelain basin—what normal people call a bathroom sink—and prepared for battle, arming myself with mint-infused weaponry disguised as toothpaste. Steam rose around me like fog on the cliffs of Everest as I stepped into the shower, conquering the icy tundra turned raging waterfall. Moments later, I stood fully armored—deodorant applied, hair fortified, outfit assembled.

Then came the treacherous journey across the minefield of clothes scattered near my bed, each step a calculated risk. I scavenged the kitchen like a wilderness explorer, hunting for something—anything—resembling breakfast. At last, I brewed my morning coffee, a liquid beacon of hope, and took the first sip like a warrior tasting victory. I was unstoppable. My morning had the makings of an epic saga—resilience, danger, survival, and... slightly stale cereal.

Okay, fine. My day wasn't *that* exciting. But that's kind of the point, isn't it? Most of life is made up of routines, habits, and small, ordinary moments. Brushing teeth, showering, making coffee, scavenging for breakfast—the *mundane* stuff.

Mundane, by definition, is "characterized by the practical, transitory, and ordinary: commonplace." It's "lacking interest or excitement; dull."[2] Yet here's the thing: the mundane isn't optional. It's woven into the fabric of everyday life; and learning to embrace it might just be the key to living with a greater sense of meaning and adventure. What if the secret to a more meaningful, adventurous life isn't about escaping the ordinary… but learning to maximize it?

Most people exhaust themselves attempting to push their life in a direction that removes as much monotonous activity as possible. The problem is that the mundane is inescapable. As humans we are creatures of habit; and we will eventually find ourselves in the middle of the mundane. Even for the world traveler, putting your boots and backpack on day after day can become mundane regardless of where you are.

Instead of fleeing the mundane, I challenge you to embrace it, anticipate it, and even celebrate it. Make the most of the monotonous and learn to cherish the small moments that seemingly lack significance. Many of life's greatest adventures are found in the mundane moments.

Believe it or not, most of your life will be spent doing mundane things. So what exactly qualifies as *mundane*?

Think about the everyday tasks that fill your time: sleeping, showering, brushing your teeth, doing laundry, cleaning the house, wiping down kitchen counters, cooking (and eating) dinner, driving to work, answering emails, grocery shopping, changing diapers, bathing kids, dropping off and picking up from school, doing homework, walking the dog, squeezing in a workout, eating meals, mowing the lawn, shoveling the driveway, getting your hair cut, and getting dressed. You get the idea.

Sure, there may be exceptions; maybe you have an unusually adventurous job or your daily life involves skydiving. But for most of us, these ordinary routines are where we live. And while you might argue that sleep doesn't count, I disagree. Unless you're sleepwalking, it doesn't get

> **MANY OF LIFE'S GREATEST ADVENTURES ARE FOUND IN THE MUNDANE MOMENTS.**

much more mundane than laying still for eight hours…

Let's talk numbers. The average life expectancy in the United States is 78 years[3]—that's 28,470 days on this earth. Of those years, you'll spend 26 of them sleeping… and another seven just trying to fall asleep.[4] That's 33 years and we haven't even gotten out of bed yet.

You'll spend 90,000 hours[5]—roughly 13% of your life—at work. Add in nine years watching TV[6], five years scrolling social media (more like fifteen if you're 18-24), and four years eating. And we're just getting started!

Brace yourself: The average person will spend over three years doing laundry, two years driving, nearly two years cooking, and fifteen days of their life wandering grocery store aisles. You'll also dedicate 38 days to brushing your teeth (hopefully) and about 180 days exercising. When it comes to getting ready, men average 42 days while women rack up 136; not counting the 287 days reportedly spent just picking out clothes.[7]

Parents: you'll change an average of 2,200 diapers in your baby's first year alone.[8] At two minutes per change, that's three days straight of just diapers.

Altogether, these mundane tasks make up around 61 years of your life. That's 78% of your existence spent doing things we often overlook or wish away. Let that sink in. Do you really want to fast-forward through 61 years? Me neither.

Instead, let's learn to see these moments differently and begin to *maximize the mundane*. In the rest of this chapter, we'll explore how to embrace the ordinary, make the most of the monotonous, and find deep meaning right where you are.

COUNTING SHEEP

When most people think of David, they picture a fearless giant-slayer or a powerful king. Few imagine a scrawny little brother, overlooked, and left in the fields with a harp in one hand and a staff in the other.

Before David stepped onto the battlefield or sat on a throne, he spent his days doing something far less glamorous—watching sheep. As the youngest in his family, tending the flock wasn't a heroic calling; it was a chore. Day after day, David wandered the hills, guiding sheep to water, fending off predators, rescuing the lost, and literally counting sheep. It doesn't get much more mundane than that.

And yet, in the quiet and the ordinary, David thrived. He wasn't just passing time; he was being formed. In the field, he developed courage, character, and communion with God. He maximized the mundane and the mundane maximized him.

Have you ever felt overlooked? Do you feel that most of your life is spent in obscurity? Do you struggle to find meaning, purpose, and significance in your daily life? You are not alone.

Whether you view your job as a means to pay the bills or you have the exhausting task of being a stay-at-home parent, you may feel overwhelmed and trapped in obscurity. I don't believe what you do from nine-o'clock to five-o'clock has to change for you to begin living with greater purpose. In fact, with a little intentionality, your nine-to-five can become a time to thrive.

David's job as a shepherd was to watch after his father's sheep. It was a thankless job that was overlooked until something went wrong. It was lonely, too, with few conversations beyond the occasional "baah." (Stay-at-home parents, you get it.)

But one story reveals how seriously David took his role. When lions or bears came looking for a snack, most shepherds—armed with nothing but a stick and some stones—would've gladly sacrificed a sheep or two to stay alive. Not David. He chased them down, grabbed them by the hair, and struck them dead.[9]

That's not dedication. That's someone who saw purpose in the mundane.

He thrived in obscurity, being fully committed even when his commitment would be unseen. His hidden seasons laid the groundwork for a deep relationship with God and unwavering faithfulness. It was in the quiet and mundane moments that he prayed many of the prayers found in Psalms. With a sheep as a pillow, he penned Psalm 23, declaring God as his shepherd. With nothing else to do, he reclined, gazing upon the star-filled sky and sang these words found in Psalm 8:3-4;

> "When I consider Your heavens, the work of Your fingers,

> The moon and the stars, which You have ordained,
> What is man that You are mindful of him,
> And the son of man that You visit him?"[10]

David's eyes were fixed on God in the midst of the mundane, but even more powerful was the truth that God's eyes were on David. Long before David defeated Goliath, God identified him as Israel's future king. God didn't wait for David to become a heroic warrior before choosing him as the next king—it was in a field, watching sheep.

When the prophet Samuel arrived at Jesse's house, following God's direction to anoint the next king, David wasn't even invited inside. Jesse paraded seven sons before Samuel, assuming one of them had to be the one. But none were chosen. Then God said to Samuel, "Do not consider his appearance or his height… People look at the outward appearance, *but the Lord looks at the heart.*"[11] David didn't look like a king and that's exactly what made him God's choice.

God has a way of using the mundane to reveal and refine what's truly in our hearts. The ordinary moments draw out what is deep inside. We can't fake the kind of heart God's after. It's not built in the spotlight but in obscurity. It's formed in the quiet, hidden places where no one is watching.

This kind of heart is built in the everyday—diaper by diaper, dish by dish. It grows when we pray for a stranger while bagging groceries or choose faithfulness in work that no one applauds. As Brother Lawrence once wrote, "We ought not be weary of doing little things for the love of God, who regards not the greatness of the work, but in the love with which it is performed."[12]

The world may overlook these moments, but God never does. He sees it all and He's using every ordinary moment to form an extraordinary heart.

THE QUINTESSENCE OF LIFE

This may be a hot take, but *The Secret Life of Walter Mitty* isn't just underrated; it's one of my all-time favorite movies.

Released on Christmas Day in 2013, the film—directed by and starring Ben Stiller—is based on James Thurber's 1939 short story. Stiller plays Walter Mitty, a quiet, daydream-prone negative assets manager at *Life Magazine*. Walter often escapes into vivid fantasies of heroism, romance, and adventure. But when a crucial photo—the one labeled "The Quintessence of Life"—goes missing, he sets off on a real-life journey more epic than anything he ever imagined.

The movie earned subpar ratings and critics gave it mixed reviews, but for me, it struck a deep chord. I saw it in theaters with my family, and while it started off feeling a little cheesy, somewhere along the way, it got me. There was nothing remarkable about Walter Mitty's job or life and that's exactly what made it so powerful. He was ordinary… like us.

Mitty's quest to track down the elusive photographer leads him on a wild, unexpected adventure. A man who once spent his days lost in daydreams now finds himself jumping out of helicopters and scaling mountains in Afghanistan—living the very life he once believed was out of reach.

He eventually finds the missing photo, the one intended for the final cover of *Life Magazine*. Expecting something jaw-dropping from a remote corner of the world, he's stunned to discover the image is of him. Ordinary, unnoticed Walter Mitty. The photo, titled "The Quintessence of Life," is a tribute to the people behind the scenes who brought the magazine to life.[13]

And that's the beauty of it. In the eyes of a world-renowned photographer who had seen the most breathtaking places on earth, it wasn't adventure or fame that defined life—it was Walter. His quiet consistency. His faithfulness in obscurity. That, somehow, was the essence of life itself.

Have you ever felt like Walter Mitty—like your life or job was holding you back from truly living? I'm guessing that many of us have felt that way. We think, *"If only I travel to X or meet Y or work for Z…"* I don't believe you need to jump out of a plane, climb a mountain in Afghanistan, or escape a volcano eruption in Greenland in order to live a life of meaning and adventure. Real adventure might just be right under your nose—right where you live, work, and fold obscene amounts of laundry.

David's story reminds us of this. Long before he defeated Goliath or became king of Israel, he was tending sheep, playing music for Saul, and carrying armor—small, overlooked tasks done with great faithfulness. He didn't wait for the spotlight to show up. He brought excellence into every corner of his work. As a shepherd, a servant, and a musician, David turned ordinary assignments into sacred offerings. He worshiped through his work. The Apostle Paul echoes this in the New Testament:

> "Work willingly at whatever you do, as though you were working for the Lord rather than for people. Remember that the Lord will give you an inheritance as your reward, and that the Master you are serving is Christ."[14]

We don't just work for bosses and paychecks. *We work for God.* And his rewards run deeper than promotions and 401(k)s. Our jobs, no matter how ordinary, can become places of sacred encounter.

Maybe you file taxes. That's not just paperwork—that's an opportunity to pray for a client, to serve them with integrity, and to steward your gift. Maybe you wait tables. God cares that the food gets there, but even more, he cares about the person sitting in front of you. Your kindness, even when it's undeserved, might be the very thing that tells them they're seen, valued, and loved. As Tish Harrison Warren reminds us, "Our task is not to somehow inject God into our work but to join God in the work he is already doing in and through our vocational lives."[15] This is worship.

One of my favorite lines from *The Secret Life of Walter Mitty* comes from the seasoned photographer played by Sean Penn. As he waits to capture a rare snow leopard on camera—a moment he's been anticipating for years—he quietly says, "Beautiful things don't ask for attention."[16] That line has stuck with me. Because neither does beautiful work. Faithfulness in the unseen corners of life often becomes the very thing God uses to shape the world—and us.

I think of my mentor and friend Brad Lewis when I think about this kind of faithfulness. For more than thirty years, he served in one ministry, not chasing attention, growth, or something more impressive, but choosing to stay rooted and present. Through that quiet consistency, hundreds of students stepped into ministry and missions, and thousands are serving Jesus today because of what was formed in ordinary, unseen moments.

This kind of quiet, ordinary faithfulness is exactly what Paul urges in Romans 12:1, when he writes, "Take your everyday, ordinary life—your sleeping, eating, going-to-work, and walking-around life—and place it before God as an offering."[17] In other words, your daily grind isn't meant to be escaped; it's meant to be surrendered. When we place even the most routine moments before God, they become sacred.

So how can your work become worship? What if every spreadsheet, carpool pickup, and errand was a holy invitation?

> "So whether you eat or drink or whatever you do,
> do it all for the glory of God."[18]

That's the invitation. Every moment matters. Every task counts. Offered to God—it all becomes worship.

INVITE GOD INTO YOUR ORDINARY

Before 1971, coffee was just… coffee. You brewed a basic cup of Folgers at home, grabbed one from a gas station, or poured it from the burnt community pot at work. It was part of the background—a caffeine fix, not an experience. Then Starbucks came along.

In *The Starbucks Experience*, Joseph A. Michelli unpacks the values that transformed Starbucks from a coffee shop into a cultural force. They didn't reinvent coffee; they reimagined how we experience it. Howard Behar, former Starbucks president, once said, "We are not in the coffee business serving people. We are in the people business serving coffee."[19]

Of course, Starbucks hasn't gotten everything right. For starters, no cup of coffee should cost six dollars. Yet here we are. Fully capable of brewing coffee at home, many of us still opt for the handcrafted latte and the curated vibe. Why? Because Starbucks took something ordinary and made it feel meaningful.

George Washington Carver once said, "When you do common things in life in an uncommon way, you will command the attention of the world."[20] That's exactly what Starbucks did and it's a picture of what's possible when we approach the ordinary with intention. If a coffee company can transform something as mundane as your morning cup into a worldwide movement, imagine what God can do when we invite him into the everyday corners of our lives.

Saint Patrick and the Christian movement he helped spark offer us a powerful blueprint for maximizing the mundane. When Patrick returned to the land of his former barbarian captors in AD 432, he didn't bring with him the rigid, institutionalized version of Christianity from England. Instead, he brought a radically relational mission—one rooted in love. He formed Christian communities that welcomed outsiders and met people exactly where they were.

> YOUR DAILY GRIND ISN'T MEANT TO BE ESCAPED; IT'S MEANT TO BE SURRENDERED. WHEN WE PLACE EVEN THE MOST ROUTINE MOMENTS BEFORE GOD, THEY BECOME SACRED.

At the time, Christianity often focused on "top-level" issues, the big questions about eternity, salvation, and the nature of God. Meanwhile, people generally handled "bottom-level" matters—daily routines, work, and survival—on their own. What Western Christianity largely ignored was the space in between.

That middle ground is where most of life actually happens. It's where we carry unresolved anxieties, navigate everyday crises, and wrestle with the demands of now. And it's this "middle" that Celtic Christianity uniquely embraced.[21] They understood that God not only dwells in the heavens or in sacred spaces, but in the fires we build, the clothes we fold, and the dishes we wash. They believed that God cared about the things that captured people's attention throughout an ordinary day.

To honor this, Celtic Christians practiced something called contemplative prayer, not confined to set hours but woven into the rhythms of everyday life. They prayed through everything. As Ray Simpson puts it, contemplative prayer is "an ongoing, or very frequent, opening of the heart to the triune God, often while engaging in each of the many experiences that fill a day."[22] They had prayers for everything: rising in the morning, tending the fire, bathing, getting dressed, and doing the dishes.

This practice dismantled the false idea that some parts of life matter more to God than others. It invited God into everything—*especially the ordinary.*

If we want to maximize the mundane, we must invite God to inhabit the middle. He's not waiting for the big moments. He's already present in the small ones. When we allow our hearts to turn toward him in life's quiet corners, the mundane becomes sacred. The middle becomes holy ground and we become more aware of God.

In *Celtic Blessings for Everyday Life*, Ray Simpson brings the ancient practice of contemplative prayer into the modern world. His beautifully practical collection includes prayers for all kinds of ordinary moments: buying a car, commuting to work, starting school, retiring, working on a computer, even taking an exam. This is what it means to invite God into the middle; to transform even the most routine tasks into sacred ground.

Don't miss the opportunity to own your ordinary and maximize the mundane. Take a look at the rest of your day and consider writing your own contemplative prayer—something simple, honest, and specific to your everyday rhythm. If you want inspiration, the appendix includes more examples to help you get started.

Every moment is an invitation. Let him in.

THE GIFT OF ANTICIPATION

I proposed to Taylor on a crisp October day at her aunt and uncle's lake place in Minnesota. In the days and weeks leading up to it, anticipation kept building. I was stepping into something sacred—asking the girl I loved to spend her life with me. It was a big day. An extraordinary day.

Is it just me, or does it feel like you need a full-on production crew to pull off a decent proposal these days? As I brainstormed ideas, I briefly considered my friend Tom's idea: we'd go fishing off the dock while he (who has no scuba diving experience) attached the ring to the end of her line from underwater. You'll be relieved to know I did not go with that plan.

Instead, I chose a simpler setup. One that, thanks to Minnesota's unpredictable fall weather, ended up with Taylor in sweatpants and a blue bomber hat. Still, I put my heart into it. I planned every detail, thought through the moment, and made sure it reflected how much she meant to me.

That's what we do with the big days—proposals, weddings, births, holidays. We circle them on the calendar. We prepare. We get excited. We make a big deal out of them and rightfully so.

But what if we started making a bigger deal out of the ordinary days too?

What if we treated today like it held something sacred?

What if we saw the potential for extraordinary even in the mundane?

Joshua Nadeau writes in *Room for Good Things to Run Wild*, "There are very few big moments in life. A handful at most, for each of us. Life is not in those big moments. The substance of life is in the every day, the Holy ordinary, the common."[23] That's where the real story unfolds—not in the highlight reel, but in the slow, faithful rhythm of everyday living.

> **ORDINARY DAYS BECOME EXTRAORDINARY WHEN WE GIVE THEM A LITTLE EXTRA.**

I'm not saying we stop celebrating the big days. I'm just saying maybe it's time we start celebrating the regular ones a little more. After all, ordinary days become extraordinary when we give them a little extra.

Every day is a blessing from God; divinely inspired and jam-packed with life and potential. There may be days on the calendar that hold greater meaning to us, but each day holds equal value to God. He doesn't categorize days like we do. Every day is a new day, overflowing with his fresh mercies.

There is an enormous gap between how we treat extraordinary days and every other day. One thing we would be wise to glean from our treatment of the extraordinary days is the anticipation they carry. I vividly remember each moment prior to welcoming each of our three children—the expectation, anticipation, joy, fear, and a bunch of other emotions I didn't know I could experience.

Anticipation has a powerful effect on us. By definition, it's the act of looking forward with pleasurable expectation[24] and it doesn't have to be reserved for holidays and highlight moments. Anticipation can be your everyday companion.

Research shows that simply looking forward to something can spark joy and boost overall life satisfaction. One study found that "the enjoyment people glean from anticipation might be an important component of life satisfaction."[25] Another noted that anticipation activates dopamine—the feel-good chemical—creating excitement, easing pain, and increasing joy. The same study showed that the anticipation of a positive experience produced similar benefits.[26] *Half the joy is in the act of anticipation.*

You don't need a plane ticket or party invitation to live with daily anticipation. The *Everyday Adventure* mindset invites you to look forward to small things—a hot shower, a good conversation, a perfectly timed cup of coffee. You don't have to wait for the next big thing to feel alive. Just start drawing your circle of anticipation a little closer.

As I write this, I'm already looking forward to our family's Friday night tradition—pizza and a movie. I'm looking forward to our youngest son's giggles during bedtime and the sweet prayers of our two oldest as we tuck them in. I'm looking forward to sitting on the deck with Taylor, reading by the fire table. I'm looking forward to the latte she'll make me in the morning with our espresso machine, and the quiet moments with my Bible, journal, and prayer. I'm looking forward to seeing my son's smile as he runs across the soccer field. The list could go on and that's the beauty of it.

> BY LOOKING FORWARD TO THE LITTLE THINGS, WE CULTIVATE AN ATMOSPHERE OF EXPECTATION IN OUR EVERYDAY LIVES.

If you want to put this into practice, take a moment to reflect on the next 24 hours. What are you looking forward to, even in the small things? The people, the tasks, the meals, the quiet moments with God. He's filled each day with moments worth anticipating. We just need eyes to see them coming. You'll find a short activity at the end of this chapter to help guide you. Don't skip it. It may just shift the way you see your entire day.

Anticipation is one of the keys that makes ordinary days extraordinary. By looking forward to the little things, we cultivate an atmosphere of expectation in our everyday lives. The second lesson is equally true: *when we build a habit of anticipation, we will live a life of celebration.*

SOMETHING TO CELEBRATE

Growing up, I spent a majority of my free time playing a sport of some kind. If a friend couldn't play, no worries, I would play by myself. We had a perfect staircase in our basement that allowed me to throw a racquetball from different angles so I could practice fielding ground balls. I'm pretty sure my parents can still hear the annoying sound ringing in their ears today.

One of my favorite parts about sports is the celebrations. There's just something about a group of full-grown men leaping ecstatically, embracing each other with tears streaming down their faces. I mean, for what other reason would a full-grown man scream, *"I'm going to Disney World!"*?

Over the course of my life, I've witnessed hundreds of unforgettable sports celebrations. As a North Dakota State Bison fan, celebrating national titles has basically become an annual tradition. I still remember the chaos in my freshman dorm when the Minnesota Twins walked off in Game 163 to clinch a playoff spot in 2009.[27] And I'll never forget the raw emotion of the 2016 NBA Finals, when LeBron James led his hometown Cavaliers to Cleveland's first championship in 52 years.

As for growing up a Minnesota Vikings fan... I remember pain. Just pain. Moving on.

One of the most iconic sports celebrations I've ever witnessed happened on November 2, 2016, when the Chicago Cubs won Game 7 of the World Series in extra innings against the Cleveland Indians.[28] It was a rollercoaster of a game filled with clutch plays, momentum swings, and edge-of-your-seat drama. Then it finally happened. Indians' shortstop Francisco Lindor hit a slow roller to third. Kris Bryant scooped it up with a grin already spread across his face and fired the ball to first. Anthony Rizzo caught it, lifted his arms in triumph, and the Cubs stormed the field.

I stood in my living room, fists in the air, jumping up and down like a kid—and I'm *not even a Cubs fan.*

What made that moment unforgettable wasn't just the game itself—it was the *wait.* The Cubs hadn't won a World Series since 1908. Their victory ended a 108-year drought. For lifelong Cubs fans, this wasn't just a game. It was a culmination of *generations* of hope, heartbreak, and holding on.

It probably meant most to Vivian Baron.[29] Born on January 28, 1908, the very year of the Cubs' last title, she became the only known fan to be alive for both championships. She waited 108 years to celebrate. Now that's anticipation in its purest form.

Here's the truth: *Heightened anticipation leads to greater celebration.* When we look forward to something with eager expectation, we heighten our joy when it finally arrives. The reason so many of us see our lives as dull or uninspired isn't because our lives lack meaning; it's because we've reserved anticipation for only the extraordinary. When we stop expecting good things in the ordinary, we stop noticing moments worth celebrating.

By making a habit of anticipation, we can build a habit of celebration in our everyday lives. If anticipation is the input, celebration is the output. Simply anticipating something happening increases our awareness of the moment when it happens. A lack of anticipation increases the likelihood that in the middle of our hurried lives, we will zoom past potential celebratory moments without flinching.

I have noticed that there is an enormous gap between a life filled with anticipation and one void of it. By anticipating my morning cup of coffee, it's the difference between my alarm clock being my enemy and it being my friend, getting me out of bed for a new adventure. Without anticipating the sweet snuggles and conversation with my kids, their early exit from their bedrooms can act as an interruption to my morning routine instead of the gift it truly is.

A habit of anticipation is the soil from which a life of celebration grows. The principle is simple: the more we anticipate, the more we celebrate. If anticipation is looking forward with joy, celebration is simply choosing to mark that joy when it arrives—and we have a lot to celebrate.

Let's circle back to that list you made earlier—the things you're looking forward to in the next 24 hours. Now, here's the next step: *prepare to celebrate those moments when they come.*

Maybe that means planning a little reward for getting out of bed on time. A donut can turn any morning into a party! Maybe it's going out of your way to genuinely greet that friend you usually just nod at in class. However it looks, small celebrations make anticipation come alive.

You can even celebrate something as simple as a meal. Our daughter Kinsley has always had a deep love for tacos. When she was younger, she had this hilarious ritual. She'd lift her taco high above her head like she was offering it to Heaven in pure gratitude. Sometimes, she'd even throw in a shoulder shimmy—her signature taco dance of joy.

Celebration doesn't require candles or confetti. Sometimes, it just needs a hallway and a chant. One of our favorite family traditions happens anytime someone gets new clothes. We turn our house into a runway. The honored family member disappears to change and then re-emerges to the raucous chant: *"Fashion show! Fashion show! Fashion show for [insert name]!"* Just tonight, our three-year-old Rowan strutted his stuff in a brand-new Lightning McQueen t-shirt—complete with a spin and a proud grin when he hit the "stage" in our living room.

There's no right or wrong way to celebrate the small moments in your day. When my wife and I were dating, she had a college exam she was absolutely dreading. She'd been studying hard all week, and I knew how relieved she'd be when it was over. I made a quick trip to Party City and grabbed balloons, party hats, and a few of those ridiculous party blowers. When we met up after her exam, we threw a tiny, ridiculous, joy-filled party, because even finishing a test is worth celebrating.

Everyday celebrations don't need to be extravagant; they just need to be *every day*. Don't wait for the next holiday to start the countdown. Any ordinary day can become extraordinary—we just have to give it a little extra.

THE MAYOR OF MUNDANEVILLE

Some of the best things in life come from the most unexpected places. Take *Dot's Pretzels*, for example. One of America's favorite snacks—now found in gas stations, airports, and major retailers across the country—didn't come from a giant food lab in New York or Los Angeles. It came from Velva, North Dakota, a town of just over 1,000 people. Dorothy "Dot" Henke started making her seasoned pretzels in her kitchen and sharing them with neighbors. By 2021, Hershey bought her brand for $1.2 billion. Not bad for a small-town snack.

Or consider Phil Jackson, one of the most successful coaches in NBA history. Before leading Michael Jordan, Kobe Bryant, and Shaquille O'Neal to a combined 11 championships, he was just a tall kid from

Williston, North Dakota, who played college ball at the University of North Dakota.

Big things can come from small places. And often, greatness begins in the mundane.

Which brings me to Cayuga, North Dakota.

Small towns are fascinating. And I don't mean "there's only one Starbucks" small. I mean "there's only one road" small. Being in a place where you are more likely to spot a stray cat than a human is a bit eerie. That's Cayuga. With a population of 37 and about as many tumbleweeds as people, it feels like you've stepped back in time.

My friend Luke grew up there. When we met in college, I quickly realized that friendship with Luke was an adventure. He's one of those people who makes you ask, *"What's his story?"* (In a good way.) Well, luckily for anyone who knows him, it doesn't take long for him to open the veil of his life and invite you in.

It's safe to say that Luke grew up in one of the most mundane places you can find (that is, if you can find it). My first trip to Cayuga was during my freshman year of college over Valentine's Day. It was a bunch of guys that were so far from having dates that we were clueless of what day it was. The moment we realized it was Valentine's Day was when we were all packed in a hot tub like a bunch of sardines. The next day, Luke gave us a tour of his hometown, which lasted about fifteen minutes. Cayuga may be small, but it helped explain so much about Luke.

We met his parents, Mark and Mary—the heart and soul of the town. Mark, a farmer, also moonlighted as the mayor. He also served as the mailman, the maintenance guy, the snowplow driver, and anything else the town needed. He is a man of few words but does let his ping pong skills do the talking. We also met Luke's mom, Mary, who happens to give the best hugs and has a smile that can light up the entire town. Fun fact: A few years ago, she took over mayoral duties from her husband. I'm sure that was a hotly contested election cycle...

To most people, Cayuga looks like a mundane small town with very little to offer, but not to the Saunders family. To them, it's a magical place that has generously offered them everything, including a beautiful life for their family. In Cayuga, a hill is a mountain, a chore is a game, and the abandoned bank is a literally racquetball court. Mark and Mary never saw it as a stepping stone before moving on to bigger and better things. It was always home.

The truth is, most of life happens in places that feel small and routines that feel ordinary. But if we learn to see the beauty in the mundane, we'll uncover that the mundane is home to life's most beautiful moments and sacred memories. Extraordinary people and things can come out of ordinary places.

We don't need to escape the mundane. We need to reimagine it. We need to become the *Mayor of Mundaneville*.

To get started, you must stop treating the ordinary like an obstacle and start treating it like the opportunity it is—an invitation to live life to the fullest, right where you are. As Mark Batterson and Dick Foth write, "Life becomes an adventure when we see the miraculous in the mundane."[30]

And it really is a choice. Every day. You can rush past the ordinary in search of something more exciting, or you can slow down and invite God into the grocery lists, the diaper changes, the emails, and errands; and discover He's already there. *Do you see the miraculous in the mundane?*

> IF WE LEARN TO SEE THE BEAUTY IN THE MUNDANE, WE'LL UNCOVER THAT THE MUNDANE IS HOME TO LIFE'S MOST BEAUTIFUL MOMENTS AND SACRED MEMORIES.

Because there is beauty in obscurity. Wonder in repetition. And adventure in the most unexpected places.

Or, as Pam Beesly says in the final moments of *The Office*,

> "There's a lot of beauty in ordinary things... isn't that the point?"[31]

Yes. That is the point.
So today—own your ordinary.
A life full of adventure can be yours *even in the mundane*.

TRAIL MARKERS

TRUE NORTH TAKEAWAY
When you invite God into the ordinary rhythms of your life, the mundane stops being something to escape and becomes the very place he forms your heart, grows your joy, and meets you with everyday adventure.

REFLECTION STOPS
1. When you think about how much of life is "mundane," how do you honestly respond—and what ordinary spaces in your daily life might God be inviting you to see as holy ground?
2. Where in your current season do you feel most "in obscurity" like David with the sheep—overlooked, unseen, or stuck in a role that doesn't feel important?
3. What are three things you're currently looking forward to—one today, one this week, and one this month—and how might anticipation reshape the way you move through the mundane?

EVERYDAY ADVENTURE CHALLENGE: EVERYDAY BLESSING
Choose one everyday routine: washing dishes, folding laundry, brewing coffee, driving to work, packing lunches, or any other ordinary part of your day.

Write a simple, honest prayer you can pray each time you do that task this week. Let it be specific to your real life and the work in front of you. For example:

- **Example 1 — Dishes Prayer**
  "Lord, as I wash these dishes, wash my heart. Thank You for the people who gathered around this table and for the home I get to care for. Help me do this with love instead of hurry or resentment and meet me here in this ordinary moment."

- **Example 2 — Commute Prayer**
  "Jesus, as I drive today, be my guide—on this road and in the day ahead. Lead me toward the work You've given me and the people You want me to love. Ready my heart for the conversations, interruptions, and unexpected turns that will come. And just as this fuel carries my car forward, be the strength that carries me into everything You've called me to today."

Use your prayer every time you do that task this week and pay attention to how it shifts your awareness of God in the mundane. For more ideas and examples, see the **Everyday Blessings** resource in the back of the book.

FOUR
Slow Down

"*I cannot live in the kingdom of God with a hurried soul.*"[1]
John Ortberg

Becoming a parent is one of life's most transformative experiences. Taylor and I had been married just over three years when we welcomed our first child—our daughter, Kinsley. The months leading up to her birth were filled with a roller coaster of emotions and a gauntlet of preparatory activities.

In the months leading up to Kinsley's birth, I learned all about nesting—the instinctual urge for a pregnant woman to prepare her domain for her hatchling. Like every mother before her, Taylor entered her nesting era, however, she knew her limits. And by "her" limits, I mean "my" limits. I'm not the handiest of men. In fact, I'm the type of guy who wants to burn down IKEA within 45 minutes of opening one of their boxes. Knowing how important the nesting process is for birds and human women, I grit my teeth and endured the most painful aspect of having a child—assembling cheap furniture.[2]

Our first go-around of parenthood opened my eyes to other cultural rites of passage. We went on a babymoon, purchased a diaper genie (who, unfortunately, did *not* grant my wishes for no more blowouts), and even attended an R-rated introduction to parenting class at our local hospital. One tradition I hadn't anticipated was the all-important task of choosing a nursery theme. Apparently, every child needs an animal motif, complete with crib sheets, wall art, stuffed animals, onesies, and trinkets. It's *obviously* an important decision.

Some parents choose a gentle herd of woodland creatures or a single beloved animal like a brave little lion or a wise owl. Parents often gravitate toward animals that symbolize qualities they hope to instill—bravery, curiosity, gentleness, or strength.

Not us. We chose a sloth.

In our defense, sloth decor was in. And if I'm being honest, I think we hoped having a child would help slow us down, as we were running at a fast pace—pastoring on a college campus, keeping up with friends and family, and trying to fill every waking hour with activity. So we bought all the sloth decor and clothes we could find.

Having a newborn dressed in sloth pajamas was not enough to slow me down. Within two weeks of Kinsley's birth, I officiated a wedding, stood as best man in another, and hauled my ten-day postpartum wife and newborn to a youth camp in the middle of nowhere to stay in a room with no air-conditioning and a bathroom we shared with other staff. A couple weeks later, we were strapped in an airplane traveling across the country for another friend's wedding. So much for slowing down.

As you can imagine, I was *not* nominated for husband of the year, although Taylor's grace toward me earned her wife of the millennium honors. The craziest part of all of this is that I didn't even recognize how insane it was until years later.

I was out of control, and I didn't even know it. I was so busy saying yes to everything that came my way that I didn't even realize what I was saying "no" to. I was driven by the desire to be a present and available pastor that I unintentionally gave my leftovers to those closest to me. I was so busy trying to make appearances in various social settings that I failed to make meaningful connections. I would go weeks without spending quality time with my closest friends because I was trying to be everyone else's best friend. I had allowed my ministry to become my identity; my value and worth rising and falling based on how "effective" I was in ministry.

Becoming a dad didn't slow me down as I expected. It magnified my unhealthy habits, propelling me to move even faster just to hold everything together. In *The Life You've Always Wanted,* pastor and author John Ortberg writes, "Hurry is not just a disordered schedule. Hurry is a disordered heart."[3] That was the reality I was living in. I didn't have a schedule problem. I had a heart problem. Covering our daughter's bedroom in sloth-themed decorations and blankets wouldn't heal my heart. I needed something far deeper than that.

Hurry quietly erodes the things we value most, including relationships, joy, gratitude, creativity, thoughtful work, spiritual depth, health, marriage, and everything else we hold dear. It's a slow and subtle thief. In *An Unhurried Life,* Alan Fadling says, "In my preoccupation with efficiency, I miss so much that God wants to do in my life and say to me in the moment."[4] That's the brutal irony of hurry. You can be in the middle of something amazing and still completely miss it.

Fadling goes on to say, "Hurry rushes toward the destination and fails to enjoy the journey."[5] And that's the heart of it. Hurry kills adventure because we never experience it while it's happening. We race from one thing to the next and only look back later, wondering where the time went. If we want to live fully, we must walk at a pace that allows us to actually *see* and *savor* life as it unfolds, otherwise we will continue to see our life as a blur.

We will keep missing out on the best parts of life if we fail to slow down. Slowing down allows you to be present to God, to people, and to the moment. It allows your heart to be where your body is. It gives you permission to embrace the goodness of your current moment instead of being in a hurry to rush to the next one.

It was Jesus' unhurried pace that allowed him to notice Zacchaeus in the tree, engage in a meaningful conversation with the woman at the well, welcome and bless children, and feel the gentle tug of the bleeding woman reaching for his robe.

Take it from me: You don't need a sloth throw pillow to fix your pace. What you really need is something far more radical: the space your soul desperately craves. You need to make room for the good stuff.

A SPACIOUS PLACE

In the summer of 2019, my family and I moved from North Dakota to a small town in southern New Jersey. New job. New home. New community. New rhythms. It was a season of transition, full of excitement and uncertainty.

Our house sat on an acre of land in the middle of farm country, nestled up to a large wooded area. Our neighbors included a donkey, a goat, and chickens who would occasionally try to cross the road. I know what you're thinking, *"You said New Jersey, right?"* Believe it or not, there is more to New Jersey than turnpikes, thick accents, and reality TV. New Jersey isn't just a big suburb of New York and there is far more to it than a bunch of Italians honking at each other in stand-still traffic on their way to the Shore (although that does happen). New Jersey is called the Garden State for a reason. While the northern part of the state leans industrial, the south is dotted with vineyards, farmland, and roadside vegetable stands. And that was the setting of the newest chapter in our life.

> IF WE WANT TO LIVE FULLY, WE MUST WALK AT A PACE THAT ALLOWS US TO ACTUALLY SEE AND SAVOR LIFE AS IT UNFOLDS, OTHERWISE WE WILL CONTINUE TO SEE OUR LIFE AS A BLUR.

My fifteen-minute drive to work brought me past farms, old Quaker churches, vineyards, and homes constructed in the 1700's. Our daily routine included walks around the big park across the street and backyard explorations with Kinsley and our dog, Kevin. At night, thanks to our defective streetlight, the night sky was filled with bright stars. I know this may be a shock, but even though I grew up in North Dakota, this was my first exposure to rural living. This was our spacious place.

Our life was suddenly filled with the very thing we didn't realize we desperately needed—*margin*. We went from sharing a bedroom wall with our townhome neighbors to living on an acre of land on the outskirts of town. Our calendar was as wide open as the fields surrounding our home. This new way of living was slowly breathing new life into our home. Our interior was beginning to mirror our exterior—a spacious place.

Margin is simply the space between. It's the buffer between your limits and your load. It's what allows you to breathe deeply instead of gasping for air. It's room to respond rather than react. And for us, this new rhythm of life was doing something sacred. It was creating space in our souls.

When we made that move, we gained more than just physical space. The margin we found wasn't just about acres and quiet roads; it began showing up in our minds and hearts. The rush started to slow and the noise began to quiet. Emotionally, I had more capacity to see and connect with Taylor. Spiritually, I was more attentive to what God was doing in and around me. And relationally, I had more time and energy to be present with the people right in front of me.

That's the power of margin: It creates the conditions for health to grow. Miracles happen in the margin. Meaning is discovered in the margin. Margin is where the good stuff happens.

But margin doesn't always show up on its own. In fact, it rarely does. In a culture that values hustle over health and productivity over peace, margin must be pursued, created, and protected.

What does it actually look like to live with margin? It looks like intentionally saying *no*—not because you're lazy or unmotivated, but because your *yes* is too valuable to be handed out to everything. It looks like scheduling breathing room into your calendar—not just back-to-back meetings or appointments, but time to think, pray, rest, and just *be*. It looks like creating distance from the constant noise so you can hear the still, small voice of God. It looks like making time for the things that matter most—not just *when* life slows down, but to *make* life slow down. It looks like putting your phone down long enough to feel boredom again, realizing that boredom might actually be a doorway to clarity—and dare I say… adventure.

Margin is *intentional spontaneity*. It's the space you create on purpose so that something unexpected and life-giving can happen. It's intentionally planning to have no plans. The reason so many of us feel stuck in the monotony of everyday life isn't because we lack opportunity for adventure, but because we've left no room for it. Our days are so tightly packed that there's no space

> **THE REASON SO MANY OF US FEEL STUCK IN THE MONOTONY OF EVERYDAY LIFE ISN'T BECAUSE WE LACK OPPORTUNITY FOR ADVENTURE, BUT BECAUSE WE'VE LEFT NO ROOM FOR IT.**

for wonder to break through. No margin to say yes to something unplanned, to explore a new idea, or to follow a nudge from the Holy Spirit. Adventure isn't just about doing wild things. It's about having the space to step into something meaningful when the moment invites you. And that starts with margin.

If you want to live with margin, you need to fight for it. You need to build it into your rhythms and resist the pressure to fill every space. Because life without margin might be full, but the question is, *"Is it full of the right stuff?"* A life without margin might be full, but it's also fragile. A full life isn't just packed with opportunities, activity, and ambition—it's also full of rest, peace, and joy.

So take a breath. Step back. Zoom out. Where do you need to create space again? What would it look like for your *exterior* and your *interior* to both feel a little more spacious?

MAKING ROOM

Now, I know what you might be thinking: *"That sounds nice, but I can't exactly pack up my life and move to the countryside."* And you're right. The truth is that margin isn't about where you live—it's about how you live. You don't need a bigger backyard to experience peace. You don't need a donkey for a neighbor to feel like you have room to breathe.

You can live in a fifteenth-floor apartment in the middle of a noisy city and still create the space your soul desperately needs. You can work a demanding job, raise kids, serve in ministry, and still find moments of rest and margin; but it takes intentionality. Because in a culture that never stops moving, margin doesn't just happen. You must make room for it.

During our time in New Jersey, we unknowingly started doing things that built margin into our everyday life. And as small and ordinary as they were, they became sacred. Weekly donut dates with Kinsley. Evening walks around the neighborhood park. Saturday breakfast at the Woodstown Diner followed by a lazy morning wandering around Barney's Bookstore across the street. Afternoons at the Amish Market in a neighboring town eating far too many pretzel logs. Mowing the lawn while Kinsley and

> THE TRUTH IS THAT MARGIN ISN'T ABOUT WHERE YOU LIVE—IT'S ABOUT HOW YOU LIVE.

Kevin ran laps in the yard. These weren't big, dramatic moments, but they were moments with *space*. Space to breathe. Space to connect. Space to slow down long enough to remember what really matters.

Margin isn't just about what you take out of your life; it's about what you purposefully add. Those donuts and diner breakfasts were not just treats—they were anchors. Rhythms. Markers of time that slowed us down and gave us something to look forward to. The goal wasn't productivity; it was presence.

Eventually, we moved back to North Dakota and re-entered the fast-paced rhythms of a larger church, a bigger community, and an increasingly full calendar. But the lessons we learned in our spacious season didn't stay behind. We carried them with us and we had to get even more intentional about putting them into practice.

Now, margin looks like a weekly Sabbath—a full day each week where we power down the productivity machine and simply rest, delight, and be. It looks like weekly date nights with Taylor that we put on the calendar the month before. It's Friday family movie nights with the kids when we order pizza, make popcorn, cuddle up under blankets, and *just be together.* It's creating boundaries in ministry to prioritize dinner and bedtime with my family as often as possible. It's "heat therapy" at the gym—time in the sauna, steam room, or hot tub—not just for the body, but for the soul. It's making space to invite friends over, to go on spontaneous donut runs and start a Saturday with nothing planned.

None of these things are flashy. They're not going to get you a round of applause. But they are the building blocks of a healthy, spacious life. A life with room for joy. Room for people. Room for God.

And here's what I want you to hear, especially if you feel like the life is being squeezed out of you right now: *you are not stuck.* You may not be able to change everything about your season, but you can change *something.* Margin doesn't start with a major life overhaul. It starts with one small choice. One intentional shift. One quiet "no" to protect a more important "yes."

Maybe for you, it looks like getting up ten minutes earlier so you can sit in silence before the day begins. Maybe it's taking a walk around the block instead of scrolling your phone during lunch. Maybe it's reserving one evening a week as untouchable family time, even if it's just for pizza and a movie. Maybe it's setting a screen time limit. Maybe it's learning to say, "I'd love to, but I can't right now."

The point isn't to imitate our exact rhythms, but to create your own. Rhythms that work for *your* life, in *your* season, and with *your* people. What matters is that you *make room* for rest, relationships, and reflection. Because without that room, even the good things in life can start to feel like burdens.

So let me ask you:

Where could you start making space again?

What small shift could open up a pocket of time for adventure in your week?

What rhythm could bring you joy *just because*?

You don't need a field or a farm. You don't need a different zip code or a different job title. You just need to believe that margin is worth fighting for and then take one small step in that direction.

The good stuff still happens in the margins.

PRIORITIZING WHAT MATTERS MOST

Margin isn't the goal; it's the means. The purpose of creating space in your life isn't just to slow down. It's to make room for what matters most.

We talked about how margin gives you the breathing room you didn't even know you needed. It opens the door for rest, connection, peace, presence, and adventure. But here's the thing: margin can only do its job if you know what you're making room *for*.

If you don't, you'll end up filling your calendar with the same noise you were trying to escape. You'll say yes to things that don't align with who you are or who you want to become. And slowly, the space you fought so hard to create will shrink under the weight of everyone else's expectations. That's why this next part of the journey is about identifying what really matters most to *you*.

Early in our marriage, Taylor and I went on a ski trip with some friends to Montana. If you're looking for a spacious place, just drive across North Dakota and eastern Montana in the dead of winter. Endless highway. Frozen fields. A spacious place. We had a lot of time in the car, and I decided to bring a book called *Train Your Brain for Success* along for the ride.

One of the chapters challenged me to do something I hadn't ever done before: identify my core values. The author included a big list of possible words to jumpstart the process, and I started circling the ones that stood out. With nothing but miles ahead of us and snow-covered plains all around, I took my time—praying, reflecting, and writing. By the end of that stretch of highway, I had written down seven words I wanted to define my life:

1. I am:
2. Jesus-Centered
3. Family-Focused
4. People-Driven
5. Authentic
6. Joyful
7. Passionate
8. Teachable

That list became more than a journal entry. It became a compass, helping me make decisions, set priorities, and come back to center when life felt out of rhythm. Those values have helped guide nearly a decade of life and leadership. They've brought clarity in moments of transition, and they've served as guardrails when things felt overwhelming.

And they didn't just help me define what mattered; they helped me build a life that reflected it. Here's why I share that: Most of us aren't living the life we desire simply because we've never taken the time to define it.

We let the loudest voices around us—our boss, our professors, our peers, our social feeds—tell us what matters. We chase after goals or build routines that sound good but leave us feeling empty. We spend our time doing things that don't reflect our actual values and then wonder why we feel like we're missing something. But what if you paused long enough to ask:

What truly matters to me?

What kind of person do I want to be?

What do I want my life to be about?

You don't have to be on a ski trip in Montana to figure this out. You just need a quiet moment and a willingness to look inward and upward. You need to ask God to help you see what he's already placed inside of you. What convictions has God stirred in your heart? What qualities do you want to be known for? What values do you want to build your life around?

This isn't about trying to impress anyone. It's not about writing a perfect mission statement or crafting a slogan for your life. It's about getting honest and asking: *What kind of life do I want to live and what matters most to me?*

When you start to identify your values, everything starts to shift. You begin to say no more confidently and yes more intentionally. You stop chasing things that look good on the outside but drain you on the inside.

And here's the beautiful part: When you get clear on what matters most, you start to build a life that reflects your heart. A life that feels like yours. A life that aligns with God's design for you. So before we talk about setting goals or shaping your calendar, let's start here: *What matters most?*

What are the non-negotiables for your life? What do you want to be true of you, even ten years from now? What do you want your kids, your spouse, your friends to know you for?

Margin gives you the space to ask those questions.

Intentionality helps you begin to live out the answers.

LIVING IT OUT

It's one thing to say what matters most. It's another thing to live like it.

I think most of us genuinely want to live with intention. We desire to build lives that reflect our values. We want to live with purpose, to honor God, to be fully present for the people we love and the life we're living. But then the days just keep coming—full, fast, and often louder than our priorities.

Before we know it, we find ourselves living out of rhythm and out of alignment. We find ourselves busy doing things that don't reflect who we are or what we believe God is calling us to be about. We're once again caught in a vicious current taking us somewhere we're not even sure we want to go.

I've felt that gap in my own life more times than I can count. I've said things like, *"I am Jesus-Centered,"* but then realized I hadn't slowed down to pray or slowly read my Bible in days. I've said *"I am Family-Focused,"* but then looked back at a week full of meetings, late nights, and missed opportunities to be present at home. And even when I was home physically, I wasn't there emotionally. I've said, *"I am People-Driven,"* yet there have been times in ministry that I've been so caught up in tasks, I haven't been able to spend quality time with the people I've been called to serve.

The hardest part? We don't end up misaligned because we *don't care* about the right things. It happens because we care about *too many* things. Good things. Important things. But eventually, we wake up and realize our life is packed full and somehow, what matters most gets squeezed out.

That's where intentionality becomes more than a nice idea. It becomes essential.

It's not about achieving balance. It's about choosing alignment.

When we lived in New Jersey, we stumbled into margin that helped bring our values back into focus. The naturally slower pace woke our souls up to a reality we hadn't realized we had been missing. Stepping out of our house on a Saturday morning with no agenda, other than to explore our little town, gave us the breathing room to experience more and see more. By needing to start over with friendships and community, we were able to spend more quality time with fewer people. We found ourselves enjoying slower evenings with friends, not thinking about other places we could be.

That season wasn't perfect, but it was formative. It gave us a glimpse of what life could look like when our rhythms matched what we said mattered most.

When we moved back to the Midwest, we quickly realized that if we weren't intentional, those values we had rediscovered would get buried again. One of the predominant thoughts I wrestled with during that time was this: *Can we still cultivate peace, presence, and purpose in a season where everything seemed to move at double speed?*

That became both a challenge and a conviction.

We knew what it felt like to live slower and breathe deeper. And even though we were extremely grateful to be closer to home, we were being pulled back into a world of packed calendars, crowded evenings, and constant motion. The question became: *How do we cultivate a slower, more intentional life—not outside the chaos, but right in the middle of it?*

That's where we had to get fully honest. If we wanted to protect the values we'd uncovered, we couldn't just wait for margin to show up. We had to create it.

We started making small choices—not huge lifestyle overhauls—just little shifts that made space for the good stuff. A protected day off. Friday night family movie nights. Intentional play time with the kids. Weekly margin for each of us to spend time with close friends.

Those choices have helped. Not perfectly. Not magically. But enough to remind us that we *can* live with intention, even in busy times. We can build in small rhythms and habits that reflect our values and make more space for adventure in our everyday lives. We can say no to things that aren't aligned; not because they're bad, but because they're just not for now.

Here's what I know: If you don't fight to live out your values, something else will fill the space.

The loudest voice will win. The most urgent task will always demand your attention. And if you're not careful, your life will start to reflect a version of success or purpose that you never actually chose.

So maybe it's time to pause and ask some honest questions:

Does my current rhythm of life reflect what I say matters most?

Do my habits and commitments support or compete with my values?

Am I making space for the things that bring life or just trying to keep up?

And if the answers to those questions are hard to hear, you're not alone. The goal isn't guilt. The goal is grace-filled awareness. Because the good news is you don't have to stay stuck and you don't need to overhaul your whole life. You just need to take one step in a new direction.

Start small. Start with one value. One rhythm. One act of resistance against the noise.

This isn't about perfection. It's about returning—coming back to who you are, who God's called you to be, and what you've already said matters most. The truth is, this is less about doing and more about becoming. It's not about setting new goals; it's about establishing new rhythms. Goals have a finish line, but rhythms build a way of life.

You won't always get it right. I certainly don't.

But maybe that's okay. Maybe intentionality isn't about *never* drifting. Maybe it's about noticing when we do and having the courage to come back again and again. Realigning. Re-rooting. Rebuilding.

Take a breath. Zoom out. Ask the question again:

Does my life reflect what I say matters most?

And if not, what's one small way I can move in that direction today?

A SUDDEN STOP

In February 2020, we welcomed our son, Summit, into the world. The birth of our second child was much different than the birth of our first. When Kinsley was born, our hospital room and home were filled with a constant flow of friends and family coming to meet her. With Summit, we lived thousands of miles away and his first week of life was spent hooked up to machines in the NICU. And then, like the plot twist no one saw coming, *the world shut down.*

It was March, and COVID-19 hit hard. Everything came to a screeching halt. In-person fundraising events? Canceled. Summer camps? Canceled. Meetings, trips, gatherings—all wiped from the calendar in the span of a week. Work, as we knew it, paused. And living on the East Coast at the time, everything felt heightened. Tension was everywhere, toilet paper was nowhere, and no one knew what day it was.

> **GOALS HAVE A FINISH LINE, BUT RHYTHMS BUILD A WAY OF LIFE.**

But in the middle of all the uncertainty, we were handed something we didn't even realize we were craving.

Time.

For the first time in a long time, our calendar was completely empty, and I was confronted with a question: *What am I going to do with this?*

Now, I'd love to say I immediately leaned into the slower pace with grace. But... no. If you need a glimpse into how deeply wired I was for hustle, let me just tell you—I helped run a virtual fundraiser *from the NICU*. Summit had been alive for less than a week and I had my laptop out, Wi-Fi connected, making things happen like a totally sane and balanced human being. (Spoiler: I was not sane or balanced.)

Eventually, though, I started to lean in.

That season, though wildly unpredictable, became fertile ground for something new. I got serious about writing this book. I launched an Instagram Live series called *Quarantine Coffee with Friends*, mostly just to stay connected with people and to help tell the ordinary stories of some of my favorite people. That little series ended up planting the seed and lighting the fire for what would later become the *Going Somewhere* podcast.[6]

I spent longer stretches of time with God—not because I had to squeeze it in, but because I actually had space to linger. I read more. I dreamed more. I processed emotions I'd pushed down for years. I soaked in as much quality time with the kids, spending hours snuggling my newborn son and adventuring with Kinsley. Taylor and I had more time to talk, reflect, and wrestle through things we'd been too busy to name. We got to know our neighbors in a way we hadn't before, forging a family-like bond with the family living next to us. We walked more. Sat more. Prayed more. Played more.

And somehow, in the middle of a global crisis, something in my soul started to breathe again. I began to wonder... *What if I don't want to go back to the way things were?*

Eventually, the world started to spin again—slowly at first, and then all at once. Meetings were back. Travel picked up. Ministry got moving. Life resumed. But deep inside, I carried this quiet conviction:

How do I keep living slower in a world that keeps speeding up?

How do I hold onto the margin, the peace, the intentionality without needing a pandemic to force it on me?

Maybe you've felt something similar. Maybe you're longing for a reset but don't exactly have a blank calendar and global shutdown to help you out. Here's the thing: You can't stop the world, but you *can* stop for a moment.

You can take a long weekend at a cabin. You can carve out a quiet morning with a cup of coffee and a journal. You can turn your phone off for an afternoon. You can take a day to walk, to pray, to reflect, to be unavailable in the best kind of way. You can look at your current commitments and ask, "*What needs to come to a complete stop?*" Not a pause. Not a maybe later. A full-on stop.

You don't need to quit your job or disappear into the woods like a modern-day monk. But you *can* choose to stop long enough to remember who you are. You *can* take a breath. You *can* return.

And maybe that's what this whole "Slow Down" chapter has been leading toward—the courage to stop, even for a moment, and ask the question: *Is the life I'm living the one I've been called to live?* You don't need a worldwide shutdown to reset your soul. You just need a little honesty and a little margin. You need to zoom out, even for an hour, and come back to what matters most.

Here's your permission slip. Cancel the meeting. Sit still. Don't respond. Turn off your phone. Take a day of PTO. Get quiet enough to hear the voice of God again.

Let this be your *sudden stop*.

LESSONS FROM A SLOTH

Turns out, a sloth was the *perfect* animal to decorate Kinsley's room because she has fully embraced the lifestyle.

As I write this, Taylor is upstairs helping her get ready for school. And by "helping," I mean issuing a series of gentle reminders while Kinsley moves at her own *very*—dare I say—slothful pace.

She puts on her pants, walks to the dresser to grab a shirt... and then notices the coloring book and markers scattered on her bedroom floor from the night before. Naturally, *that* becomes the priority. After doodling for a few minutes, Taylor reminds her about the shirt. She heads to the bathroom to brush her teeth but emerges instead with a bath toy in hand, eager to tell a long-winded story about a friend at school. Still no toothbrush.

After a series of patient (and not patient) nudges, we make it to the car. I park in the drop-off lane, and our sweet little sloth takes her time unbuckling her seatbelt. She climbs up front for a hug, I pray over her and send her off.

Two steps out of the car, she stops. She turns. She waves. She blows a kiss.

Every single day.

We often joke about our decision to decorate her nursery with sloths. At the time, it was just a fun theme—something cute and simple. But looking back, it feels more like a setup. Like God knew exactly what he was doing.

Because Kinsley *is* our daily reminder to slow down.

She reminds us that not everything has to be rushed. That joy is found in the pauses and in the margin. That the best parts of life aren't found in the hurry, but in the moments we linger.

Of course, we still forget. We still rush. We still find ourselves prodding and pushing and trying to keep pace with the world around us. But then Kinsley stops. Turns. Waves. Blows a kiss. And we remember.

We remember that life is not measured in how fast we move, but in how present we are. We remember that hurry is not only a disordered schedule, but a disordered heart. We remember that hurry kills.

And whether or not you have a seven-year-old sloth of your own, the invitation is the same.

To stop. To notice. To slow down.

Because when we do, we just might find that the very things we were rushing past were the things that mattered most all along.

A few weeks ago, Taylor and I found ourselves buried under what felt like a small mountain range of laundry.

With three young kids—one in the throes of potty training and all of them spending summer days covered in sunscreen, mud, and popsicle drips—the dirty clothes had gotten the best of us. One load turned into five, and before long we had an Everest of clean-but-unfolded laundry piled in the living room.

As we sat on the floor surrounded by dinosaur t-shirts, flower dresses, and Lightning McQueen pajamas, Taylor paused mid-fold and said, *"It never stops."* Then after a moment of reflection, she added softly, *"But someday it will."*

That one sentence hit me like a freight train. It captured everything I've been learning about intentionality.

The laundry mountain, as ridiculous as it felt in that moment, was a sign of life. And not just chaos—but joy, family, adventure, and growth. This is what it means to *maximize the mundane*. To recognize that the ordinary *is* the adventure, and that the slow, repetitive tasks of life are where love and legacy are formed. The mountain of laundry is as much of an adventure as the mountains in Alaska. Folding laundry becomes sacred when we remember what it represents.

Intentionality isn't just about appreciating what is, but it's also about choosing where we want to go. As we explored in *Place Your Pins*, intentional living starts by identifying where you are, where you want to be, and what it takes to move forward. Life doesn't drift toward purpose on its own. It requires direction. But direction doesn't mean rushing. That's why we must learn to *Slow Down*—to actually notice the beauty right in front of us before it becomes a memory.

There's a line tucked away in the acknowledgments of Donald Miller's *Scary Close* that has always stayed with me. He thanks his in-laws "whose adventure wasn't an ocean or a mountain, but a family."[7] That's it. That's the quiet beauty of intentionality—not chasing the next thing, but fully showing up for *this* thing. This family. This job. This season. This moment.

> **THE MOUNTAIN OF LAUNDRY IS AS MUCH OF AN ADVENTURE AS THE MOUNTAINS IN ALASKA. FOLDING LAUNDRY BECOMES SACRED WHEN WE REMEMBER WHAT IT REPRESENTS.**

Ecclesiastes 9:9 says, "Enjoy life with your wife, whom you love…"[8] That verse has quietly become a guiding motto in our marriage. It reminds us that intentionality isn't always a grand strategy. It's often about choosing joy in the daily grind. It's learning to enjoy life rather than just endure it.

I once read an article about a young mother who, upon finding out she was terminally ill, began writing hundreds of letters for her daughters to open throughout their lives. It was a powerful expression of love, but it also made me wonder: what if we didn't wait until the end to live with that level of intention? What if we lived *today* like it really mattered? We don't need to wait for a diagnosis or a wake-up call to start living this way.

Here's your invitation: Live the kind of life you'd be proud to leave behind. Be present. Be purposeful. Be aware. Make small choices that lead to big impact. Rekindle a forgotten friendship. Bless your kids during a diaper change. Eat dinner without your phone. Fold laundry with gratitude. Start a neighbor night. Pray while you drive. Celebrate small wins.

Life is happening. Right now. And it won't always be like this. So don't miss the beauty in front of you.

Be intentional.

Adventure isn't out there—*it's right here, right now.*

TRAIL MARKERS

TRUE NORTH TAKEAWAY
Life to the fullest isn't found in doing more, but in slowing down enough to live in step with God, your values, and the people right in front of you.

REFLECTION STOPS
1. Where do you see hurry quietly eroding what matters most right now—your marriage, your kids, your friendships, your health, your walk with God?
2. What are the non-negotiable for your life? What do you want to be true of you, even ten years from now? What do you want your kids, your spouse, your friends to know you for?
3. Does your current rhythm of life reflect what you say matters most or are some habits and commitments pulling you away from your values? Take a moment to identify where you need to create space again for the things that bring life.

EVERYDAY ADVENTURE CHALLENGE: BE A SLOTH
Sloths don't rush. They move at the pace their life requires. This week, you're going to borrow their wisdom.

1. **Review Your Calendar**
   Look at the last two weeks like it's a map of your life. Circle anything that clearly reflects what matters most (faith, family, health, calling, rest). Put a "?" next to anything you only said yes to out of guilt, habit, or fear of disappointing people.

2. **Release One Thing**
   Choose one recurring commitment you can release or reduce this month. Big or small—it all creates space.

3. **Protect One Thing**
   Choose one life-giving rhythm (Sabbath, family night, quiet mornings, exercise, prayer, date night) and treat it like a non-negotiable by putting it in your calendar before everything else.

That's it.

Three small steps that help you slow down, breathe again, and make room for the good stuff.

RESIST COMPLACENCY
Part Two

RESIST COMPLACENCY
Part Two

Cast Away, starring Tom Hanks, tells the haunting story of Chuck Noland, a FedEx executive stranded on a deserted island after a plane crash. With only a handful of scattered packages and a future volleyball companion for company, Noland endures more than four years of isolation, surviving on coconuts, trial and error, and sheer will.

What makes this nearly silent film gripping isn't just the setting—it's the struggle. The daily tension between giving up and going on. Between wasting away or doing whatever it takes to keep moving. Noland's story keeps going because he *refuses to settle*. He chooses, however painfully, to resist stagnation.

That's the core of this section: **Resist Complacency**.

Not all of us are stranded on a literal island, but many of us feel stuck. Maybe you feel isolated in your job, routine, or stage of life. You're not alone. But the truth is, adventure ends where complacency begins. You don't have to change your location to reawaken your life—you must change your posture.

Complacency quietly kills growth. And while your season might feel limiting, your spirit doesn't have to be. Stagnation is less about where you are and more about what you've stopped reaching for.

Ask yourself: *Have I become complacent, or am I still growing?*

I've been there. I remember sitting in my final year of college, feeling stuck, even though the semester had barely begun. At that point, I felt God calling me into full-time ministry, which meant I was likely walking away from the career path my degree had prepared me for. That made it hard to stay motivated. I kept thinking, *"What's the point of studying all this if I'm never going to use it?"*

On top of that, I was feeling the weight of my financial reality. I had racked up over $25,000 in student debt for a degree I wasn't planning to use, and my income was practically nonexistent. Meanwhile, many of my older friends had already graduated, landed jobs, and were starting what looked like real lives. I felt like they were moving forward, and I was stuck, just waiting for the next eight months to pass.

It didn't take long for God to awaken my heart to the beauty of the season I was in, opening my eyes to opportunities I'd never have again after graduation. He invited me to view the final months of my college experience through a new lens. No longer was I able to coast through the finish line of my senior year, with my heart already fixed on a future season. My eyes were fixed on Jesus and the opportunities he laid before me. Looking back at my final months of college, I see God's grace. Over the course of my final months of college, I not only leaned into what my professors were teaching me, but I leaned into what God was teaching me. A season that I was rushing away became one I wanted to rest in just a little while longer.

When we refuse complacency and reject stagnation, we never have to be stuck, even if the season we are in isn't changing anytime soon.

I believe there are three powerful postures that will help you fight back against complacency and keep you moving toward a life of everyday adventure:

1. Cultivate Curiosity
2. Become a Lifelong Learner
3. Ditch Your Comfort Zone

Curiosity allows you to see the beauty and wonder in the world around you—even in the mundane. A commitment to learning turns ordinary moments into opportunities for growth. And stepping beyond your comfort zone is where adventure begins to take root.

Complacency will always lure you back toward comfort. But the life Jesus is inviting you into is a life of movement, discovery, and transformation.

Even if your surroundings don't change anytime soon, you can still move forward. A commitment to curiosity, learning, and embracing discomfort will prevent stagnation and create a life of adventure wherever you find yourself to be.

So grab the nearest volleyball, give it a name, and let's get off this island called Complacency.

Adventure awaits—and Wilson's coming with us.

FIVE
Cultivate Curiosity

"*Each day we're presented with an unending parade of wonders, should we not be too busy to notice.*"[1]
Brad Montague

Every good North Dakotan knows the story of Lewis and Clark. When your state isn't exactly a hotspot for national headlines, you hold tight to any brush with fame—and the fact that Lewis and Clark once spent a winter here basically makes them everyone's honorary great-great-great-great uncles. I mean everyone knows Lewis, Clark, Sakakawea, and Teddy Roosevelt are the four most influential human beings in American history.

In 1803, President Thomas Jefferson commissioned Meriwether Lewis to lead an expedition into the vast, uncharted territory of the Louisiana Purchase. Lewis recruited William Clark as his co-captain, and together they assembled a team of 45 men to explore the unknown West. They set off from St. Louis on May 14, 1804, paddling up the Missouri River with a simple but daunting mission: map the new land, study its resources, build relationships with Native American tribes, and try to find a water route to the Pacific Ocean.

Over the course of 28 months and nearly 8,000 miles, the expedition faced brutal weather, treacherous terrain, illness, injury, and uncertainty at every turn. But they pressed on, eventually returning as national heroes. Their journey opened the door to westward expansion and produced groundbreaking maps, journals, and over 120 newly documented animal species, including the prairie dog, coyote, and grizzly bear.[2]

What made Lewis and Clark so successful wasn't just grit or survival skills—it was curiosity. They weren't just traveling across the land; they were discovering it. A plant that looked slightly different? Worth inspecting. An unfamiliar sound in the trees? Worth investigating. Their mission was built on a relentless desire to learn, explore, and see what others had never seen.

Their success wasn't accidental. It was fueled by wonder.

What drove Lewis and Clark, and countless other explorers, into uncharted territory? Curiosity. Every great adventure begins with someone asking, "I wonder what's out there?" Someone stared at the ocean and thought, "What's down there?" and that question has taken us to the ocean's deepest trenches. Someone looked up at the moon and asked, "Is that really cheese?" so naturally, we built a rocket ship to go find out. Or something like that.

Lewis and Clark's journey began in St. Louis, a city now marked by the iconic Gateway Arch and known as the "Gateway to the West." In the same way, curiosity is the gateway to adventure. It's where every great journey begins.

But this kind of curiosity isn't reserved for history books or heroic expeditions. Curiosity is the gateway to *everyday adventure*. It's what turns routine into discovery. It's the difference between someone who walks into the same office, sits in the same cubicle, and dreads the same old day, and someone who enters with eyes wide open, eager to solve a problem, spark a new idea, or learn something meaningful about a coworker. Curiosity keeps us awake to the wonder all around us. It keeps us growing and it keeps us going.

CHILDLIKE WONDER

A few years ago, I took my daughter—or I should say my daughter took me—on a backyard adventure. We taped together two empty toilet paper rolls to make a pair of binoculars, and she grabbed a small notebook to start charting a map. But when we opened the back door, we weren't just stepping into the yard, we were stepping into a grand expedition.

Over the next thirty minutes, I watched her creativity and curiosity come alive. It pulled me in and she started to lead me out of my stuffy grown-up world with countless to-dos and into her wide-open haven of wonder. I tried my best to see through her eyes, resisting the adult urge to focus on overgrown weeds, common birds, and unfinished work projects, and instead marveling at her discoveries. With cardboard binoculars pressed to her face, she gasped at every "new" sight, eagerly handing them to me and pointing so I wouldn't miss it. Of course, those toilet paper roll binoculars didn't really make anything appear closer. But somehow, they did magnify life. That little backyard adventure helped me see the beauty of the world—and of that moment—a little more clearly.

Children are natural-born explorers. They seem to see the world through wonder-tinted glasses, where everything is new, exciting, and worth investigating. And there's a reason for that. As the early childhood development organization Zero to Three

> THOSE TOILET PAPER ROLL BINOCULARS DIDN'T REALLY MAKE ANYTHING APPEAR CLOSER. BUT SOMEHOW, THEY DID MAGNIFY LIFE.

puts it, "Babies are born learners, with a natural curiosity to figure out how the world works. Curiosity is the desire to learn. It is an eagerness to explore, discover and figure things out."[3] From the very beginning, we are wired for curiosity.

When I see rocks near a lake's shore, I don't think twice. When my young son sees the same rocks, he wonders (and asks), *"I wonder how far I can throw those rocks? How did these rocks get here? Did someone leave them here? Can it rain rocks? Should I wear a helmet in case it starts raining rocks? Can fish eat rocks? I'm going to throw a rock into the water to see if a fish will eat it."* Although we can both see the same rocks, his curiosity drives him to a much more engaging experience.

In his book, *Becoming Better Grownups,* Brad Montague (founder and creative mind behind *Kid President),* summed it up perfectly:

> "When we take time to see life with childlike wonder, we are reminded how life is relentlessly remarkable. I used to think

life was relentless and occasionally remarkable, but now I know better. Each day we're presented with an unending parade of wonders, should we not be too busy to notice…In all the everydayness of life, we forget the everythingness of life."[4]

A child's curiosity is a beautiful thing. They see the world in full color: vibrant, new, and alive. Around every corner is a fresh mystery, each one marked by a dozen floating question marks just waiting to be explored.

What's interesting is that as we grow older, our curiosity often fades. The more we think we know, the less we tend to seek. We settle in, comfortable with what's familiar, content with what we've already figured out. But children show us a better way. Their constant chorus of "Why?" may wear on our patience, but it leads us back to wonder. That persistent questioning opens doors to discovery. If we adopted even a fraction of that mindset, we'd uncover fresh meaning in the most familiar places: at work, in our routines, even in our relationships.

Throughout his ministry, Jesus often welcomed children, even when others saw them as a distraction. He went so far as to say, "Unless you turn from your sins and become like little children, you will never get into the Kingdom of Heaven. So anyone who becomes as humble as this little child is the greatest in the Kingdom of Heaven."[5]

Jesus wasn't calling us to immaturity, but to humility—to see the world with childlike faith, awe, and wonder. Children are unassuming, wide-eyed, and full of trust. Jesus invites us to recover that posture of wonder and curiosity.

TURN ON WONDER

As we enter adulthood, many of us lose that childlike wonder and begin to grow too accustomed to our surroundings, failing to notice the beauty all around us. Taylor Hughes, an entertainer and author of *The Road to Wonder*, said, "Wonder opens the door to possibility."[6] By turning on wonder in your everyday life, ordinary moments can become extraordinary, and you can begin to taste life to the fullest.

In order to turn on wonder, Hughes suggests making an appointment with your eight-year-old self. Step back and create space to look at your life through those younger eyes. What would stand out in your surroundings? Would your current worries feel as overwhelming or would your attention shift to the possibilities and wonder around you?

As a parent, I've spent a lot of time at parks. The moment we arrive at our kids' favorite playground, you can see the anticipation light up their faces. As soon as it's in sight, it's like they've been released from captivity. I look at a playground and see a bunch of plastic and metal that presents a thousand ways for my children to get hurt. But my kids? They see a thousand possibilities for fun, adventure, and imagination. Watching how they see the world helps me unlock a little wonder of my own.

A few years ago, my family took a trip to Orlando, Florida. My in-laws graciously watched our young daughter while my wife, her sister, and I spent a day at Disney's Hollywood Studios. The moment we stepped inside, something shifted. A wave of childlike wonder swept over us. Within minutes, a security guard yelled at us to stop running, but even that brief adulting reality check couldn't stop us from being filled with wonder. Our eyes bounced from one attraction to the next, soaking in the architecture and hidden details. For a full day, we felt like kids again.

> IF CURIOSITY IS THE GATEWAY TO ADVENTURE, THEN CHILDLIKE WONDER IS THE KEY THAT UNLOCKS IT.

But as we walked out of the park that night, I was struck with a thought: *Why don't I experience this kind of wonder in my everyday life?* Conviction settled in. I realized how often I rush past opportunities for awe without even noticing.

When we got home, I made a choice. I began to pay attention. The more I looked, the more I saw: butterflies overhead, our dog Kevin's tail wagging, the breeze in the trees. When you begin to prioritize wonder, even the ordinary starts to come alive.

I've always been fascinated by the story of Walt Disney and the world he set out to create. With every ride, movie, and detail, Disney has a way of awakening something inside us. But that shouldn't surprise us. As Walt once said, "We keep moving forward, opening up new doors and doing new things, because we're curious… and curiosity keeps leading us down new paths."[7]

Curiosity is the fuel that keeps us moving forward. And if curiosity is the gateway to adventure, then childlike wonder is the key that unlocks it.

WHY SO CURIOUS?

Some of the world's greatest discoveries began with one simple question: *Why?*

Take Sir Isaac Newton's theory of universal gravitation. During an outbreak of the bubonic plague, Cambridge University temporarily shut down, forcing Newton to return to his childhood home, Woolsthorpe Manor. It was there, in the quiet and stillness, that legend has it he observed an apple falling from a tree. Most people would have shrugged it off. But Newton paused and asked, *"Why does it fall straight down and not sideways or upward?"*[8]

What seemed like a childish question led to one of the most significant scientific breakthroughs in history. As financier Bernard Baruch once said, "Millions saw the apple fall, but Newton asked why."[9]

Wonder and curiosity made all the difference.

Lean into the life happening around you and don't be afraid to start asking "Why?" again and again. Your why's make you wise. A good string of questions won't just spark insight; it will keep you from becoming stagnant or stuck. As Ellen Parr said, "The cure for boredom is curiosity."[10]

If you're feeling bored or burned out, don't rush to escape your season. Get curious about it. What might God be trying to show you right where you are? Curiosity might not change your circumstances, but it will change how you see them. Just like Newton, you might discover something life-changing in the most ordinary moment.

When our lives are on autopilot, we are rarely able to see the intricate things that God is doing around us. When we allow God to grip our hearts with a sense of wonder and curiosity, we gain access to everyday adventure like never before. Curiosity allows us to lean in a little closer to the mundane and ordinary moments of our lives. Curiosity has a way of helping us experience more of life. Curiosity points us to the Creator and has a way of reminding us of the beauty all around us.

That's the power of curiosity. It can lead us back to God.

Curiosity invites us to explore the depths of God's power and love. One of the places I feel most connected to God is outdoors. Something about nature quiets my soul and shifts my focus back to him.

On a camping trip in Montana, I found myself standing on the edge of a cliff, overwhelmed by the beauty before me. Across the canyon, I spotted mountain goats scaling the impossibly steep rock face. I found myself asking, *"How can they even do that?"* That simple question turned into wonder. I realized their feet were divinely designed to grip the narrowest cracks in the cliffside. God created them for that very purpose and even made vegetation grow in unlikely places so they could eat. In that moment, I wasn't just admiring creation, I was being drawn closer to the Creator.

When we lived in New Jersey, our home sat on the edge of a quiet little town, where nights were truly dark. No city glow. No streetlights. One evening, as I took our dog outside, I couldn't help but pause because the stars were stunningly bright. I grabbed a hammock, wrapped Kinsley—two years old at the time—in a blanket, and we laid there staring up at the sky. She was mesmerized. I asked, "How do you think those stars got up there?" Without hesitation, she answered, "Jesus." Sure, that was her go-to answer for most things; but in that moment, it stopped me. Tears welled up in my eyes as I told her how God knows the number of stars in the sky and how that same God created and knows her, too.

Curiosity invites us into that kind of awe. It opens our eyes to the greatness of God and the depths of his love. That's exactly what Paul prayed for the early believers in Ephesus and it's my prayer for you, too:

> "And may you have the power to understand, as all God's people should, how wide, how long, how high, and how deep his love is. May you experience the love of Christ, though it is too great to understand fully. Then you will be made complete with all the fullness of life and power that comes from God."[11]

My prayer for you is that wonder would lead you to worship. That curiosity would stir your soul. That the everyday moments of your life would become sacred glimpses into the heart of a very big, very loving

God. That you would begin to see the world through a new lens—one of wonder and curiosity.

Let curiosity lead you to that kind of discovery. Take a moment right now to look around you. What grabs your attention? What sparks awe in your heart? Let it point you to our wonderful, loving, and endlessly creative God.

CURIOSITY'S DARKSIDE

Like most good things, curiosity has a darkside too. It can lead to awe, discovery, and growth; but without boundaries, it can also lead us into trouble. Curiosity has its dark side. I mean, it did kill the cat.

We've all seen it: a curious toddler sticking something in an outlet, a teenager pressing a red button labeled "Do not touch," or an adult clicking on a shady link in their email that promises a hefty inheritance from a Nigerian prince. (Yes, Americans still fall for that one to the tune of $700,000 a year.)[12]

Curiosity can open doors to wonder, but if we're not careful, it can also lead us down paths of regret. Historically, it has fueled both world-changing inventions and catastrophes. It has pushed explorers to the peak of Mount Everest; but it has also left more than 300 people on the side of the mountain.

> CURIOSITY ISN'T INHERENTLY GOOD OR BAD, BUT IT IS POWERFUL. IT CAN BE A SPARK FOR GROWTH, OR A GATEWAY TO TROUBLE.

Even in the Garden of Eden, it was curiosity that the serpent exploited. Eve didn't eat the fruit simply out of rebellion. She was curious. She wondered what she might be missing. That same unchecked curiosity still whispers to us today. Curiosity is powerful, but without discernment, it can become dangerous.

The world we live in is filled with enticing invitations and promises. The internet is filled with messages that promise happiness, fulfillment, and wealth with one click. When our curiosity runs wild, it can often lead us into situations that are difficult to get ourselves out of. As a teenage boy, it was curiosity that invited me into the trap of pornography that would hold me captive for years. What started as adolescent curiosity and wonder turned into a sin habit that was impossible to shake in my own power. That story is all too familiar in our world today.

So, is curiosity good or bad? The short answer is both. This is what Barnabas Piper said in his book, *The Curious Christian: How Discovering Wonder Enriches Every Part of Life*:

> "Proper curiosity about the world opens our eyes to the wiles of the world and provides the discernment we need to fight against them. Curiosity about God anchors us in God's strength as we learn more, seek more, and see more of him. Curiosity drives us to seek out truth and discern right from wrong. Curiosity isn't a dangerous trap; it's the thing God uses to make us wise so we can avoid the traps of sin and live freely for him."[13]

Curiosity about God is the anchor that keeps us fixed on him. The combination of curiosity and the truth found in God's Word help us navigate what is and isn't from him.

The adventures of Curious George have always left me a little conflicted. I was watching an episode with my kids recently, and as usual, George's curiosity led to chaos—spilled paint, broken dishes, and a trail of well-meaning destruction. And yet, by the end of the episode, his curiosity had also helped solve a mystery or fix a problem. It struck me: Curiosity isn't inherently good or bad, but it is powerful. It can be a spark for growth, or a gateway to trouble.

In our own lives, curiosity can be a tool that helps us see life in new ways or a trap that leads us down paths we were never meant to walk. The key is where we anchor it. When our curiosity is rooted in the God who created the universe, it becomes a catalyst for life to the fullest.

HOW TO SPARK CURIOSITY

Curiosity is the spark that lights the path to everyday adventure; but like any fire, it needs fuel. While wonder may come naturally to children, most of us find it harder to access in the middle of real life—between work deadlines, parenting chaos, school demands, and grocery runs. So how do we reignite it? How do we intentionally cultivate curiosity in the middle of our ordinary, overloaded days?

1. **Learn from a child's perspective.**
   If you're a parent, take time to intentionally observe your child. If not, find a non-creepy way to do this. I'd suggest asking to hang out with a friend who has kids over showing up at a random park or school. Listen to the way kids describe the world around them. Notice how their imaginations transform a playground into a mountain or a backyard into a castle. Ask them questions about what they see and think.

2. **Join in their imaginary world.**
   Don't just watch—play! Join them in whatever imaginary game they're playing. Jump from couch cushion to couch cushion while avoiding the scorching lava that imaginarily flows beneath your feet. Something remarkable happens when you step down from your adult perch and fully embrace play. Play reawakens wonder.

3. **See ordinary moments as if it's your first time.**
   In college, I became friends with a Vietnamese student named Khuong. One winter morning, he burst through our front door, eyes wide with joy, shouting, "It's snowing!" That same morning, I had grumbled at the forecast and dreaded scraping off my car. But for Khuong, it was magic because he had never seen snow before. We followed him outside and spent the morning playing like kids again. He made his first snow angel, built his first snowman, caught snowflakes on his tongue, and launched into his first-ever snowball fight. His joy was contagious! That morning reminded me how quickly wonder returns when we choose to see the familiar with fresh eyes.

   What if you looked into your spouse's eyes like it was the first time again? What if you smelled a flower with fresh wonder? Or ran your fingers through a dog's fur as if you'd never felt it before? Wonder would awaken and run wild in your heart.

   I recently watched a video of a young boy hearing his mother's voice for the first time through a new hearing device. His face lit up with pure joy and I instantly teared up. Why? Because for a moment, I imagined myself in his shoes. I closed my eyes and imagined hearing my mom's voice for the very first time—a voice I've taken for granted my whole life.

4. **Ask better questions.**
   Get in the habit of asking deeper, more thoughtful questions. Instead of "How was your day?" ask, "What surprised you today?" or "What made you smile?" Instead of asking, "What do you do for work?" ask, "What do you enjoy about your work?" Instead of asking, "Where are you from?" ask, "What was your favorite thing about the place you grew up?" Curiosity thrives in conversation when we move beyond surface-level talk. This applies to prayer too. Ask God why, how, and what if more often.

5. **Learn something new—just because.**
   Pick up a book outside your usual genre. Watch a documentary on something you know nothing about. Try a new recipe, art style, or language. Curiosity needs exercise, and novelty wakes up our brains. Even five minutes of purposeful learning per day builds a lifelong posture of curiosity. Lean into the moment you come across something unfamiliar.

6. **Embrace silence and solitude.**
   We often crowd out curiosity with noise. When we give ourselves moments of silence—on a walk, during chores, or in prayer—we create space for wonder to surface. Questions arise. Beauty breaks through. Curiosity grows in quiet soil. We must make a habit of eliminating the bombardment of distractions and noise in order to follow the prompts of curiosity that are bursting at the seams within us.

7. **Expect wonder.**
   Start each day with the anticipation that God might show you something beautiful—even in the most ordinary places. Ask God to open your eyes to what's already around you. Look for awe-inspir-

ing moments. Be ready to ask "why" when something doesn't make sense. And don't overlook the people you pass by because even strangers carry stories worth hearing. Curiosity is often the bridge between stranger and friend.

I'll never forget walking through downtown St. Louis with a group of friends when a man approached us to ask for help. Most of us politely smiled and kept walking. But my friend Sean stopped. He asked the man's name. He looked him in the eyes and saw him the way Jesus does. That moment of curiosity turned into a shared meal at a nearby restaurant and a conversation that ended with Sean praying for the man to know Christ.

Sean lives that way. He wakes up expecting God to lead him toward meaning and his curiosity helps him find it. Today, he and his wife serve as missionaries, using that same spirit to turn strangers into friends and friends into followers of Jesus.

Curiosity isn't just a personality trait; it's a habit, a rhythm we can cultivate. When we build curiosity into the fabric of our everyday lives, we train our eyes to see more clearly. We notice the good, pay attention to the beauty, and discover the presence of God right in the middle of the ordinary.

FIND THE GOOD AND FIND GOD

Cultivating curiosity is like stepping into a treasure hunt—not the kind filled with treasure maps and gold coins, but an everyday search for hidden goodness. It's the posture of someone determined to find beauty in the ordinary, joy in the routine, and meaning in the moments most people rush past.

When you live with curiosity, even a trip to the grocery store becomes an adventure. You might notice the elderly man in aisle seven who just wants someone to say hello. Or the teenager bagging groceries who's trying hard and just needs to hear, "You're doing great." You might think of the farmers responsible for harvesting your produce and develop a sense of gratitude.

Whether it's in your family, your workplace, your city, or your season, there's treasure to be found. You just need to look for it.

Finding the good might look like celebrating a small win at work that no one else noticed, cheering on a coworker's progress, or spotting potential in a project others wrote off. In your city, it might be chatting with a neighbor you've always passed by or supporting a local business run by someone chasing a dream. In your family, it could mean noticing a moment of growth in your child or pausing to appreciate a quiet act of love from your spouse. If you are single, it might simply mean embracing the freedom to explore new places, build meaningful friendships, and grow in ways you couldn't otherwise.

But this treasure hunt isn't just about discovering what's good. It's about discovering *God*. In his book *See the Good*, author Zach Windahl writes, "the more we give thanks to God, the more we see him moving in our lives."[14] Gratitude sharpens our vision. It slows us down long enough to notice the fingerprints of God in places we once rushed past.

That's where curiosity comes in.

When you live with curiosity, you start to ask deeper questions. You start to look beneath the surface of your life. You wonder, "Why am I here?" "What's really worth living for?" "Is there something more?" That kind of curiosity doesn't distance us from faith. It draws us toward it. I've seen this firsthand while being a part of Alpha, a space designed for people who are curious about life, purpose, and faith. There's no pressure, no sermon—just good food, honest conversation, and a chance to ask real questions in a judgment-free space.[15]

CURIOSITY ISN'T JUST A PERSONALITY TRAIT; IT'S A HABIT, A RHYTHM WE CAN CULTIVATE.

What amazes me every time is how God meets people right where they are—in their curiosity. I've seen skeptics become seekers and seekers become followers of Jesus, not because they got all the right answers, but because they finally felt safe enough to ask the right questions.

That's the power of curiosity. It helps us find what's good. It leads us to the people and places where joy and beauty live. And it leads us back to the God who wired us to wonder in the first place.

In *The Light in the Heart*, Roy T. Bennett said, "Enjoy every step you take. If you're curious, there is always something new to be discovered in the backdrop of your daily life."[16] You don't have to wait for your presidential invitation to explore a new uncharted territory like Lewis and Clark. Your daily life provides the backdrop needed for adventure.

You don't need a magnifying glass to cultivate curiosity in your everyday life, but you will need to start seeing life through a different lens. Just like a magnifying glass makes what you're looking at appear a little bit closer, to cultivate curiosity, you need to lean in a little closer to life around you.

Curiosity may have killed the cat, but it also scaled Mount Everest, walked on the moon, and sailed the ocean blue. Curiosity may just be the missing link between you and a life of everyday adventure. In your everyday life, curiosity can drive you to befriend a stranger, learn a new and helpful skill in your career, reconnect with your spouse, unearth new passions, and explore the depths of God's character, love, and grace.

Wake up tomorrow like it's the start of a great treasure hunt. Look for the good in your spouse, your kids, your job, your neighborhood, even your hardest circumstances. And as you do, don't be surprised when you stumble across something even greater—the God who's been with you all along.

Curiosity is the gateway to adventure.

TRAIL MARKERS

TRUE NORTH TAKEAWAY
Curiosity wakes us up to the wonder woven through our everyday lives. When we slow down enough to look closer, the ordinary becomes meaningful, the familiar becomes sacred, and we begin to see God's goodness everywhere.

REFLECTION STOPS
1. What is one ordinary place in your life that you've stopped noticing? What might you see if you looked at it with childlike eyes again?
2. Where do you feel bored, stuck, or on autopilot? What would happen if you approached that area with curiosity instead of resignation?
3. What is one small shift you can make this week to slow down enough to notice the wonder woven into your everyday world?

EVERYDAY ADVENTURE CHALLENGE: TINY TREASURE HUNT
Choose one ordinary place you'll be today—your kitchen, your drive to work, your office hallway, the grocery store, or your neighborhood sidewalk. Slow your pace just a little and move through it with fresh eyes.

1. **Notice five things you normally overlook.**
   This could be a sound, a color, a texture, a person's expression, a small act of kindness, a detail in creation, or something that simply makes you smile.

2. **Choose one "treasure" to pause with.**
   Take ten seconds to appreciate it. Ask yourself: Why did this stand out? What does it reveal about beauty, goodness, or God?

3. **Turn your treasure into gratitude.**
   Say a quick thank you—to a person if appropriate, or to God in prayer. Let that moment anchor your attention and joy.

You'll be surprised how much life you find when you start looking for it.

If you're ready for more practical steps like this, check out the Everyday Adventure Challenge—a simple weekly challenge designed to help you practice intentionality and embrace the adventure in your everyday life. You can learn more at **everydayadventurebook.com**.

SIX
Become a Lifelong Learner

"Anyone who stops learning is old, whether at twenty or eighty.
Anyone who keeps learning stays young."[1]
Henry Ford

Not long ago, I was invited to be the guest reader in my daughter's kindergarten classroom. I walked into the room with my son, Summit, and one of our favorite children's books in my hand. After reading the book, I sat down to answer five questions from a room full of wide-eyed five-year-olds. They asked me about my favorite color, my go-to pizza toppings, and my favorite sports team.

But as I looked around the classroom, I was transported back. The cubbies, the alphabet on the wall and curiosity in the air—it was all still there. And in that moment, I realized how much we lose when we leave these places behind.

Let's get a little nostalgic. Do you remember your kindergarten classroom? If yours was anything like mine, it had a row of cubbies with names above them, jackets hanging inside like little trophies of independence. The desks popped open to reveal pencils, glue sticks, and treasures only a five-year-old would value. The walls were bursting with color, the alphabet was stapled proudly above the whiteboard, and the air smelled unmistakably like a mixture of Elmer's Glue, Crayola markers, and magic.

But as we progressed through school, something began to fade. The colors dulled. The inspiration waned. The cubbies disappeared along with the story corner. The shelves once filled with toys became filled with books about chemistry and geometry. Desks became rigid, books got heavier, and learning started to feel less like a playground and more like a pressure cooker. The joy of discovery was slowly replaced with the stress of performance and by the time we graduated, many of us unintentionally packed up our appetite to learn and left it behind with our last textbook.

This is the real loss.

Learning was never meant to end with a diploma. Somewhere along the way, many of us swapped curiosity for certainty. We stopped asking questions and started clinging to what we already knew. But here's the truth: The most adventurous people I know aren't the ones with the most credentials; they're the ones who never stopped learning. Life is their classroom and everyone and everything is a teacher.

To live a life of everyday adventure, you must see life as the classroom it really is. The walls are no longer square, and the teachers no longer stand at the front of the room. They're all around you, disguised as conversations, challenges, parenting moments, or even mistakes.

The question is, *"Are we going to show up for class or are we going to keep playing hooky?"*

What does being a lifelong learner look like? I believe it looks like seeing every day as an opportunity to grow, every place you enter as a classroom, and every person as a teacher. Being a lifelong learner means choosing growth long after the report cards stop coming. It's about consistently committing ourselves to growth in every aspect of life—in your career, your relationships, your faith, your hobbies—even your failures. Lifelong learners don't get bored. They don't settle. They stay curious and keep moving forward.

CREATING A LEARNING ENVIRONMENT

I have a lot of friends who are teachers. They are some of the most selfless, dedicated people I know. Whenever I get a chance, I love asking them, "Why did you want to become a teacher?" Their eyes always light up. Most respond with something about their passion for education, investing in the next generation, or creating a space where kids feel safe and seen. I know that teaching is not always a glamorous job, and it is definitely not fairly compensated. That is one of the reasons teachers who care deeply are so special.

One summer evening, my wife and I visited a friend who teaches elementary school. It was one of her last nights before school started, and her living room had been transformed into what could only be described as an adult craft explosion. She was joyfully cutting, taping, gluing, and prepping materials for her classroom. We found out later that she paid for most of the materials and decorations with her own money. She was invested in the details because she was invested in her students, and she was committed to creating an environment that would help them learn.

> SOMEWHERE ALONG THE WAY, MANY OF US SWAPPED CURIOSITY FOR CERTAINTY. WE STOPPED ASKING QUESTIONS AND STARTED CLINGING TO WHAT WE ALREADY KNEW.

Teachers understand the importance of creating a space for students to learn, grow, and thrive. Not only do they fill their room with decorations, posters, and materials that promote curiosity and learning, but they also meticulously eliminate distractions and any roadblocks to learning.

As lifelong learners aiming to live a life of everyday adventure, we must aim to create an environment for learning and growth in our daily lives. You don't need to plaster motivational quotes on your walls (unless that's your thing), but you do need to pay attention to the space around you: the mental, emotional, and spiritual environments you live in every day. Are they helping you grow? Or are they filled with distractions, noise, and clutter that choke curiosity?

To become a lifelong learner, we must first become aware of some common weeds that prevent us from learning and ultimately pursuing a life of everyday adventure. In *The Key to Everything,* Matt Keller lists pride, fear, and insecurity as roadblocks to teachability. Each one of these is a weed that, if left unattended, will stunt our growth, and push us in the direction of complacency and stagnation. We must first become ruthless in our attempt to uproot them from our lives.

Weed #1: Pride

Pride is mentioned over fifty times in Scripture, and Jesus speaks directly to its danger in the lives of his followers. Some of his strongest rebukes were aimed at the Pharisees because their pride blinded them to the truth. Pride isn't just arrogance; it's a stubborn commitment to our will over God's. Sometimes it shows up in outright defiance, but other times it takes root quietly through complacency and stagnation. This passive pride can be just as destructive, convincing us that we've arrived, dulling our hunger to grow, and tuning out the wisdom of others. Scripture leaves no ambiguity: God takes pride seriously.

> "But he gives us more grace. That is why Scripture says,
> 'God opposes the proud but shows favor to the humble.'"[2]

Pride chokes out help from others, including God. Leadership expert John Maxwell puts it this way: "Pride deafens us to the advice and warnings of those around us."[3] It clings tightly to what we know and the way things have always been done. Prideful people often find new ideas, especially when they come from someone "less qualified," more annoying than helpful. I saw this in myself during my time in college ministry. Slowly and subtly, pride began to take root. As a campus pastor in my mid-twenties, I grew overly confident in my way of doing ministry. I can only imagine how difficult I was to work with at times. Eventually, through some honest conversations with trusted people, I came to see how my pride was stunting my growth, our team's growth, and ultimately, the ministry's effectiveness.

> A HUMBLE HEART MAKES ROOM FOR NEW IDEAS, WELCOMES NEW PERSPECTIVES, AND KEEPS YOUR LIFE FERTILE GROUND FOR LEARNING.

If you want to remain teachable and open to growth no matter your season, you must pursue humility. Humility honors others and the wisdom they bring, regardless of age, background, position, or perspective. It doesn't mean putting yourself down; it simply means lifting others up. A humble heart makes room for new ideas, welcomes new perspectives, and keeps your life fertile ground for learning.

Weed #2: Fear
Fear, like pride, can quietly choke out our ability to grow. Not all fear is bad. Some fear is protective. A healthy fear of a Midwest thunderstorm will get you off the golf course and into shelter. But fear of change, failure, or the unknown? That kind of fear keeps you stuck. It's the voice that says, "What if this doesn't work?" or "What if I'm not good enough?" and convinces you to stay put when God is calling you to move forward. Matt Keller writes, "Change is inevitable. To reach your full potential in life, you must be willing to embrace it. But change inevitably brings risk and its next-door neighbor, fear."[4]

Fear keeps us anchored to the familiar, even when the familiar is no longer fruitful. It convinces us that comfort is safer than obedience. But spiritual growth requires movement—often through discomfort, risk, and even rejection. Has fear taken root in your heart, causing you to resist a necessary step forward? Maybe it's fear of failure, criticism, or simply losing control. Whatever its form, fear will always offer you safety; but it will never offer you fullness. And fullness is what God has in mind.

Weed #3: Insecurity
Another weed that often grows in the soil of our lives and quietly chokes out our potential is insecurity. Like a persistent fly buzzing around your head, insecurity swarms the mind with lies: *You're not good enough. Not smart enough. Not qualified enough.* It's that nagging "less than" feeling we've all experienced. Insecurity wears many faces: inferiority, imposter syndrome, self-doubt, or unworthiness. It often takes root in comparison, and when left unchecked, it will hold you back from stepping into the life God created you for.

Have you ever walked into a room and thought, *"I don't belong here"*? I have. While working for a non-profit in the Philadelphia area, I was tasked with planning a large-scale Christmas event alongside leaders from city government and major community organizations. I felt completely out of place, underqualified, inexperienced, and like I had nothing to offer. But in that moment of doubt, I sensed God whisper, "I have you right where I want you. Just be yourself and learn from those around you."

That simple reminder shifted everything. I stopped trying to prove myself and started asking questions. I leaned into others' expertise instead of being intimidated by it, and the event turned out better than we could have imagined. I also walked away with mentors who continue to encourage me. Insecurity could have kept me quiet and closed off, but humility opened the door to growth.

Be ready when insecurity creeps in. Matt Keller writes, "One of the most empowering strategies for fighting off feelings of insecurity is to remind yourself that you are in process. In other words, you're not there yet, and that's okay."[5] You don't need to have it all figured out to stand confidently where you are. Life is a journey and insecurity, if left unchecked, will try to convince you to stay stuck. But you have nothing to prove, and no one to prove it to. Just keep showing up, stay teachable, and let God do what only he can.

Just as a great teacher shapes the classroom to inspire learning, we must shape the environment of our lives to stay teachable. That means recognizing and relentlessly uprooting the weeds of pride, fear, and insecurity that silently choke our growth and stifle our potential.

REDEFINING TEACHER

Have you ever had a teacher who left a deep, lasting impact on your life? Who comes to mind? What made them so unforgettable?

I've had several incredible teachers, but for some reason, my fifth-grade teacher, Mrs. Hoffman, always rises to the top. It's been over two decades since I sat in her classroom, but I still remember the way she made us feel seen, celebrated, and believed in. I remember her patience, her warmth, and the way she handled hard moments with grace and strength. One day, a student in our class was being picked on. Mrs. Hoffman stood up for him firmly, but what struck me most was how she also embraced the student doing the bullying. She didn't just correct behavior. She saw the potential in both of them.

That's what great teachers do. They refuse to let students settle for less than they're capable of. They challenge, encourage, inspire, and believe. They pull the best out of us even before we know it's there. They lead with conviction and compassion, making learning both meaningful and fun.

You might be thinking, *"Great teachers like that are rare."* I disagree.

Great teachers are all around us. We just have to learn to recognize them.

To become a lifelong learner, you must redefine what "teacher" means to you. In *The Key to Everything*, Matt Keller writes, "The ultimate goal is to see everyone, everywhere, every day as a teacher you can learn from."[6]

That's what it means to build a lifestyle of teachability. The classroom is everywhere. If you're paying attention, every person, every moment, and every season can become your teacher.

I am always amazed at how much I can learn from the most unlikely sources. My dog, Kevin, has taught me how to make someone feel special and valued. Stay with me. If you have a dog, you get it. I can leave the house for one minute to get the mail, but when I return, he greets me as if I've been gone for months. There is something about a dog greeting you at the door that makes you feel like a million bucks.

> IF YOU'RE PAYING ATTENTION, EVERY PERSON, EVERY MOMENT, AND EVERY SEASON CAN BECOME YOUR TEACHER.

Jimmy Fallon has taught me about charisma and being fully present and engaged with the person you are with. He has a way of authentically making every guest on his show feel like they are the most interesting person on the planet.

A stranger named Chris who sat next to me in seat 21F on an airplane from Alaska to Minnesota, taught me about joy and the beauty of kingdom relationships… *for six hours.* By the time we landed, my neck was sore, but my heart was full.

A sunrise teaches me that a new day rises along with new opportunities. It serves as my daily reminder to stop dwelling on the past and to open my eyes to everything a new day brings.

Many of life's greatest lessons don't come from books, classrooms, or conference stages. They come from the little humans sitting in your backseat or spilling juice on the kitchen floor. My three kids have become some of the most surprising and profound teachers I've ever had.

In fact, I should start carrying a notebook around when I'm with them, not just to jot down their hilarious one-liners but to capture the unexpected wisdom they drop on a regular Tuesday.

One morning when my daughter was two, we were on a daddy-daughter donut date at a nearby grocery store. Our plan was to run in, grab some donuts and a coffee before heading to the park. From the time we got to the checkout counter until the time we walked out the door, she made three new friends. She cheerily greeted the woman checking us out, insisting on showing off her Elsa doll. When the computer froze up (pun fully intended), my precious two-year-old assured the woman saying, "It's fine!" When we got to our next checkout counter, the new clerk gave Kinsley four stickers, which made her very excited. As we stood in line for my coffee, she befriended the girl behind us in line, giving her one of her stickers and asking if she would like to dance with her. Kinsley's new friend spun her in circles as they danced. When we got our coffee, she made me hold her things, and then she ran back to her new friend to give her a big hug around the leg. She was teaching me about being an easy friend. She made friends with more strangers in fifteen minutes than some people do in fifteen years. I want to be more like her when I grow up.

IDENTIFY YOUR TEACHERS

Who are the everyday teachers already around you? Who in your life could you intentionally begin learning from?

The truth is that our teachers aren't limited to professors or mentors, or even people. If we're willing to pay attention, people, pets, nature, and even life's interruptions can become some of our greatest instructors. Wisdom is everywhere, but only the curious and teachable will find it.

Being a lifelong learner means choosing not to coast through life with your head down. It means living with eyes wide open and a heart ready to receive. Complacency walks past the moment. Curiosity stops, leans in, and asks, *"What can I learn from this?"*

The best learners aren't necessarily the smartest people in the room. They're the ones most tuned in to what life is trying to teach them. So take a look around.

A lifelong learner can lean into every experience, every success, every failure, and every relationship. In the wake of success, we can ask, "Why was I successful? What paved the way for this success?" In the aftermath of failure, we must ask, "How can I allow this failure to shape me for the better? What must I do to not end up in this place again?"

In *The Divine Mentor*, pastor and author Wayne Cordeiro writes, "If you can figure out how to learn from the bad as well as from the good, you'll learn twice as much in life. That's why God put into the Bible raw, unedited accounts of men and women behaving both wisely and foolishly."[7] We aren't limited to our own experiences. Why learn everything the hard way when we can learn from those who've gone before us? That's why I love reading, especially Scripture. Through stories of David, Paul, Rahab, and Moses, we gain mentors for life.

One of the greatest habits you can form is reading the Bible daily. It's filled with teachers—real people whose lives, both triumphant and tragic, speak truth across generations. But more than that, the Bible is the living, infallible Word of God. It is the ultimate standard by which all other lessons are measured. When Scripture becomes the core of your life's curriculum, you gain the wisdom to discern which voices are worth listening to. You can learn from anyone, but not everyone is teaching the right thing.

When I was in college, I would ask upperclassmen which professors to take and which to avoid. Why? Because I wanted the right guidance for the degree I was pursuing. In life, my goal isn't a diploma. It's a full, meaningful, abundant life in Christ. The Bible points the way. But I still must stay alert, because If I'm willing to learn, the right teachers are all around me.

A STUDENT OF JESUS

There is one teacher that stands out from all the rest—Jesus. Yes, Jesus is far more than just a teacher. Of course, he is our Savior, our Redeemer, the miracle worker, the Son of God, and our friend; but that doesn't take away the fact that he is our *Teacher.*

Those who followed Jesus often referred to Jesus as *rabbi,* or *teacher.* From the onset of his earthly life, Jesus was more than a religious teacher simply teaching the way to Heaven. *He was the way.* The disciples were not handed a stack of textbooks to study; they were presented with a person to observe and follow. Jesus was his own curriculum.

The word *disciple* didn't originate with Christianity. In Jesus' day, it was a common term that meant learner, pupil, or student. To be someone's disciple was to study their life up close—to follow them, observe them, and imitate their way of living. That's exactly what the first followers of Jesus did. They walked with him, listened to him, and watched how he treated people, constantly learning along the way. In his classic book *The Master Plan of Evangelism*, theologian and author Dr. Robert Coleman writes, "Having called his men, Jesus made a practice of being with them. This was the essence of his training program—just letting his disciples follow him."[8] It was in his presence that they learned everything they needed to know.

> JESUS WAS MORE THAN A RELIGIOUS TEACHER SIMPLY TEACHING THE WAY TO HEAVEN. HE WAS THE WAY.

The same invitation is extended to each one of us. We are invited to walk with Jesus, observing his teachings and imitating his way of living. In *Practicing the Way*, author and pastor John Mark Comer summarizes the aim of being an apprentice to Jesus with three goals: be with Jesus, become like Jesus, and do what he would do if he were you. Simply put, discipleship to Jesus is learning from Jesus. Being an apprentice to Jesus is to model all of life after him.

Most of Jesus' followers weren't standout religious scholars. They were fishermen, tax collectors, and everyday people. After Jesus' resurrection and ascension, his followers began spreading his message boldly, which caught the attention of the religious elite.

> "When they saw the courage of Peter and John and realized that they were *unschooled, ordinary men*, they were astonished and took note that *these men had been with Jesus*."

These "unschooled, ordinary men" were turning the world upside down and the defining factor wasn't their education or status but their proximity to Jesus. Being with Jesus had changed them. And it can change you and me too.

Dr. Robert Coleman described them as "impulsive, temperamental, easily offended, and prejudiced toward their environment"—hardly the ideal candidates for world-changing impact. But they were willing to learn. And though the process was messy and slow, their lives began to look more like their teacher's. That's the power of walking closely with Jesus. It transforms ordinary people and prepares them for the adventure of a lifetime.

That's the point. A life of everyday adventure cannot be unlocked if we are unwilling to give attention to what is happening around us, especially to Jesus. John Mark Comer commented, "The mind is the portal to the soul, and what you fill your mind with will shape the trajectory of your character. In the end, your life is no more than the sum of what you gave your attention to."[9] The question is: *What are you giving your attention to?*

Every single day is a fresh invitation to apprentice under Jesus; to walk with him, learn from him, and be shaped by his presence. It begins in prayer, simply talking to God and making space to listen in the stillness of a quiet moment and through the truth of his Word. One prayer I try to pray each morning is, "God, what do You want me to notice today, and what do You want me to do?" And as I move through the day, I often ask, "What would Jesus do if he were in my shoes right now?"

Living this way has proven to be an adventure.

In your quest to embrace a life of everyday adventure and to become a lifelong learner, start by becoming a student of Jesus. He is one teacher that will always get rave reviews from every student that chooses to learn from him.

THE PRICE OF ADMISSION

Learning isn't cheap. Just ask any college graduate staring down their student loan balance. The average cost of college in the U.S. is over $35,000 per year, and that number has tripled in the last two decades[10]. If you want to learn, you need to be willing to pay the price.

The same is true for becoming a lifelong learner. It may not drain your bank account, but it will likely cost you something even more valuable: *your comfort.* True growth demands humility, courage, and a willingness to confront insecurity. It requires us to let go of what's familiar in exchange for what's forming us.

There is no shortcut to transformation. If you want to step into the life God is calling you to live, you'll need to release the grip on life as it is. The price of admission isn't always measured in dollars, but it will always cost you something. Here are some of the real price tags of learning:

1. **Comfort**

   Growth almost always starts where comfort ends. Whether it's having a hard conversation, facing insecurity, or stepping into the unknown, learning stretches us beyond what feels easy.

   As a parent, it's easier to raise my voice and assert control when my kids misbehave. But I've learned that doing so can rob me of the opportunity to patiently invest in their growth. The cost of learning patience? A few extra moments and a deep breath—but it's worth every second.

2. **Time**

   Learning takes time to reflect, engage, and practice new habits. Whether it's striking up a conversation with a stranger or picking up a new skill to connect with someone in your life, learning demands your calendar's attention. It takes time to reflect each day on what God is teaching you. It takes time to grow.

3. **Emotional Energy**

   Another common price tag is emotional energy. Coasting through life requires the least amount of energy. Allowing God to teach you a new way to respond to hurt in your life comes with an emotional cost. Learning how to forgive and rebuild a relationship with a loved one has a cost. Learning how to say no to good things so you can say yes to the best things has a cost.

4. **Finances**

   Sometimes learning really does cost money. I've spent years setting aside part of my budget for books, conferences, online courses, and coffee with mentors. Whether I'm investing in parenting resources, theology, minimalism, or leadership, those dollars have helped shape who I've become.

The price of growth may feel high, but the cost of not growing is even greater.

Stagnation can rob us of restored relationships, meaningful opportunities, and the future God has for us. A relationship might be restored if you're willing to learn humility and forgiveness. A new, purpose-filled career may become a reality if you embrace discomfort and step through inconvenient doors. God may be inviting you into more than you think, but you'll never know if you're not open to growing.

Choosing not to grow is one of the most expensive decisions you can make.

SET THE COURSE

Like any great adventure, the journey of becoming a lifelong learner calls for both direction and flexibility. We need a map to give a sense of where we're going as well as the curiosity and courage to embrace the unexpected turns along the way. Like we discussed earlier, wise travelers don't just wander aimlessly; they chart a course with intention. They ask, "What do I need to learn to get where I believe God is leading me?"

Just like a syllabus helps a student navigate the path to mastering a subject, a learning map can help us stay focused in our pursuit of a full, meaningful life in Christ. It provides clarity, purpose, and perspective—not rigid structure, but helpful guidance. Because while the destination matters, so does how we grow along the way.

At the start of each new year, I set aside intentional time to reflect on the past and prayerfully look ahead. This rhythm helps me take inventory of where I am and realign with where I sense God is leading me next.[11] One of the core practices I've built into that space is curating a reading list for the year ahead. Through prayer and reflection, I ask, *"God, what do you want to teach me this year? In what ways are you calling me to grow?"*

It was during one of my year-end reflection practices that God opened my eyes to how hurried and overloaded my life had become. I was doing good things, but I was running on empty. The pace was affecting my health, my marriage, and my family. In that sacred moment of clarity, I began to chart a new course. I rearranged my schedule, made space for rest, and sought out wisdom. That's when I stumbled upon *The Ruthless Elimination of Hurry* by John Mark Comer, cracking open a new way of living and introduced me to voices that would deeply shape my journey.

I had found my syllabus—a learning path rooted in prayer, Scripture, and wise mentors. And over time, it reshaped me.

What might God want to teach you in this season? I challenge you to carve out a few hours this week to pause, reflect, and ask, "God, what do I need to learn to become who You've created me to be?" With his guidance, set a course. Pay attention to the breadcrumbs he provides through books, podcasts, conversations, and mentors, and stay open to divine detours. They often lead to the best adventures.

Lifelong learners don't grow by accident. They pursue it on purpose.

Where is God leading you right now?

What do you need to learn to follow him there?

If you want to live a life of everyday adventure, you must reject complacency and embrace a rhythm of learning. Your pursuit of learning isn't just for you. It's for the people you love, the calling you carry, and the story God is still writing through your life.

TRAIL MARKERS

TRUE NORTH TAKEAWAY
A life of everyday adventure grows in teachable soil. When you stay curious, uproot pride, fear, and insecurity, and learn from every person and season, you create the kind of humble, open heart God can shape and lead.

REFLECTION STOPS
1. Where do you see pride, fear, or insecurity showing up in your life right now? How might each one be quietly choking your growth?
2. What are you giving your attention to most consistently right now (news, social media, work, hobbies, Scripture, prayer)? How is that shaping who you're becoming?
3. Who are the everyday teachers already around you—people, kids, coworkers, mentors, even pets or interruptions? Identify one, and name what they're teaching you right now. How could you become more intentional about learning from them?

EVERYDAY ADVENTURE CHALLENGE: CREATE A LEARNING MAP
Set aside 30–60 minutes this week to chart a simple "learning map" for your next 3–6 months.

1. **Start with two questions:**
   God, what do You want to teach me in this season?
   Where do I most need to grow to become who You've created me to be?

2. **Identify 3–5 learning tools in the areas you sense God highlighting.**
   These could be books, podcasts or sermons, a mentor or friend you can learn from, a course or class, or a section of Scripture to study deeply.

3. **Write them down like a mini syllabus.**
   Keep it simple. No pressure. You're not creating homework; you're creating direction.

4. **Pick a start date and begin with the first step on your map.**
   This is your personalized route toward growth—a way to stay curious, stay teachable, and stay aligned with where God is leading you.

If you're ready for more practical steps like this, check out the Everyday Adventure Challenge—a simple weekly challenge designed to help you practice intentionality and embrace the adventure in your everyday life. You can learn more at **everydayadventurebook.com**.

SEVEN
Ditch Your Comfort Zone

"A comfort zone is a beautiful place, but nothing ever grows there."[1]
John Assaraf

In college, I was invited to be part of an improv comedy team through our campus ministry. At first, we hosted small events called H.Joy, filled with ridiculous improv games and spontaneous sketches, all in front of about 200 of our fellow students. Over time, those gatherings grew. What started as a small crowd of familiar faces turned into one of the biggest outreach events on our campus. Eventually, we packed out our university's largest auditorium, with over 1,000 students crammed in shoulder to shoulder, ready for a night of laughter and unexpected moments.

Everything in me wanted to say "no" when I was first invited. Performing on a stage and making up skits on the fly was *way* outside of my comfort zone. I wasn't a theater kid. I didn't think of myself as the funniest person in the room. I'd never done anything like this before. But something happened when I stepped out of my comfort zone and onto the stage. I found joy—not just in making people laugh, but in showing up fully, taking a risk, and discovering there was more in me than I thought. And I would've missed all of it had I stayed in my seat.

Our ridiculous improv act grew on campus, and we eventually had the opportunity to take the show on the road. We performed at other universities, conferences, and events, sharing laughter and chaos with crowds well beyond our own. It was surreal, hilarious, and wildly outside my comfort zone.

But it was also where something else started.

H.Joy is where my wife, Taylor, and I became friends. She was on the team, too. Before we ever started dating, we spent hours creating skits, talking in absurd accents, and laughing until we cried. In that space of creativity, risk, and unfiltered joy, a real friendship formed—one that would eventually grow into something much deeper.

All of it—the growth, the joy, even meeting my future wife—came because I said yes to something uncomfortable.

When's the last time you let yourself fully step out of your comfort zone?

IN THE (COMFORT) ZONE

You don't have to look far to see that our culture values comfort. From the coffee shop I'm sitting in, I see ads promising deeper sleep with a new mattress, more room in a luxury SUV, and a retirement plan that claims to land you on any beach you choose. We're drawn to comfort and marketers know it. They feed our desire for ease and sell us the dream of a life without friction.

The gravitational pull of culture is always toward comfort and convenience. We get our groceries delivered and pre-order coffee just to avoid standing in line. But comfort isn't the real problem—complacency is.

Complacency is the quiet villain that poses as rest but slowly robs you of purpose. It uses convenience as a leash and convinces you to settle for less than what God has for you. The danger isn't comfort itself. It's never leaving your comfort zone.

And without discomfort, you'll never taste the adventure God made you for.

Our pursuit of an easy life often causes us to miss the best parts of it. In our culture's obsession with minimizing pain, we've also minimized our potential for growth. At the first sign of discomfort, we retreat to our comfort zones, searching for a quick fix. We'd rather send a text than make a call. Instead of reading, we binge Netflix. We skip the effort of cooking a healthy meal and opt for fast food, or more often, we tap an app and have it placed on our doorstep. Discomfort is avoided at all costs, but in doing so, we forfeit the transformation it brings.

Staying in your comfort zone impacts every area of your life: your health, relationships, career, and most significantly, your faith. That's because your spiritual life sits at the center of who you are. It shapes how you relate to others, how you engage with the world, and how you respond to challenges. When we settle for comfort, our spiritual growth stalls. Pastor and author Craig Groeschel puts it plainly: "You can never fulfill your calling in your comfort zone."[2] The comfort zone may feel safe, but it's a breeding ground for complacency—not for calling, not for conviction, and certainly not for the kind of bold faith that leads to everyday adventure.

OUR PURSUIT OF AN EASY LIFE OFTEN CAUSES US TO MISS THE BEST PARTS OF IT.

From the safety of our comfort zones, we will never share about Jesus with a co-worker. We will never pray for someone in public. We will never give generously to meet a need in our community. Discomfort is a prerequisite to spiritual growth.

When I was in high school, some students from my youth group went on a mission trip to Spain where they spent a week taking turns perching themselves on top of a red box in the city square, preaching to bystanders. They didn't return to our youth group alone. They brought the red box back with them. This group of students, now filled with a new conviction for evangelism, took to the streets of our hometown to share the gospel with anyone who could hear them.

They invited me to join them, and I made every excuse not to. *"I have baseball practice. I work that day. I promised my grandma I'd alphabetize her spice rack."* I would have rather been stuffed inside that red box than stand on top of it. I was afraid. Afraid of embarrassing myself. Afraid of not knowing what to say. Afraid someone I actually knew would hear me.

Eventually, I caved and I joined them. We parked and rolled our red box to the busiest, most central street corner we could find. I would have preferred to set it up on a deserted island. A few of my friends went first, hopping up on the box and sharing short gospel messages. Then came my turn. My heart pounded like a bass drum as I stepped up, legs trembling, voice shaking, and preached a three-minute message about God's love. No one booed. No tomatoes flew. Revival didn't break out in the streets, but something did happen *in me.* Something shifted.

When I stepped on to that red box, my faith felt more alive than ever. I found myself atop the red box a few more times that summer, growing in confidence and conviction each time. That summer, we prayed with several people who made decisions to follow Jesus and prayed with several others for healing. Since that summer, I have stepped onto stages hundreds of times to boldly proclaim God's love to thousands of people. But first, my shaky legs reluctantly stepped onto a red box to preach my very first message to a group of fifteen bystanders just trying to get to lunch.

Life to the fullest requires making hard decisions to push yourself past the place of comfort and ease. Your first step may not be onto a red box in downtown, but I can guarantee your first step won't be your last. Getting beyond your comfort zone and into the abundant life God is offering requires a first hard step. Adventure requires action.

THE EDGE OF BREAKTHROUGH

One of the key characters in the story of God and his people is a man named Abraham. God chose Abraham to be the patriarch of his people. But before God could do something great through Abraham, he asked him to do something deeply uncomfortable: *leave everything familiar behind.* No map. No destination details. Just a simple instruction—"Go to the land I will show you."[3] That's it.

God didn't give Abraham all the answers. He gave him an invitation.

And Abraham said yes.

Abraham's willingness to step out of his comfort zone became the launching point for a story that would change history. He didn't know where he was going, but he trusted who was leading him. And because of that, God was able to fulfill his promise: to build a people who would bless the world.

Obedience and comfort rarely go hand in hand. Sometimes the only way to step into God's purpose is to first step into the unknown.

The same invitation is extended to us as well. Life to the fullest begins where your comfort zone ends. If we choose to stay where we are comfortable, we will not be able to say yes to some of the best God has to offer. In fact, we won't even hear the invitation.

In the spring of 2018, my wife and I started to sense that God was moving us in a new direction. We had an unexplainable feeling that our time in Fargo was coming to an end. What was troubling was that I loved my job as a campus missionary and deeply loved the community God had placed us in; and to top it all off, my wife and I were expecting our first child. As we prayed, we felt even more strongly that God was calling us beyond our comfort zone. About a year later, we packed up our lives and moved across the country, leaving behind everything familiar.

On the eve of our cross-country move, I tossed and turned all night. Everything was packed, the vehicles were loaded, and the U-haul was in the driveway. There was nothing left to do. The next morning, I'd wake up and hit the road on an epic journey. I needed rest, but sleep was nowhere to be found.

You've probably been there. The night before a big move, a final exam, or a first date. Anticipation and anxiety join forces, and adrenaline keeps you wide awake. Right before a new chapter begins, our minds race with reflection and imagination. We replay what brought us here and wonder what's ahead. That's life on the edge of breakthrough.

The edge of breakthrough is where anticipation turns into courageous action or cowardly retreat. We either charge the hill or shrink back into our comfort zone. But let's be clear: The path of least resistance is also the path of least abundance. If we stay safe, we risk missing the full, rich, and satisfying life God invites us to live.

Abraham's obedience set a path into motion that would echo for generations. That path led him to cradle his miracle son, Isaac, at age 100. It led him to an altar he built with his own hands, where he prepared to offer that same son in obedience, only to discover God had already provided a ram in the thicket. That path led his descendants through both blessing and hardship; from wandering in unfamiliar lands to centuries of slavery in Egypt. It led to Moses, a de-

> OBEDIENCE AND COMFORT RARELY GO HAND IN HAND. SOMETIMES THE ONLY WAY TO STEP INTO GOD'S PURPOSE IS TO FIRST STEP INTO THE UNKNOWN.

scendant of Abraham, returning to the land where he was once an outlaw to deliver God's people. It led the Israelites to the edge of the Red Sea, where God parted the waters and made a way where there was none.

But before seas split and miracles unfolded, Abraham stood at the edge of breakthrough and stepped out of his comfort zone.

OPPOSITION OR OPPORTUNITY

Decades after Abraham took his first obedient step toward the land God promised, his descendants stood on the edge of that very promise. Moses had sent twelve spies to explore the land God had pledged to Abraham generations earlier.[4] This mission wasn't just about strategy; it was about preparation. They were on the edge of breakthrough.

The land Abraham had only imagined was now in sight. But when the spies returned, ten of them were paralyzed by fear. Though they had witnessed God's power firsthand, they caved at the sight of giants and claimed, "We seemed like grasshoppers in our own eyes." They let fear dictate the narrative.

Two of the spies, Caleb and Joshua, saw the same giants but also remembered the same God. They tore their clothes in grief and declared:

> "The land we traveled through and explored is a wonderful land! And if the Lord is pleased with us, he will bring us safely into that land and give it to us. It is a rich land flowing with milk and honey. Do not rebel against the Lord, and don't be afraid of the people of the land. They are only helpless prey to us! They have no protection, but the Lord is with us! Don't be afraid of them!"[5]

But the people listened to fear instead of faith. They walked away from the adventure of a lifetime and missed their moment. Of the entire generation present that day, only Caleb and Joshua would live to step into the promise. While fear disqualified the rest, their faith carried them forward.

Ten of the spies saw only opposition. Caleb and Joshua saw opportunity—a moment for God to show up. They weren't inherently braver than the others. They simply had a clearer lens, one shaped by God's promises and power. They had a more accurate perspective of what was really happening. While the ten saw towering walls and called them impenetrable, Caleb and Joshua said, *"They have no protection."* What made the difference? Caleb and Joshua's final plea to the people to take the land says it all:

"…but the Lord is with us. Don't be afraid of them."⁶

Maybe you're standing at the edge of breakthrough, too. The future is within reach, but fear is whispering lies, trying to hold you back. If you want to step into the life God has for you, you must first step out of your comfort zone. The journey will stretch you, and there will be giants, but you have a choice: will you see it as *opposition or as an opportunity?*

The Israelites made their choice. On the verge of the Promised Land, they begged to return to Egypt. At the edge of breakthrough, they longed for slavery. Why? Because it was familiar, comfortable, and safe.

Can you relate? Your "Egypt" might not look like theirs, but we all have one—a place we're tempted to retreat to when things get hard.

I'm convinced that much of the loneliness, frustration, and boredom we experience in life stems from our inability to see opportunity in the face of opposition. When we lose sight of purpose, we settle and grow numb in miserable routines. We tolerate stagnant marriages, dread Mondays, and count down the days until a vacation we won't even fully enjoy. But it doesn't have to be this way. What if the very thing you see as an obstacle is the invitation God is using to lead you into something greater? It starts by asking him to shift your perspective; to help you see opportunity where you once saw opposition.

> **IF YOU WANT TO STEP INTO THE LIFE GOD HAS FOR YOU, YOU MUST FIRST STEP OUT OF YOUR COMFORT ZONE.**

My wife and I are in the throes of parenting. We have three kids under seven, meaning we are not averse to tantrums, sibling fights, and messes. It takes longer to go places and most nights end in utter exhaustion. It can be challenging to sneak in a shower some days, let alone a date night or an evening with friends. We often feel a gravitational pull toward a life of ease and comfort because who wants to be the parents dragging screaming kids out of Target?

Simply put, we are in a season that seems like every time we open our eyes, we see opposition. Opposition to deep friendships. Opposition to pursuing dreams and ambitions. Opposition to intimacy with each other. Opposition to intimacy with God.

Yet, time and time again, we have allowed God to reveal opportunity where we see opposition. Instead of sinking into shallow friendships, we advocate for each other to carve out time for friends. I have not allowed this season of parenting to prevent me from pursuing my dreams, in fact, it has propelled me to write this book with greater enthusiasm and purpose. We refuse to allow our marriage to drift in this season, so we plan and budget for date nights. We even invested in cozy deck furniture, where we look forward to spending time together most summer evenings. Even when finding a moment of stillness feels impossible, we have prioritized habits of coming to God, especially in our exhaustion and frustration. He is always faithful in meeting us there.

> THE COMFORT ZONE MAY FEEL SECURE, BUT THERE IS NOTHING MORE DANGEROUS THAN A COMFORT ZONE BECAUSE IT KEEPS US IN BONDAGE TO FEAR AND SHACKLES US TO SECURITY.

You may be in a season where you feel like a grasshopper in a land of giants. Starting over in a new city with a new job is intimidating. It's easy to retreat into nights of Netflix and occasional calls home. But what if you stepped out of your comfort zone, invited coworkers to dinner, or joined a small group at church? Stay-at-home parenting can feel isolating and exhausting. Try making a local adventure bucket list with a friend and create memories your kids will never forget. Stuck in a job that drains you? Have the hard conversation. Update your résumé. Pursue something new.

Settling for what's comfortable is like begging God to take you back to Egypt. He has more for you.

How often have we stood on the edge of God's promise, only to retreat to the safety of our comfort zone? The comfort zone may *feel* secure, but there is nothing more dangerous than a comfort zone because it keeps us in bondage to fear and shackles us to security.

The best of life is on the other side of your comfort zone.

SAYING YES

I share a birthday with Michael Jordan, which felt especially fitting the year I turned 23—my so-called "Jordan Year." But what made that birthday unforgettable wasn't just the fun fact; it was the leap of faith I took that night, one that launched one of the greatest adventures of my life.

It was Monday, February 17, 2014. I had celebrated with friends the night before, spent the morning at work, and the afternoon cashing in on every free birthday freebie I could. But by evening, I found myself pacing my apartment because I had a wild idea rattling around in my head:

"What if I asked Taylor Monk out on a birthday date?"

Taylor and I had been friends for a few years. Our paths kept crossing, and lately, my interest had been piqued.

So I did what every guy does when he's about to call a girl and ask her out—I stared at my phone for an hour. Her number was right there, mocking me. The closer my finger got to the call button, the faster my heart beat. I was excited. I was nervous. My heart pounded, and my brain kept whispering: *"What if she's not interested? What if she says no?"*

Then, in a moment of courage, I made the call.

"Hey! It's my birthday, and I was wondering if you'd like to go to Tutti Frutti with me? I'll buy yours, since mine is free." I know—smooth.

To my delight, Taylor said yes. Less than thirty minutes later, I picked her up in my 2001 Pontiac Bonneville, and we headed off for frozen yogurt. We talked for hours; telling stories, sharing dreams, and laughing until we shut Tutti Frutti down. After dropping her off, I drove away grinning from ear to ear.

Fifteen months later, we said "I do" in front our family and friends. Today, we have three amazing kids—all because of one call I almost didn't make.

I can't help but think how close I came to letting fear win. I put my phone back in my pocket a dozen times that night. I distracted myself with other things. But something in me wouldn't let it go. I said yes to something outside of my comfort zone, and it changed my life forever.

Stepping out of your comfort zone requires a habit of saying yes to things that make you slightly uncomfortable. Before I asked Taylor to pick up our family and move across the country, I asked her to be my wife. Before I asked her to be my wife, I asked her to be my girlfriend. Before I asked her to be my girlfriend, I asked her to get frozen yogurt with me on my birthday. Living life to the fullest requires building our *yes* muscles. A habit of uncomfortable yeses leads to a lifestyle of adventure.

Today is the day to begin saying yes to everyday opportunities that will stretch you and help you become comfortable being uncomfortable. It's time to seek discomfort, intentionally putting yourself in situations that make you squirm. What can we do in our everyday lives to step out of our comfort zone?

I believe that every day presents countless opportunities to stretch beyond our comfort zone. If you just think about your day so far—the places you've been, the people you've encountered, and the tasks you've completed—you can probably think of multiple times you retreated to the confines of your comfort zone. Many of us take the same route to work, eat at the same places for lunch, talk to the same people, and watch the same shows.

One of the best decisions I made in college was taking out my headphones while walking to class. My headphones were a comfort zone, silently signaling, *"I'm in a hurry—don't talk to me."* It's hard to say yes to anything when your posture screams no. Removing them made me more aware and more available. I started having conversations with classmates, stopping to connect with friends in passing.

One day, I walked beside a classmate who was often overlooked and mocked behind his back. We talked briefly before he headed to class. It was awkward, nothing special. But later, while studying in the student union, another classmate asked to sit with me. After a few minutes, she said, "Are you a Christian?" Surprised, I said, "Yes, why?" She replied, "Everyone avoids him—but you seek him out." That moment led to prayer, tears, and her experiencing the love of God in a personal way. My small insignificant decision to say yes to walking without headphones led to a significant moment I would have otherwise missed.

Later in college, two of the football team's star players walked into our campus ministry's weekly worship service. I watched as students gawked at them. I mean these guys were legends, having recently led our school to a national championship. Something in me urged me to introduce myself. That introduction led to an invitation and a few days later, they were in our living room enjoying pheasant nuggets with me and my roommates as we shared our testimonies. I didn't have much to offer, but it was the vulnerability and safety for them to be themselves that sparked deep friendships that have opened countless unique doors, ministry opportunities, and new relationships.

> LIVING LIFE TO THE FULLEST REQUIRES BUILDING OUR YES MUSCLES. A HABIT OF UNCOMFORTABLE YESES LEADS TO A LIFESTYLE OF ADVENTURE.

On another occasion, I met a student from South Korea. Like many international students, he had us call him by his "American name" which happened to be *Kevin*. Being an international student is challenging. There are cultural and language barriers that often make it difficult to connect with other students, usually meaning many international students spend most of their time in America with students from their home country. God had been stretching me and pushing me out of my comfort zone and when I met Kevin, I aimed at being a *real friend* by inviting him to my apartment, taking him grocery shopping, and sharing meals together.

On his final day in the U.S., as we packed his bags, he looked at me and said, "Thank you for being my friend and for showing me Jesus." That day, I prayed with him to give his life to Christ before he flew back to Korea.

The trail of uncomfortable yeses almost always leads to a pasture of significance and adventure.

For me, becoming relationally available is the most common way to step outside my comfort zone. Walk without headphones. Ask someone where they're headed. Sit with someone new. Skip mobile ordering and have a real conversation with your barista. Strangers are just friends you haven't met yet.

Think about relationships in your life that feel distant, strained, or forgotten. The uncomfortable yes might be a text, a coffee invite, an apology, or even a plane ticket. Discomfort is often the path to growth and healing.

Keep your eyes open. Respond to what you see. And say yes even when it's uncomfortable.

LIVING DANGEROUSLY

Do you want to know one of my biggest pet peeves? It's when people say, "Drive safe!" I don't know why that phrase irritates me so much, but it triggers my inner middle schooler. Every time I hear it, I want to blurt out, "Nope! Planning on driving with my knees while texting and eating a burrito." Too far? Maybe. And for the record, I'd like to formally apologize to my parents, the chief offenders, who have heard my sarcastic replies well into my thirties.

"Drive safe" has a twin: "Travel safely." Especially when flying. I mean, short of choosing between pretzels and cookies, there's not a lot I can control once we're in the air. I've flown dozens of times and still don't know how to activate the life vest under my seat.

Now, as a parent, I understand the importance of safety. I've spent plenty of time protecting my children from impending danger. But here's my concern: in our obsession with safety, we may be unintentionally robbing the next generation of the very experiences that help them grow.

With "Safety First" as the battle cry of modern parenting, we've elevated safety over resilience, growth, and adventure. And it's not entirely our fault. One study shows that 90% of media coverage is negative.[7] The New York Times once reported that 87% of U.S. Covid coverage was negative—compared to just 51% internationally.[8] Why? Because bad news sells. We literally crave bad news, so it's no surprise we find it everywhere.

> **THE TRAIL OF UNCOMFORTABLE YESES ALMOST ALWAYS LEADS TO A PASTURE OF SIGNIFICANCE AND ADVENTURE.**

That bad news doesn't just own the headlines; it owns our heads and our hearts. In the name of safety, we've shut down the very opportunities that shaped us. And for those mad at me for writing this, I can tell you never rode your bike without a helmet as a kid.

This isn't about removing airbags or letting your kids ski off the roof. It's about putting safety back in its proper place. Because *risk* is required if you want to live life to the fullest.

It's impossible to play it safe and live a spiritually vibrant life. You can either put safety first or Jesus first, but not both.

In his book *All In*, Mark Batterson writes:

"Jesus didn't die to keep us safe. He died to make us dangerous. Faithfulness is not holding the fort. It's storming the gates of hell. The will of God is not an insurance plan. It's a daring plan. The complete surrender of your life to the cause of Christ isn't radical. It's normal. It's time to quit living as if the purpose of life is to arrive safely at death. It's time to go all in and all out for the All in All."[9]

Our goal isn't to hold the fort; it's to storm the gates.

Whole-hearted Christianity requires us to be on offense, not defense. Following Jesus requires us to take ground. Because of Jesus' perfect sacrifice we can move forward in confidence:

Therefore, since we have such a hope, we are very bold.[10]

Our boldness comes from Jesus, not ego. He is our example. If self-preservation was his goal, he wouldn't have traveled with a ragtag group of ordinary and unschooled men. He would've had bodyguards and a press secretary.

The disciples left everything—careers, family, stability—to follow Jesus. They walked dusty roads without guarantees or hotel reservations. Ironically, those three years were the most "comfortable" they'd ever be. Most of them would later face beatings, imprisonment, and martyrdom. But they didn't die playing it safe, they died turning the world upside down.

When David offered to fight Goliath, Saul gave him armor. But David wasn't interested in survival; he was aiming for victory. He ditched the armor, grabbed five smooth stones, and ran toward the giant. No backup plan. Just faith.

If we choose to play it safe, we might as well not play at all.

In *The Key to Everything*, Matt Keller writes, "When you choose to play it safe, everything will plateau in your life, and a plateau is never where a preferred future takes place." A plateaued faith is a passive faith. Comfort will never lead to your calling. Playing it safe doesn't protect you; it paralyzes your potential.

So how do we break free? One uncomfortable step at a time.

Eleanor Roosevelt is often quoted as saying, "Do one thing every day that scares you."[11] Her invitation is one of discomfort. It's a daily challenge to take a courageous step beyond the comfort zone. Why? As Ralph Waldo Emerson is often quoted saying, "He who is not everyday conquering some fear has not learned the secret to life."[12]

The secret to life to the fullest is to do hard things daily.

There was a guy named Larry at the church I grew up in. Every time I saw him, he'd say, "I know who you are..." It wasn't as creepy as it sounds. We loved Larry. One Sunday, my dad and I saw Larry and my dad told him that his shoe was untied. Without skipping a beat or even looking down at his foot, Larry responded, *"I know, I like to live dangerously."*

I think we all need to be a little more like Larry.

Because playing it safe isn't safe at all.

And I don't know about you, but *I like to live dangerously.*

DISCOMFORT: GOD'S GROWTH PLAN

Our move to the East Coast in 2019 changed everything. We left behind everything familiar—friends, rhythms, even the ability to pump our own gas[13]—and said yes to adventure's first cousin: *discomfort.* We outed ourselves as Midwesterners; greeting people we didn't know, trying to pump our own gas, nervously walking into a new church without knowing a soul, and making friends with neighbors twice our age. Everything was new, awkward, and uncomfortable.

Five months later, we welcomed our son, Summit, three weeks early. He spent his first week in the NICU. Just weeks after bringing him home, COVID-19 shut down the world. Travel plans were canceled. Support systems disappeared. Like many others, we found ourselves isolated, overwhelmed, and stripped of any sense of stability.

But that season taught us something important: discomfort is fertile soil for growth and transformation.

We often want to protect ourselves and those we love from trials. But if our goal is to avoid discomfort, we'll end up avoiding the very circumstances God uses to shape us. Trials are not signs that God has abandoned us; they're invitations to press in and rely on him more deeply.

> "Consider it pure joy, my brothers and sisters, whenever you face trials of many kinds, because you know that the testing of your faith produces perseverance. Let perseverance finish its work so that you may be mature and complete, not lacking anything."[14]

Discomfort and difficulty grow us. God uses trials to test our faith. They strip away our self-reliance and lead us to refuge in God. Sincere and lasting faith is forged in the fire. Like a skilled blacksmith, God uses suffering to shape us for fruitful and faithful living.

The full life we long for doesn't come from staying safe and comfortable. It's found in surrender—through trials, tears, and trust.

Abandoning your comfort zone doesn't mean you pursue a reckless and careless life, deceived to believe there are no consequences for your actions. That's stupidity. Going beyond your comfort zone simply means you no longer value your comfort over your calling. It means willingly accepting hardship and trials, not as punishment from an unloving god, but as a gift from a gracious and loving Father. It means joyfully enduring suffering, knowing God will produce good things through hard times. Discomfort is God's growth plan; so learn to embrace it, not despise it.

Think about a trial you are currently walking through or one you recently endured. In what ways do you think God is inspiring you to grow and mature? The trial you're up against is not evidence of God's absence. It's an invitation into his presence and his purpose. The discomfort is momentary, but the fruit is eternal.

We recently visited New Jersey for the first time since moving back to the Midwest in 2021. We spent most of our time revisiting our favorite places, reconnecting with dear friends, and eating all our favorite food. As we stood outside our little mint-green house across from the park and drove along the familiar country roads, we were overwhelmed with gratitude.

That season, though difficult, gave us a new perspective. In the isolation, we discovered a slower, more intentional pace of life, which we've fought to protect since returning. With our usual support systems gone, Taylor and I leaned into each other. It exposed insecurities and old wounds, but it also created space for healing. My priorities shifted, and God gave me fresh vision for who I was as a husband and father. With fewer distractions, dormant dreams (like this book) began to wake up, and I had room to pursue them. God became my closest companion. I learned to bring my fears, disappointments, and anger to him in prayer. In doing so, my relationship with him deepened in a way I hadn't known before.

Those two years in New Jersey changed everything.

That's the power of discomfort. It produces what comfort never will. God may not be calling you to move across the country, but he is calling you to step beyond what's familiar, into places where you don't have all the answers and moments that stretch you toward growth.

Discomfort is God's growth plan.

It's time to ditch your comfort zone once and for all.

In *Zootopia*, Judy Hopps is a small-town rabbit from Bunnyburrow who dreams of becoming the first rabbit police officer in the big city. While Judy is determined to chase her dream, her parents, Stu and Bonnie Hopps, have different hopes for her future. They'd prefer she stay close to home, live a quiet life, and carry on the family carrot farm legacy—safe, simple, and predictable.

After a school play where young Judy plays the role of a police officer, her parents try to gently talk her out of her ambitions:

> **Stu:** "Judy, you ever wonder how your mom and me got to be so darn happy?"
> **Judy:** "Nope!"
> **Stu:** "We gave up on our dreams and we settled, right Bon?"
> **Bonnie:** "Oh yes, Stu, we settled hard."
> **Stu:** "See that's the beauty of complacency, Jude, if you don't try anything new, you'll never fail."[15]

In the words of Gen Z, Stu "said the quiet part out loud." And let's be honest; he's not totally wrong. If you never try anything new, you'll never fail…

You'll also never grow, never stretch, and never experience the full, abundant life God created you for.

Don't buy what Stu Hopps is selling. It's a cute carrot-farming pitch, but it's a slow drift into complacency. And complacency? It's a dream killer. It stunts growth, suffocates potential, and drowns out the voice of God by cranking up the volume on comfort.

That's why I'm so passionate about resisting it. Because I believe with everything in me that the best stuff in life—the stuff that's rich, meaningful, and God-sized—is waiting on the other side of your comfort zone.

But there's the cost of staying put. When we let comfort call the shots, we end up missing out on things like:

- Freedom
- Forgiveness
- Healing
- Hope
- Love
- Growth
- Restored Relationships
- Deep Joy
- Clear Purpose
- Meaningful Friendships
- New Careers
- Ignited Passions
- Fresh Beginnings
- Bold Ideas
- God-sized Dreams and Opportunities
- Greater Dependence on God
- Better Stories
- Life to the Fullest
- Adventure

By drifting toward complacency and seeking out comfort, we bypass another one of God's blessings: *his divine comfort*. We settle for Arby's when he offers Fogo de Chao. We settle for the cheap stuff, when what God offers has no limits. We bypass the comfort only God can bring when we conjure up our own comfort, by clinging to the path of least resistance, and barricading ourselves in with the false security of more money and more things.

> "Praise be to the God and Father of our Lord Jesus Christ, the Father of compassion and the God of all comfort, who comforts us in all our troubles, so that we can comfort those in any trouble with the comfort we ourselves receive from God."[16]

The God of all comfort desires to come near you, surround you, and care for you. When we create our own comfort, we trick ourselves into thinking we don't need his. Bob Goff said it this way:

> "It would be great if we could recognize how dependent we are on God in the high times, too, when we're healthy or have a little extra in our savings account. But the discomfort brought by fear and uncertainty in our lives can become blessings. Here's the reason why: comfortable people don't need Jesus; desperate people do."[17]

Discomfort breeds desperation, and desperation leads to Jesus.

During our time in New Jersey, there were more than a few nights when my wife and I ached for the comfort of home. Raising two kids under two without family nearby left us longing for a knock on the door and a night off. When the winter heating bill arrived (thanks to an ancient oil-burning system), we missed our old apartment where utilities were included. Every missed exit on the Jersey Turnpike made us nostalgic for the straight, simple roads of North Dakota.

But it was in those hard, stretching moments that God met us. He drew near, comforted us, and provided in ways that still amaze us. He gave us neighbors who became like family. He led, guided, and showed up again and again.

Jesus offers life to the fullest; not just when it's easy, but especially when it's not. If you commit to cultivating curiosity, becoming a lifelong learner, and stepping beyond your comfort zone, you'll discover that life with God is never boring. Adventure awaits.

TRAIL MARKERS

TRUE NORTH TAKEAWAY
Life to the fullest is found beyond your comfort zone. When you trade safety for surrender and start saying courageous yeses to God, discomfort becomes the place he grows your faith, deepens your character, and leads you into adventure.

REFLECTION STOPS
1. Are there any areas where you've been valuing comfort more than your calling? What's one concrete change you sense God inviting you to make?
2. When you look at your current season, what feels most like "Egypt"—familiar but spiritually stagnant or limiting?
3. Think about a time you did step outside your comfort zone. What shifted in you, your faith, courage, relationships, or sense of calling?

EVERYDAY ADVENTURE CHALLENGE: THE DAILY BIG "GULP"
Choose one small, good thing today that pushes you just beyond comfortable. It could be starting a hard but needed conversation, inviting someone to coffee, sharing your story, trying something new, or simply saying yes where you'd normally retreat.

Rate your fear (1–10) before and after.

Then thank God for meeting you in the stretch.

Do this once a day for a week and you'll feel your "yes muscles" grow stronger with each step of courage.

If you're ready for more practical steps like this, check out the Everyday Adventure Challenge—a simple weekly challenge designed to help you practice intentionality and embrace the adventure in your everyday life. You can learn more at **everydayadventurebook.com**.

DEVELOP RESILIENCE
Part Three

DEVELOP RESILIENCE
Part Three

Hugh Glass was an American frontiersman and fur trapper who signed on for a fur-trading expedition from St. Louis in 1823. A seasoned outdoorsman, Glass made his living in the wild; but it was extreme adversity that made him a legend.

That June, the expedition led by General William Ashley was attacked by Arikara warriors, leaving many injured or dead. Glass survived, though wounded by a gunshot to the leg. Just weeks later, while scouting ahead, he surprised a mother grizzly bear with her cubs. The bear mauled him brutally, leaving him with a broken leg, a punctured throat, ripped scalp, and deep gashes across his body.

For two days, the crew tried to carry Glass, but he slowed their pace. Eventually, two men, John Fitzgerald and Jim Bridger, volunteered to stay behind with him until he died. But they grew impatient. Fearing for their own safety, they placed Glass in a shallow grave, took his weapons and gear, and left him for dead.

But he didn't die.

Over the next two months, Hugh Glass crawled and limped over 200 miles toward Fort Kiowa, near present-day Chamberlain, South Dakota; fueled by survival, sheer grit, and a desire for revenge. His story became the stuff of legend and inspired the 2015 Oscar-winning film *The Revenant*, starring Leonardo DiCaprio.

Perseverance is defined as *continued effort to do or achieve something despite difficulties, failure, or opposition.*[1] That's exactly what Hugh Glass embodied. He endured external trials such as violent attacks and a brutal bear mauling, as well as internal ones like abandonment, betrayal, and the will to keep going while crawling across 200 miles of wilderness.

You may never face a grizzly bear, but you will face hardship. Obstacles will rise both externally and internally. Each one will whisper the same tempting lie: *"It's not worth it. Just give up."*

Maybe a devastating breakup has made you question whether deep relationships are worth the risk. Maybe a loved one's death has shaken your belief that anything good lasts. Maybe the loss of a job or dream has left you emotionally numb, drifting through life with nothing but distraction and disappointment.

But to be an everyday adventurer, you must decide there's more to life than just surviving. True living demands perseverance. A life of purpose, joy, and meaning isn't something you accidentally stumble into. It requires grit, vision, and courage to keep going when comfort tells you to quit.

You were made for more than passive existence. You were made for a vibrant life. A life filled with connection, adventure, spiritual depth, and resilience.

The life you long for is possible, but it's only found on the other side of perseverance.

To gain the life you're made for, you must be willing to bypass the world's invitation into lesser, easier pursuits. Simply chasing wealth, accumulating toys, and retiring on a beach won't deliver what it promises. You might end up with a stunning view, but you'll struggle to enjoy it because your soul feels hollow and detached.

I worry that in the waiting—for a better season, a clearer path, a little more ease—we'll do everything we can to avoid the very pain and discomfort meant to shape us. In the mundane, the hidden, and the hard, we're tempted to zone out, waiting for a future moment that may never come and certainly won't look like our daydreams.

The path of the everyday adventurer is slow, gritty, and often marked by trials. It weaves through adversity, not around it. Living a life of everyday adventure is a marathon, not a sprint. And perseverance is the difference between a fleeting moment of adventure and a life that overflows with adventure.

It takes perseverance to grind through the early years of building a career. It takes grit to stay present in the long days (and nights) of parenthood. But on the other side is growth, purpose, and joy you won't find anywhere else.

To embrace the meaningful life God invites us into, we must learn to keep going, especially when things get hard. Thankfully, we're not alone. We have a cloud of witnesses cheering us on, and a perfect example to follow:

> "Therefore, since we are surrounded by such a huge crowd of witnesses to the life of faith, let us strip off every weight that slows us down, especially the sin that so easily trips us up. And let us run with endurance the race God has set before us. We do this by keeping our eyes on Jesus, the champion who initiates and perfects our faith. Because of the joy awaiting him, he endured the cross, disregarding its shame. Now he is seated in the place of honor beside God's throne."[2]

This race takes endurance. It takes grit. And the only way to keep going is to fix our focus on Jesus. He paved the way and paid the price so that we could run free.

The reality? We can't control every trial we'll face. We can't guarantee what the road ahead will look like. But we can choose how we respond. Perseverance isn't about pretending it's easy; it's about choosing not to quit.

In the next few chapters, we'll unpack what it really looks like to run this race well. We'll explore how to:

1. **Lighten Your Load**
   Identify what's weighing you down.

2. **Fix Your Focus**
   Learn to keep your eyes on Jesus.

3. **Refuse to Quit**
   Cultivate the grit to keep showing up.

Hugh Glass shouldn't have survived. But he did. Because he crawled forward when others would've stayed buried. That same resilience—gritty, stubborn perseverance—is what we're called to develop in our own lives.

Martin Luther King Jr. said it best:

> "If you can't fly then run, if you can't run then walk, if you can't walk then crawl but whatever you do you have to keep moving forward."[3]

That's the heartbeat of perseverance.
Keep moving forward.

EIGHT
Lighten Your Load

"If you wish to travel far and fast, travel light. Take off all your envies, jealousies, unforgiveness, selfishness and fears."[1]
Cesare Pavese

I am a serial over-packer.

Every trip, I start with the same noble intention: *"This time, I'm packing light."* And every time, without fail, I find myself staring at a mountain of bags thinking, *"This is all for two days?"*

It starts small. I toss in a couple extra sweatshirts and pairs of jeans. One book turns into four, just in case I finish the first. I count my underwear... then grab seven more pairs because you never really know.

Please tell me I'm not alone. Don't act like you've never been that person at airport bag check, redistributing weight like you're working on a NASA payload. I've stuffed my shoes in my backpack, layered on sweatshirts, and even sacrificed perfectly good possessions at the altar of Delta, all to avoid a $100 overweight baggage fee.

Although packing nine t-shirts for a two-day trip is borderline psychotic, there's a bigger overpacking issue we need to address. My habit of overpacking for travel pales in comparison to the way I overpack for life. The longer I live, the more I carry. Every experience, every heartache, and every failure gets stuffed into my emotional luggage. Only, the consequences aren't just a $100 overweight baggage fee. They're far worse: missed opportunities and a life that falls short of all God has for me.

We all carry baggage. A broken relationship? We carry bitterness. A missed promotion? Envy. Abandonment? Resentment. Loss? Doubt. Mistakes? Shame. Burned bridges and regrets? Hopelessness.

It's time to lighten the load.

Resilience and perseverance often begin with letting go of what's weighing us down. The writer of Hebrews urges us to "strip off every weight that slows us down, especially the sin that so easily trips us up."[2] If we want to go far, we need to travel light.

So what's slowing you down? What doesn't belong in your bag anymore? What are you still carrying that's incompatible with where you're going?

The answers to those questions might bring discomfort. Digging through your baggage might stir up pain. But it's necessary, because freedom, growth, and the full life Jesus offers await you on the other side of what you're willing to release.

PAST HURTS

Playing high school baseball in North Dakota had its challenges. While most places kick off the season around mid-March, "spring" in North Dakota is more of a rumor than a reality. You could pretty much count on a late blizzard to show up and crush your dreams.

Every year, our season began in a stuffy gym, running pointlessly long distances; part training, part tryout, and mostly a roster-clearing strategy. Without fail, guys would quit mid-run. Our "spring training" also involved shoveling snow off the infield of our local diamond in hopes of speeding up the melt. By the time we could use the field, we had three weeks to cram in an entire season.

That was the good part. A compressed season meant skipping more school for doubleheaders and makeup games.

One of those travel days during my sophomore year got rerouted because our destination field was still unplayable, so our coaches arranged a scrimmage between our two JV squads.

I was playing shortstop when someone hit a lazy pop-fly over my head. I turned, sprinted into shallow center, stretched for the catch… and collided full speed with our centerfielder. I missed the ball and the crash snapped both my tibia and fibula.

Lying on the grass, foot flopped at a grotesque angle, my mind raced. First thought? *"Oh no… my dad's going to see my car stereo is on a secular music station."* Second? *"My season is over."*

Baseball was my world. Every dream and plan I had revolved around it. And in one moment, those dreams felt as shattered as my shin bone. The pain in my leg was nothing compared to the one in my heart.

When you look in the rearview mirror of your life, chances are you've got some pain back there too. And odds are, the pain you've experienced far exceeds my broken leg. The fix goes way beyond surgery, a metal plate, six screws, and a few months on crutches. The wounds from a loved one's death, a breakup, a divorce, a traumatic accident, or a diagnosis cut much deeper.

You've probably heard the phrase, "Time heals all wounds." I don't buy it. Losing a parent as a child isn't something you "get over" in a few years. Being diagnosed with an incurable disease doesn't just fade away. Some wounds change the trajectory of our lives forever.

My friend Giovanni Hamilton was born with a rare genetic disorder called Schwartz-Jampel syndrome, which affects his muscles, bones, and ability to walk. Fewer than 1,000 people in the U.S. have it. Giovanni is just eighteen years old and has already endured more than 30 surgeries. He's spent most of his life in a wheelchair. His childhood has been anything but normal. He has suffered immense physical pain, and he's faced deep emotional wounds, disappointment, and bullying.

In every way, Giovanni's past has shaped his future. No surgery will restore his body to "normal." No effort can completely shield him from the cruel words of others. But Giovanni has made a powerful choice to not allow his pain to define or defeat him. He can't erase his diagnosis, but he chooses what he carries into the future.

> **WHATEVER PAIN, TRAUMA, OR DISAPPOINTMENT YOU'VE BEEN CARRYING, HE INVITES YOU TO PLACE IT IN HIS HANDS.**

He keeps his pain in its proper place. He sees it not as an anchor, but as a launching pad. His dream of becoming an NFL reporter is alive and well. His optimism, joy, and kindness are the fruit of a heart surrendered to God's greater purpose.

I'm not here to compare your pain to mine or to Giovanni's. I don't pretend to know what you've endured. But I do know this: God can redeem it. Whatever pain, trauma, or disappointment you've been carrying, he invites you to place it in his hands. He heals. He restores. He binds up wounds and leads us into life more beautiful than we imagined.

As Paul wrote to the church in Philippi: "Forgetting the past and looking forward to what lies ahead, I press on to reach the end of the race and receive the heavenly prize for which God, through Christ Jesus, is calling us."[3]

Keep pressing on. There's more ahead.

UNFORGIVENESS

Some of the emotional weight we carry feels justified, especially when it comes to unforgiveness. Unforgiveness is holding on to anger, bitterness, or resentment toward someone who hurt us. It can stem from cruel words, betrayal, neglect, or deep personal wounds. Letting it go can feel like letting them off the hook—like we've lost.

That's the trap of bitterness. It gives the illusion of power. We think that by clinging to it, we're maintaining control or winning some moral battle. But in reality, bitterness doesn't empower us; it poisons us.

> TO FORGIVE IS TO RELEASE AND LET GO OF SOMETHING THAT YOU WERE HOLDING. TO FORGIVE IS TO OPEN THE DOOR OF THE INTERNAL PRISON YOU SENTENCED YOUR OFFENDER TO, ONLY TO REALIZE THAT YOU WERE THE ONE INSIDE THE CELL

It's been said that holding on to unforgiveness is like drinking poison and expecting the other person to die. We rehearse the hurt in our minds, convincing ourselves that our pain is proof we're in the right. But in the end, unforgiveness has no real effect on them and a lasting effect on us.

I don't pretend to know your story. Some of you have been wronged in real, painful, and unfair ways. This isn't about minimizing what happened or telling you to just move on.

Forgiveness is not approval. It's not pretending it didn't hurt. And it doesn't always mean reconciliation. Forgiveness is choosing to release the weight of resentment so you can walk in freedom. It's trusting God with justice and choosing healing over hostility.

Forgiveness is a conscious, deliberate decision to release feelings of resentment or vengeance toward a person or group who has harmed you, regardless of whether they truly deserve your forgiveness.[4] To forgive is to release and let go of something that you were holding. To forgive is to open the door of the internal prison you sentenced your offender to, only to realize that you were the one inside the cell. To lighten your load, let go of bitterness. Forgiveness brings freedom. It may not happen overnight, but remember: forgiveness is a process. Wake up and choose forgiveness again and again every day.

I will never be able to walk in your shoes and I can't fully empathize with what you have experienced, but Jesus can. Jesus was falsely accused, mocked, ridiculed, tortured, and crucified. He had every right to spew his wrath on his accusers and those who carried out his crucifixion. Instead of retaliating blow for blow, he boldly forgave them.

> "Jesus said, 'Father, forgive them, for they do not know what they are doing.' And they divided up his clothes by casting lots."[5]

We have an opportunity to follow in the example of Jesus. To experience the abundant life Jesus offers, we must embrace the lifestyle of Jesus. An abundant life is filled with abundant love. To walk in the fullness of life, we must release the weight of bitterness.

> "Get rid of all bitterness, rage and anger, brawling and slander, along with every form of malice. Be kind and compassionate to one another, forgiving each other, just as in Christ God forgave you."[6]

To persevere on the path of everyday adventure, we must empty our bags of bitterness, resentment, and unforgiveness.

Remember Hugh Glass? After surviving a brutal bear attack, he was left for dead by members of his own crew. Fueled by the pain of betrayal and a thirst for revenge, he crawled over 200 miles across unforgiving terrain—often on hands and knees—with one goal in mind: to find the men who abandoned him.

And he did.

But the story takes an unexpected turn. Though justified in seeking vengeance, Glass chose forgiveness. He laid down revenge and walked away.

You can too.

You don't have to keep crawling through life, weighed down by bitterness. You don't have to let the past keep stealing from your present. Letting go won't erase what happened, but it will free you from its grip.

Lighten your load. Forgiveness doesn't excuse the pain, but it makes space for healing.

And healing is where freedom begins.

REGRET

We all have regrets.

Some are harmless; like going to the midnight premiere of *The Hobbit* the night before your most important college final. Or texting your crush what you meant to send to your best friend. Or begging your dad to stop fishing so you could go tubing… only to get wrecked on a choppy lake five minutes later. Totally hypothetical examples, of course.

But other regrets cut deeper.

Maybe yours popped into your head the moment you started reading. Maybe it keeps you up at night, haunted by what you did (or didn't do). And maybe it has convinced you that a full and meaningful life is no longer possible for you.

Regret wears many disguises. It shows up as something we did that we wish we hadn't or something we didn't do but wish we had. It can stem from missed opportunities, poor decisions, reckless words, or silence when we should have spoken up.

The truth is: We all get it wrong sometimes. We act on incomplete information. We speak before thinking. We rush instead of reflecting.

But here is the good news: Your life doesn't have to be defined by regret. Sure, someone else may take the job you passed up and find wild success. Another guy might ask out your crush and end up with the love story you dreamed of. You might skip a trip your friends talk about for years.

But none of that disqualifies you. Regret is inevitable. Living in it is optional.

Regret can either be fuel to your purpose or your pain. It will cause you to feel inadequate because you believe the lie that you missed out on a better life, or it will give you the perspective you need to embrace what you do have and the opportunities you said yes to. Regret does not have to hold you back. It can propel you forward, informing you of decisions you hope to say yes to in the future. It can inspire boldness to act in moments you let fear override in the past.

Regret is meant to be temporary.

If you say something hurtful to your spouse or a friend, regret invites you to make it right. If you fall back into a pattern of sin, regret nudges you toward repentance, forgiveness, and healing. But regret becomes a problem when we let it tell us *who we are*. It holds us back when it convinces us that our life is worse than it could have been.

There are rarely do-overs in life. We've all done things we can't undo and said things we wish we could take back. But living in regret doesn't have to be one of the consequences. You can trust that God is sovereign and that you are in the perfect place to move forward into what he still has for you.

We only get one life. Make it count. Deal with what's behind you and then leave it there. What happened yesterday doesn't have to define what happens today. God is a redeemer of regrets. He offers fresh mercy, a new day, and a new beginning.

Peter denied Jesus three times, the very thing he swore he would never do. The weight of regret crushed him in the moment, but it didn't keep him down. He got past his past and stepped into the bright future God had for him.

Regret begets regret. It builds on itself, turning a mismanaged moment into a mismanaged life. But it doesn't have to. You have the power to put regret in its place—behind you. Don't let yesterday's failure rob you of tomorrow's calling.

WORRY

My dad was a "stay awake until you get home" kind of dad.

I have vivid memories of trying to sneak into the house late at night. I was smart about it. Shoes off in the garage. Doorknobs twisted slowly to avoid the "click." I would tiptoe toward the stairs like a Navy SEAL. And yet, there he was. Casually waiting for me in his bathrobe.

Now, with three kids of my own, I get it. His love for me kept him up. I'm already feeling it and mine are still young. It's hard to rest when the nest isn't secured. Honestly, I think it's time I bought a bathrobe.

That kind of worry feels familiar. And if we are honest, it rarely stays contained.

What begins as protective love often grows into something heavier.

We worry about our kids, but it goes beyond that. We worry about money. About the future. About whether we're measuring up. About what others think. About what we wear or what we drive—even our fantasy football lineup.

Worry doesn't need a big reason; it just needs a crack in the door. And once it's in, it touches everything.

What about you?

What's weighing on your mind?

What makes you feel stretched thin or overwhelmed?

For me, work often fuels my worry. As one week ends, my brain races ahead to what's left undone or what's coming next. Then I start worrying that my worry is keeping me from being present with my family. I'm anxious about robbing them of my attention.

And then there's the world. It's hard not to feel the pull. One scroll through the headlines and you can feel your heart rate rise. The news knows exactly how to prey on our fears because doom sells and fear keeps us clicking.

People are worried. They're concerned about what's being taught in schools, about inflation and interest rates, and about what might happen if one party takes the White House or the other stays in it.

It's easy to see that stress and worry are everywhere, especially in our own hearts. Just because worry feels normal doesn't mean it's what we were made for. In his gospel, Luke writes, "Who of you by worrying can add a single hour to your life?"[12] Ask yourself that. Worry doesn't add anything. In fact, it only takes away.

Worry convinces us to choose safety over growth. It builds walls around abundant life and chains us to fear about a future we can't control. Worry is not the enemy, but it is one of the enemy's favorite tools to derail God's plans for our lives.

A life completely free from worry may not be possible, but a life where worry doesn't control you is possible. The key is to learn how to release it quickly, to place God back in his rightful place, and to trust him with the days ahead—no matter what they hold.

> "So humble yourselves under the mighty power of God,
> and at the right time he will lift you up in honor. Give all your
> worries and cares to God, for he cares about you."[8]

Let go of what's weighing you down and place yourself under his mighty care. He will provide for you because he deeply cares for you.

Did you catch that? The God of the universe cares about you. He cares about your future, your family, and the things that matter most to your heart. He is trustworthy, and he wants you to live freely and lightly. The next time you reach for worry, remember: You don't have to carry it. Let him carry it for you. Turn your worry list into a prayer list.

> "Don't worry about anything; instead, pray about everything.
> Tell God what you need, and thank him for all he has done.
> Then you will experience God's peace, which exceeds anything
> we can understand. His peace will guard your hearts and minds
> as you live in Christ Jesus."[9]

Worried about your finances? Pray. Worried about the election? Pray. Stressed about school or your job or your family? Pray. Prayer is the pathway to peace.

God promises a peace that doesn't make sense. A peace that shows up in the middle of chaos. When we hand him our stress and trust him with the unknown, worry no longer controls our hearts. His peace stands guard.

It doesn't mean the storms disappear, but it does mean you don't have to face them alone. Like a loving Father steadying your bike as you learn to ride, he is with you. Guiding. Encouraging. Holding you up.

So give your worries to God. You're not alone and you're deeply loved.

EXPECTATIONS OF OTHERS

One of the heaviest weights we carry is the expectations of others. And often, we carry them everywhere we go.

Not all expectations are bad. Many begin with well-meaning parents or authority figures who want to see us succeed. But when love or acceptance feels attached to our performance, expectations can quietly become pressure. If a child believes their worth depends on grades, or an employee feels their value hinges on productivity, a brick is added to their backpack. Over time, that pressure piles up.

If you think this isn't a big deal, just look at college campuses. The American Psychological Association reports that rising parental expectations have fueled a spike in perfectionism, which is now linked to increased rates of anxiety, depression, self-harm, and eating disorders.[10] Students are breaking under the weight of needing to "measure up."

If we live by the expectations of others, we'll die by them.

Crushing expectations can paralyze confidence, sabotage progress, and send us spiraling into disappointment. As leadership expert John Maxwell says, "Disappointment is the gap that exists between expectation and reality."[11] When disappointment becomes identity, we lose ourselves in the pursuit of someone else's version of success.

We must be careful not to heap blame on our parents, teachers, or coaches. The goal isn't to hold grudges against those whose expectations have weighed us down. The goal is to live freely and lightly, and that's impossible if we replace the weight of unmet expectations with bitterness and blame.

What's the solution?

You may never be able to silence the expectations others have for you, but you can choose not to carry their weight. A parent may continue projecting expectations well into your adulthood; shifting from grades and sports to career, parenting, or finances. But their expectations don't have to define your direction.

Run the race marked out for you.

Get clear on what you are aiming for. Surround yourself with people who encourage you, not control you. And learn to recognize others' expectations for what they are—just someone else's opinion. Value what is helpful, but don't let it dictate your worth.

As a young parent, I have experienced this firsthand. Both my parents and in-laws have offered wisdom, and we're genuinely thankful for their insight. They've raised amazing kids (humble brag), and their experience is valuable. But at times, their well-intended expectations have had too much influence, leaving us parenting to please instead of parenting with peace.

> WHEN DISAPPOINTMENT BECOMES IDENTITY, WE LOSE OURSELVES IN THE PURSUIT OF SOMEONE ELSE'S VERSION OF SUCCESS.

We have learned to communicate directly when needed: "We appreciate what worked for you, but we've chosen a different approach. We're grateful for your support." And in some cases, we've had to process those expectations internally and move forward anyway.

You cannot stop others from forming expectations. But you can stop them from holding you back.

Your identity is not found in meeting others' standards. It's found in living the life God uniquely marked out for you.

SIN AND SHAME

My kids love setting up booby traps. Many mornings, I hear the sound of giggles and clattering toys just outside my bathroom door. These traps are elaborate and they often involve monster trucks, Magnatiles, and plastic animals. If fatherhood has taught me anything, it's this: When faced with a booby trap, go all in!

Here's how it usually goes down.

Moments after stepping out of the shower, I get a text from my wife: "Heads up... booby trap." It's not really a warning—it's a cue. She's telling me to prepare for the performance of a lifetime. After getting dressed, I open the door and dramatically step onto the pile of toys. I flail and dramatically crash. My kids erupt with laughter and cheer. Their trap worked. Dad is down. On a good day, I'd say my performance deserves an Oscar.

The funny thing is that the enemy's tactics aren't all that different.

Satan sets traps hoping we will fall, tripping us up and derailing the life Jesus has called us to. That's what sin does: it entangles. It deceives. It takes our feet out from under us.

> SIN TRIPS US UP, AND SHAME KEEPS US DOWN. IT'S A VICIOUS CYCLE; LIKE AN AWFUL CARNIVAL RIDE WE CAN'T ESCAPE. AND ON OUR OWN, WE CAN'T.

Simply put, sin is disobedience to God. It first entered the world through Adam and Eve, who were deceived by Satan—disguised as a serpent—and doubted God's goodness. They gave in, took the fruit, and invoked the consequences: shame, separation, pain, and eventual death.[12]

But the fallout didn't end with them.

Their sin tripped them up, and they took all of us down with them. The stain of sin now marks all of us. As the psalmist writes, "For I was born a sinner—yes, from the moment my mother conceived me."[13] Sin broke the perfect world God created, and we have all been born into that brokenness.

> "When Adam sinned, sin entered the world. Adam's sin brought death, so death spread to everyone, for everyone sinned."[14]

> "For everyone has sinned; we all fall short of God's glorious standard."[15]

Like a disease, sin has spread to every one of us. And just like in the Garden of Eden, the enemy still uses the same deceptive tactics to trip us up. He sets booby traps designed to take us down—traps baited with pride, greed, rage, lust, gossip, drunkenness, and envy. Like that juicy fruit on the tree, Satan dangles what looks good in front of us, tempting us to believe we know better than God.

As a teenager, I stumbled into pornography. I was staying at a friend's house when he flipped to a channel I had never seen before. What appeared on the screen was something I had never seen before either. My mind started racing. Deep down, I knew I wasn't supposed to look, but I kept watching. A new path was etched in my mind and heart and I would walk that road again and again for years. A trap had been set, and I kept stepping into it.

It became a pattern: A trap was set, a choice was made, momentary pleasure, deep sorrow, and then a wave of shame.

Shame can be defined as "a painful emotion caused by consciousness of guilt, shortcoming, or impropriety."[16] If sin trips us up, shame is what pins us to the ground.

Over time, shame became more than something I felt; it became what I wore. It distorted how I saw myself. It caused me to hide, to cover up, to pretend. And this isn't new. The moment Adam and Eve ate the fruit, they were overwhelmed with shame.

> "At that moment their eyes were opened, and they suddenly felt shame at their nakedness. So they sewed fig leaves together to cover themselves."[17]

Adam and Eve weren't suddenly naked; they were suddenly aware of their nakedness. And with that awareness came shame. So they covered themselves. When they heard God walking through the garden, they hid. Shame still works the same way today. It drives us into hiding, convincing us we have something to prove, something to cover up.

Sin trips us up, and shame keeps us down. It's a vicious cycle; like an awful carnival ride we can't escape. And on our own, we can't.

That's where God steps in.

Our sin brings separation and leads to death. But in his mercy, God made a way.

> "But God showed his great love for us by sending Christ to die for us while we were still sinners."[18]

This is the Good News. And not just good news—the best news! Through Jesus, God has made it possible for us to live freely and lightly. You don't have to stay trapped in the cycle. You don't have to carry the weight anymore. Sin doesn't have to define you, and shame doesn't get the final word.

You and I are carrying some things that can't come with us anymore—not if we truly want to experience the full life Jesus offers. Some of what we carry is no longer compatible with the future God has designed for us. And we won't experience God's best if we simply grit our teeth and try harder. We have to let some things go.

When I was thirteen, my baseball team traveled to Van Buren, Arkansas, for the Babe Ruth World Series. It was my first time flying without my parents, and it felt like a dream. We were treated like kings—parades, free Louisville Slugger baseball bats, even signing autographs.

After the tournament, we packed up and headed home; now loaded down with trophies and keepsakes. At the airport, I sent my backpack through security. But it didn't come out.

A group of TSA agents huddled around the screen and then approached me. My stomach dropped. One of them pulled out a pair of scissors I had accidentally tossed in my backpack at the last minute. I was convinced I was headed to prison. Thankfully, they confiscated the scissors and let me go. Evidently, the kid with soiled pants isn't a threat. Unfortunately, they didn't find an extra pair of underwear in my backpack, because I could have used them...

I learned something that day: Not everything you pack can come with you. Some things need to be left behind.

That's true in life, too.

There are burdens you've picked up that God never asked you to carry. There are patterns, habits, regrets, and lies that are weighing you down and keeping you from taking flight. And here's the good news: You don't have to carry them anymore. God is inviting you to surrender what doesn't belong in your bag.

> "Give your burdens to the Lord, and he will take care of you.
> He will not permit the godly to slip and fall."[19]

And listen to this promise from Jesus:

> "I won't lay anything heavy or ill-fitting on you. Keep company with me and you'll learn to live freely and lightly."[20]

That's not just a poetic idea; it's a real promise. There is a way of life with Jesus that is marked by peace, by freedom, and by release. It may take time. It may be uncomfortable. But it's worth it. You were never meant to carry it all.

One way to practice this is through a simple daily rhythm I call a "Bag Check." Each morning, pause and ask yourself: What's in my bag? Am I carrying anything that can't come with me today? Make it part of your prayer, echoing Psalm 139:23–24:

> "Search me, God, and know my heart; test me and know my anxious thoughts. See if there is any offensive way in me, and lead me in the way everlasting."[21]

It's a small but powerful habit—a chance each day to let God show you what needs to stay behind so you can step into the life he has for you.

So let me ask again: What do you need to give to God? What are you carrying that has reached its final destination?

It's time to unpack. It's time to lighten your load.

TRAIL MARKERS

TRUE NORTH TAKEAWAY
You can't run toward the life God is calling you to if you are weighed down by hurts, regrets, unforgiveness, worry, expectations, or hidden sin. Lightening your load begins by naming what you're carrying and releasing it into Jesus' hands.

REFLECTION STOPS
1. What's slowing or weighing you down—past hurt, unforgiveness, regret, worry, expectations, or hidden sin/shame? Which of these no longer belongs in your bag, and why is it incompatible with where God is leading you?
2. Think of a specific past hurt or loss. How has it tried to define you? What might it look like to let God use it as a launching pad instead of an anchor?
3. As you read Jesus' promise to help you "live freely and lightly," what specific burden do you sense him inviting you to hand over today?

EVERYDAY ADVENTURE CHALLENGE: THE DAILY BAG CHECK
For the next seven days, take five minutes to lighten your load. Follow these simple steps:

1. **Pause.**
   Find a quiet spot and ask: "What's in my bag today?"

2. **Identify one weight.**
   Choose just one from the chapter's list that's showing up today: past hurt, unforgiveness, regret, worry, expectations, or sin/shame.

3. **Name it clearly.**
   Write a single sentence finishing this phrase: "Today, I'm carrying…"

4. **Release it to God.**
   Pray Psalm 139:23–24 in your own words and say: "God, I give this to You. Lead me forward."

5. **Take one small action.**
   Send a text, journal a prayer, have a conversation, breathe deeply, repent, or simply choose gratitude—whatever helps you set it down.

Do it daily, one weight at a time. You will be amazed at how much lighter you begin to walk.

NINE
Fix Your Focus

"The trick is this: keep your eye on the ball. Even when you can't see the ball."[1]
Tom Robbins

We have a sixteen-year-old goldendoodle named Kevin. We didn't name him. His original owners did—hilariously choosing a name that sounds more like your uncle than a dog. But honestly, I cannot imagine him being called anything else.

Having a dog named Kevin creates some awkward moments. Within the first week of bringing him home, I let him out into the backyard to do his business. After several minutes of his pacing back and forth, I grew impatient and shouted, "Kevin, go poop!" At that moment, I noticed a neighbor standing on his deck with a cigarette in hand and the most bewildered expression on his face. I have always wondered if his name was also Kevin.

I get nervous talking about Kevin in public. Saying things like, "Kevin's been humping the furniture again," or "Kevin shredded another poopy diaper," sounds a lot worse if people don't realize I'm talking about a dog...

When we adopted Kevin, his previous owners warned us, "Kevin will play fetch until it kills him." We obviously never let it go that far, but I believe them. Some of my favorite memories are of Kevin sprinting after tennis balls in an open field—living his best life.

Greyhounds take that kind of drive to a whole new level. They can hit speeds up to 45 miles per hour[2], bred and trained to chase an artificial lure—usually a mechanical "rabbit"—that stays just ahead of them.[3] They run with singular focus.

We may not be able to run 45 miles per hour, but we each have a race to run. And if we want to run with endurance, we've got to fix our focus and keep our eyes on the prize.

> "And let us run with endurance the race God has set before us. *We do this by keeping our eyes on Jesus*, the champion who initiates and perfects our faith. Because of the joy awaiting him, he endured the cross, disregarding its shame. Now he is seated in the place of honor beside God's throne."[4]

How do we run our race with endurance? How do we persevere through life's setbacks and surprises? How do we go the distance without burning out or giving up?

We keep our eyes on Jesus.

By staying focused on him, we can overcome obstacles, weather storms, and endure trials. He's not just the key to our perseverance; he's the source of our strength and the anchor of our resilience.

But what does it really mean to keep our eyes on Jesus? Does it mean hanging pictures of him in every room like your grandma probably did? Maybe. Does it mean wearing a cross necklace and kissing it before stepping up to the plate like Sammy Sosa? I mean, if it helps, go for it; but that's not the heart of it.

To keep our eyes on Jesus means we choose to stay focused on him in every moment, especially the hard ones. It means we lift our gaze above what's temporary and lock in on what's eternal. As Paul wrote, "Think about the things of heaven, not the things of earth. For you died to this life, and your real life is hidden with Christ in God."[5]

Fixing our eyes on Jesus shifts our perspective. It reminds us that our real life is not defined by what we see, but by the One we follow.

WALKING ON WATER

It's one thing to talk about fixing our eyes on Jesus; it's another thing entirely to actually *do* it. I wish I could say I always live with unwavering focus, but most days I find myself relating more to Peter in one of his most infamous moments.

You might know the story. Peter and the disciples were out in the middle of a lake when Jesus came walking toward them—on the water. Naturally, they freaked out, assuming it was a ghost. But Peter, ever bold, called out, "Lord, if it's really you, tell me to come to you, walking on the water."[6] Jesus simply replied, "Yes, come."[7]

And Peter did. He stepped out of the boat and, for a moment, he actually walked on water.

> "So Peter went over the side of the boat and walked on the water toward Jesus. But when he saw the strong wind and the waves, he was terrified and began to sink. 'Save me, Lord!' he shouted."[8]

Peter didn't sink because he forgot how to walk on water. He never knew how in the first place. What held him up was his lack of faith. When he stepped out of the boat, his eyes were locked on Jesus. But the second his attention shifted to the wind and waves, fear took over, and down he went.

What changed? The wind didn't suddenly pick up. The waves didn't grow. The difference was Peter's focus. One moment, his eyes were locked on Jesus—his faith steady. The next, he was staring down a storm. And that's when he sank.

I get it. Not the walking-on-water part, but the losing-focus part. I'll start my day centered on Jesus—faith stirred, heart full—and then one of my kids comes out of their room too early. My eyes shift from Jesus to frustration, and instead of responding with patience, I bark, "Go back to bed!"

Sometimes, I don't even get out of the boat. I roll over, check my phone, and start my day focused on headlines, emails, or someone else's curated highlight reel. And just like that, I'm stuck in a loop of distraction, self-reliance, and low-grade discouragement.

Maybe you've felt it too. You want to live a life of purpose and adventure. You wouldn't be reading this if you didn't believe it was possible.

> **WE MUST DEVELOP PERSEVERANCE IN OUR FAITH IF WE DESIRE TO EMBRACE ALL GOD HAS FOR US.**

But the waves keep rising. Bills pile up. A relationship breaks down. Work gets overwhelming. Life feels heavy. You want to persevere, but you feel like you're sinking. That's the human struggle. Even with the best intentions, we lose focus and start to drown in the chaos around us.

Great explorers like Ferdinand Magellan, Nellie Bly, and John Muir didn't become famous because their journeys were easy. They are remembered because they pressed on. They kept moving forward, even when everything screamed for them to turn back.

That's the call for us too—to develop perseverance and keep our eyes fixed on Jesus.

We must develop perseverance in our faith if we desire to embrace all God has for us. We will experience setbacks and disappointments; in fact, Jesus guarantees it.

> "I have told you these things, so that in me you may have peace. In this world you will have trouble. But take heart! I have overcome the world."[9]

The trouble we experience in this world doesn't have to derail or destroy us. Our confidence doesn't need to be dependent on our circumstances or even our own strength. Our faith is in Jesus who has overcome the world. As we keep our eyes fixed on him, he will lead us into unfathomable peace, joy, and adventure.

MILE MARKER 213

Spring Break 2011 is one I will never forget. Five of my friends and I decided to make the 1,900-mile trek from Fargo, North Dakota, to Fort Myers, Florida, to watch our beloved Minnesota Twins at MLB Spring Training. After a long, soul-crushing Midwest winter, we were desperate for vitamin D.

Before cramming into one of our friend's mom's minivans, we first had to drive south to drop off my friend Steve's Toyota Echo in South Dakota. If you have never seen a Toyota Echo, just picture the next size up from a Hot Wheels car. I'm barely exaggerating.

It started snowing not long after we left Fargo; just light flurries at first, but it quickly picked up. Steve and I were in the Echo; the rest of the crew rode in the minivan. We pulled up a weather report and saw the word "squall." Apparently, that's a real word. But this was not a squall, whatever that is. It was a full-blown blizzard. Visibility tanked, roads got slick, and eventually the interstate was closed.

That should have been the end of the road. But Steve is a real-life adventurer (he now lives in Alaska and regularly finds himself in harrowing situations). He is also very stubborn. Nothing was going to stand between him and some baseball games that didn't even count for anything…

After a quick call to a friend for an amateur weather update, we left the closed interstate and continued via backroads. Because obviously, if the freeway is unsafe, backroads are a great alternative.

A few miles in, we came to a hill. The Echo gave it everything it had, but we slid right back down. As we sat defeated, the wind picked up and spun the Echo a full 180 degrees while parked. Still, we pressed on in whiteout conditions. And I don't mean difficult visibility. I mean, *"Get out of the car to see if we're still on the road"* zero visibility.

Somehow, we stumbled across a rest area. We ran inside and looked back through the window and couldn't even see the Echo parked ten feet away. The rest of our friends joined us in the rest area. We were safe, at least for the moment.

Now, you'd think that would be the end of our idiotic adventure. But after just a couple hours in the warm safety of the rest area, Steve started doing some mental math. If we didn't leave soon, we might miss first pitch. *At a spring training game. That doesn't count.*

So Steve delivered a Braveheart-style speech and rallied the troops for a vote. It ended four to two in favor of pressing on. If you couldn't guess, I was part of the two. My vote wasn't just "no," it was "absolutely not." I went into the rest area bathroom and called my brother crying—*actually crying*—asking him to tell my mom and dad I loved them.

Back in the Echo (which now doubled as a death machine), Steve and

I made it a whopping four miles; two out, two back. A suburban stopped us and essentially blocked the road, making us turn around. When we pulled back into the rest area, Steve and I *exchanged words.*

After trying to sleep on the rest area floor surrounded by strangers, the storm finally let up. We ditched the Echo at a friend's house, loaded all six of us into the minivan, and continued the journey to Florida. We missed the national anthem but made it before the end of the first inning.

So why tell this story?

It's definitely not to show you how brave I am. Remember, I was the one in the bathroom crying like we were on the Titanic.

I tell it because the *struggle* became the *story.*

I have no clue who the Twins played that day. I don't know the score or who won. But I remember the Wilmot Rest Area is at mile marker 213. I remember the wind catching Steve's door and bending it so it never sealed properly again. I remember the pure relief of trading the Echo for an overcrowded minivan full of my best friends.

Because that's what we remember. That's what makes a story worth telling.

We think we want the view from the top, but what actually shapes us is the journey to get there. It's the frustration, the wrong turns, the fear, and the survival that make a memory. The struggle *is* the story. *The joy is in the journey.*

A life of everyday adventure is no different. The faith stories that live on—the ones we carry, the ones that mark us—are never about the easy moments. They're forged in the chaos, in the storms, in the prayers whispered through tears on a bathroom phone call.

The memories that shape us and the faith that sustains us are born in the middle of the mess, not just in the destination.

JOY IN TRIAL

The adventure is not the destination, but the journey along the way. Although we keep our focus on the destination, we can't miss what is happening in the journey.

We are invited to consider it joy whenever we face trials. This is definitely one of those "upside down" biblical themes. In a natural sense, trials do not equal joy. Trials equal pain, setback, heartache, delay, and disappointment—pointing to suffering, hardship, and loss. How could those things add up to equal joy? Let's revisit the words of James:

> "Consider it pure joy, my brothers and sisters, whenever you face trials of many kinds, because you know that the testing of your faith produces perseverance. Let perseverance finish its work so that you may be mature and complete, not lacking anything."[10]

We are encouraged to consider it pure joy whenever we face trials because the testing of our faith produces perseverance. Through perseverance, God grows a deep resilience in our faith and we grow in maturity, integrity, and wholeness.

This does not mean God produces trials in our life to grow our faith. He does not inflict us or a loved one with cancer in order to develop our grit. *God redeems broken things.*

> "God causes everything to work together for the good of those who love God and are called according to his purpose for them."[11]

Don't grow discouraged when life doesn't go as planned. God often uses pain as a tool for our formation, maturity, and growth. But when tragedy strikes, it's easy to question God's goodness or doubt his love. In the middle of hardship, we can lose our bearings, forgetting where we have come from and losing sight of where we are going.

We are not the first to do this. The Israelites had the same struggle.

The story of God and his people is cyclical: They get into trouble, God rescues them, they forget, and the cycle repeats. After Moses led the Israelites out of slavery in Egypt, they found themselves trapped with mountains on one side, the Red Sea on the other, and Pharaoh's army in pursuit. And what did they do? They begged to go back to Egypt. Back to slavery.[12]

> **GOD'S DELIVERANCE DOESN'T ALWAYS COME BEFORE THE STORM; IT OFTEN MEETS US IN IT.**

But God came through. He parted the Red Sea, and they walked through on dry land. The kind of story we tell for generations only happens in the face of trials. God's deliverance doesn't always come before the storm; it often meets us in it.

Most of us would rather skip the struggle. We want to blink and arrive in the *promised land*. But as author Alan Fadling put it, "God's goal may not be our arrival at a destination but our formation along the way."[13] The struggles we walk through are part of our holy adventure. These are the stories we tell, not to glorify pain, but to glorify the God who meets us in it.

When I broke my leg in high school, I was devastated to miss the baseball season. But God used that time to reveal how much I had idolized baseball. That injury became a turning point in my relationship with God.

Years later, in my early twenties, I walked through a painful breakup. I was convinced I was going to marry the girl and like a rug pulled out from underneath me, our relationship ended. I was confused, disappointed, and heartbroken. I was embarrassed and afraid of starting over. But in that season, I gave my disappointment to God, and he met me there with healing and comfort. Eventually, my path crossed with Taylor's and the rest is history.

> "Blessed is the one who perseveres under trial because, having stood the test, that person will receive the crown of life that the Lord has promised to those who love him."[14]

I don't know about you, but I desire God's blessing for my life. Even when circumstances are not joyful, we can find joy because God is forming something deep within us. He never wastes our pain.

FAILURE IS NOT FATAL

I have always been afraid of failing. For most of my life, I played it safe by avoiding situations with a higher likelihood of failure. I stayed away from classes that would threaten my GPA. I stayed in the friend zone, unwilling to risk asking a girl I liked out, because what if she said "no"? To me, failure was not an option.

I remember sitting in a job interview in college and being asked,

"What is a time you failed and what did you learn from it?" I froze. I scanned my life for an answer, but nothing came. Eventually, I landed on a cheesy story about making three errors in a baseball game and how I learned to keep my glove down. The interviewer nodded and moved on, but I couldn't shake it. I kept thinking, *"Have I really never failed at anything meaningful?"*

That question haunted me. I started replaying my life and noticed a pattern: If I thought I would succeed, I jumped right in. If I feared I might fail, I drifted to the background. In high school gym class, we went ice skating and I could barely stand. I was so embarrassed I swore off ice skating forever. I decided, *I'm just not someone who skates.*

Somewhere along the line, I embraced a lie: *Failure is the enemy.* And for nearly three decades, that lie held power over me. In my mind, failure wasn't an event—*it was an identity.* I believed there was no difference between failing and being a failure.

So I played it safe. I avoided anything that carried risk, not because I wasn't curious or interested, but because I didn't want to lose. I didn't want to fall. I didn't want to fail.

In his book, *Failing Forward*, leadership expert John Maxwell said, "If you're not failing, you're probably not really moving forward."[15] My allergy to failure had some unintended side effects. I had unknowingly settled for mediocrity by removing myself from the game before I could lose. And if I'm being honest, that same temptation still lingers. I have stopped writing this book more than once because of the nagging fear: *What if no one reads it? What if I pour years of my life into something and no one cares?*

It's time to rethink failure. Failing does not make you a failure. Failure is not the end of the road. It's often the beginning of a new one. Thomas Edison is famously quoted as saying, "I have not failed once. I have discovered ten thousand ways that don't work."[16] When asked how it felt to fail 1,000 times while trying to invent the lightbulb, he replied, "I didn't fail 1,000 times. The lightbulb was an invention with 1,000 steps."[17] Edison had a remarkable ability to mine failure for direction. For him, each failure was one more step in the right direction.

He is not alone. A healthy view of failure is a common trait among many of the world's most successful people. Walt Disney was fired for "lacking imagination." Steven Spielberg was rejected from film school three times. Henry Ford's first two car companies went under. Albert Einstein's school records labeled him "mentally slow." Jerry Seinfeld got booed off stage during his first stand-up gig.[18] Failure wasn't the end of their stories; it was a necessary chapter in their success.

Now imagine you are back in that interview chair: "Tell me about a time you failed. What did you learn?"

Some of you, like I once did, might struggle to answer because you've avoided risk at all costs. Others may feel buried under the weight of failure. Somewhere along the way, your mistakes became your identity. Maybe someone unfairly labeled you a failure, and you've carried that weight ever since. You've convinced yourself that you are not cut out for deeper relationships, meaningful work, or a life of adventure because of what didn't work in the past.

But I am here to declare: you are not a failure. And this is not the end of your story.

Author and speaker, Zig Ziglar once said: "Failure is an event, not a person."[19] You are not defined by what didn't work. Life to the fullest is still possible.

Don't stay stuck in a bad experience. Learn from it and move forward. Sometimes failure requires repentance or reconciliation, but don't waste your pain. Mine it for wisdom.

In his book, *Straight to the Top and Beyond*, author and adventurer, John Amatt, said, "The only failure in life is when we fail to learn the lessons from our experiences."[20] Our failures build resilience and develop perseverance, giving us the grit to keep going. It's on us to decide if we will let them.

Failure is not fatal. It's formative. And it may just be the first step toward your next great adventure.

GETTING BETTER AT FAILING

Over the past few years, I've been learning how to fail better. My instinct is still to avoid failure at all costs, but I am beginning to recognize that fear of failure is often the biggest thing holding me back. For years, I quietly worked on this book in secret. It lived in a private corner of my life, tucked away in the "maybe someday" box. That secrecy made it easy to delay, stall, and keep tinkering without ever risking anything real.

But everything changed when I went public. I started telling people I was writing a book, and suddenly, it became real. Real enough to fail. Before, no one held me accountable because no one knew. I could always pretend it didn't matter because there was no chance of public disappointment. But once I named the dream out loud, the potential for failure entered the picture. And strangely enough, that's been good for me. I've had to redefine what failure truly means. Failure isn't trying and falling short. It's feeling the nudge to do something and never acting on it. The only way I can truly fail at writing this book is by never writing it at all.

In his devotional, *Live in Grace, Walk in Love,* Bob Goff says, "God hopes we'll develop a greater fear of inaction than of failure, because then, we'll experience with wide-eyed excitement what it's like to cruise, doing what we were made to do."[21] If our fear of failure is greater than our fear of inaction, we won't even get a sniff of the life God has designed for us. If we begin to elevate the obstacles that stand in our way and lose sight of the prize itself, we don't stand a chance at experiencing life to the fullest.

I think that is why so many of us struggle to see our everyday lives as an adventure. We tend to view life as more of an assignment than an adventure; something we have to get through rather than something we get to enjoy. In doing so, we end up robbing ourselves and holding ourselves back. By chasing a life of minimal resistance, we might earn a good paycheck, take a few nice vacations, and snap some beautiful family photos; but will those things hold real life in them? Life that's truly life?

Let me be clear: I am not saying you should quit your job to chase a music career, sell everything to live in a van, or walk away from your marriage just because things feel stale. I believe real adventure starts right where you are. It begins with small steps of courage. You may have an opportunity today to push past the fear of failure and step into something more meaningful.

For you, that might mean sitting down with your spouse to apologize and pursue counseling together. It might look like finally telling someone about a dream you have buried for years. It could mean reaching out to a friend you have grown distant from, even if you are not sure how they'll respond. I don't know exactly what it means for you, but I do know this: *If you never try, it will never happen.* The life you long for will not be found in avoiding risk. It will be found in stepping forward, even when the outcome is uncertain.

When Taylor and I packed up everything and moved across the country in 2019, we didn't have all the answers. What we knew was that we were leaving our community, families, and a career we loved to step into what we believed was God's next adventure. Our daughter had just turned one, and we had recently found out we were expecting our second child. We were scared. It was the biggest risk we'd ever taken.

Over the next few years, we experienced all kinds of highs and lows. We made new friends, discovered new places, and even weathered a global pandemic. I had the chance to work with some incredible people and take on once-in-a-lifetime opportunities. In 2021, our organization was going through major changes, and I had the opportunity to move back to Fargo and continue working remotely. It was a huge gift to be close to family again while staying committed to the work I cared about.

Then in April 2022, I found out that my role would be dissolved. I was devastated. I was embarrassed. I was angry and confused. In that moment, it felt like everything we had sacrificed was for nothing. I felt like I had failed my family.

But with time and perspective, I began to see the bigger picture. I realized how difficult the decision had been for my leaders and how necessary it was for the longevity of the organization. It still stung, but I had a deep confidence that God wouldn't waste anything. And most of all, I saw how God was using the pain to shape me. What felt like failure became a turning point. Losing my job opened the door to new God-sized dreams and a deeper dependence on him.

I am getting better at failing. And that's not a bad thing at all.

RUN YOUR RACE

One of the keys to developing perseverance is keeping our eyes on the prize. As followers of Jesus, we are called to fix our focus on him. But that's easier said than done. We know storms and setbacks can throw us off course, but there's another, sneakier distraction that derails our focus just as quickly: comparison.

Hebrews 12:1 urges us to "Run with perseverance the race marked out for us."[22] Not someone else's race. Ours. But how often do we glance sideways, wondering if we are falling behind, missing out, or measuring up?

Comparison is a subtle thief. It convinces us that the good life is what someone else is living. It causes us to chase after what others have instead of staying faithful to where God has placed us. And when we do that, we lose sight of the race God has called us to run.

Comparison doesn't just make us feel small; it robs us of joy, contentment, and clarity. It tricks us into thinking that a "rich and satisfying life" comes from looking like someone else, living like someone else, or achieving what someone else has. But your fullest life is not going to look like mine, and that's exactly how God designed it.

Our culture has shaped our view of the good life more than we realize. We're told it's found in wealth, status, and nonstop achievement. It's about climbing the ladder, hitting the right milestones, building the perfect life, and chasing whatever feels good in the moment. From 401(k) s and college acceptance letters to vacation homes and viral posts, we are constantly sold a version of life that appears full but often leaves us feeling empty.

But as followers of Jesus, we must resist the urge to buy into whatever the world is selling. A rich and satisfying life isn't found in bigger paychecks, busier calendars, or newer gadgets. Comparison will always leave us discontented and distracted.

> "Do not conform to the pattern of this world, but be transformed by the renewing of your mind. Then you will be able to test and approve what God's will is—his good, pleasing and perfect will."[23]

God doesn't just invite us into a new way of living—he transforms us from the inside out. He renews our minds so we can recognize and embrace his good, pleasing, and perfect will. But when we conform to the patterns of this world, we end up reaping the fruit of that pattern: discontentment, envy, loneliness, pride, and emptiness. We will never fill a God-sized hole with anything other than God himself.

My wife and I have been married for over a decade, and in recent years, we have watched peers walk through heartbreaking seasons of infidelity and divorce. A recurring theme in their stories is that the monotony of everyday life produces boredom and discontentment. Some of the stories we have heard involve poor decisions made after several years of discontentment and longing for what they used to have or what their single friends currently have. Along the way, what was once their dream—marriage and family—began to feel like the thing holding them back. They chased something new: freedom, excitement, or happiness.

> A RICH AND SATISFYING LIFE ISN'T FOUND IN BIGGER PAYCHECKS, BUSIER CALENDARS, OR NEWER GADGETS. COMPARISON WILL ALWAYS LEAVE US DISCONTENTED AND DISTRACTED. COMPARISON WILL ALWAYS LEAVE US DISCONTENTED AND DISTRACTED.

But the happiness they are chasing won't be found in a new partner or more freedom. The enemy loves to whisper that what we have isn't enough. His goal is always to steal, kill, and destroy.[24]

We must kill comparison before it kills us. If we're not careful, it will pull our eyes away from Jesus and onto the lives of others. The only remedy is to fix our focus again on the One who never changes and always satisfies.

After Jesus' death and resurrection, he began appearing to his disciples and other followers. One morning, Peter was out fishing with several of the disciples. As they struggled to catch anything, a voice called from the shore, instructing them to cast their net on the other side of the boat. They obeyed and their net overflowed with fish. At that moment, Peter realized it was Jesus. Without hesitation, he threw himself into the water and swam to shore.

Not long before this, Peter had denied Jesus three times. Now, Jesus lovingly restored him and spoke of the unique path Peter's life (and death) would take. But rather than staying focused on his own call, Peter turned and pointed to another disciple, John, and asked, "What about him, Lord?"[25]

"Jesus replied, 'If I want him to remain alive until I return, what is that to you? *As for you, follow me.*"[26]

In that powerful response, Jesus reminded Peter—and us—that our job is not to compare stories, but to faithfully follow. We cannot keep our eyes fixed on Jesus if we are constantly looking over our shoulder at everyone else. Jesus gives the same invitation to you and me: *As for you, follow me.*

FIX YOUR EYES

To develop perseverance, we must fix our eyes on Jesus. Our attention determines our endurance. Running with perseverance requires an unwavering focus on what God is calling us toward, not on the distractions trying to pull us away. Like a racehorse with blinders, we need to block out anything that tempts us to drift.

So let me ask:

What has been stealing your focus?

What has left you feeling disheartened or discontent?

What has caused you to feel like giving up?

THREE TRAPS WE MUST LEARN TO RESIST

1. **Don't grow disheartened by obstacles**

    Trials will come. Tragedy will strike. Life will not go according to plan. But just because it's hard doesn't mean you're on the wrong path. Don't let setbacks throw you off course. Remember: The stories worth telling are rarely the smoothest ones. The challenges you are facing today may become the stories of faith, grit, and growth you'll tell tomorrow. So what trial are you in right now? Where do you need to keep going, even if it is uphill?

2. **Don't grow discouraged by failure**

    Failure isn't final, and it isn't fatal. Failing does not make you a failure. Maybe you've tried before and it didn't work. Maybe you're scared to try again. But could it be that what feels like failure is actually forming you? What dream have you buried out of fear? What is something God put on your heart that you've been too afraid to pursue?

Remember: Real failure isn't falling—it's refusing to move. Or as Alfred once said to Bruce Wayne: "Why do we fall, Bruce? So we can learn to pick ourselves up."[27]

3. **Don't grow distracted by comparison**

You are called to run the race marked out for you, not someone else. Resist the urge to chase the life someone else is living when God is calling you to something different. Keep your eyes on your own paper and kill comparison before it kills you. The world promises happiness through more—more money, more stuff, more status—but its fruit rarely delivers on its promise. Who or what are you comparing yourself to? What expectations are weighing you down that God never asked you to carry? Don't worry about them. As for you—follow Jesus.

Jesus is inviting you into a deeper, more meaningful life—one that is marked by endurance, joy, and eternal perspective. He isn't just calling you to run the race; he ran it first. Scripture describes him as "the champion who initiates and perfects our faith."[28] Jesus endured the cross, scorning its shame, not because it was easy, but because he kept his eyes on the joy set before him. He knew the end of the story. He stayed the course.

That same joy—real life with God, now and forever—is available to us. Jesus didn't quit when things got hard. Even when his soul was overwhelmed with sorrow, he chose the Father's will over his own.[29] And now, he sits at the right hand of the Father, having made a way for you and me to do the same.

When you feel weary, disheartened, discouraged, or distracted, think of Jesus. When obstacles block your view, think of Jesus. When failure whispers lies, think of Jesus. When comparison clouds your vision, fix your eyes once again on him.

He has gone before you. He has paved the way. And now, he invites you to follow.

Keep your eyes on Jesus. Run your race.

TRAIL MARKERS

TRUE NORTH TAKEAWAY
Perseverance doesn't come from avoiding trials, failure, or comparison. It comes from fixing your focus on Jesus. As you run your race, resist distraction, learn from struggle, and keep your eyes on the One who has already overcome.

REFLECTION STOPS
1. What has been stealing your focus lately? Where do you feel most disheartened, discontented, or tempted to give up?
2. Where are you most afraid of failing right now? Is there a dream or step of obedience you've buried because of fear?
3. In this season, what does it practically look like for you to "run with perseverance the race marked out for you"—not someone else's race?

EVERYDAY ADVENTURE CHALLENGE: THE FIRST FOCUS
Your day always follows your first glance. If the first thing you look at is noise, you'll carry noise. But if your eyes land on Jesus first, your whole day shifts—your thoughts, your pace, and your perspective.

For the next three days, give Jesus your first focus instead of your phone.

1. Before reaching for your phone, pause for 15 minutes.
2. Read a grounding passage like Hebrews 12:1–2 or Colossians 3:2–3.
3. Pray: "Jesus, help me fix my eyes on You today. Lead my thoughts, my steps, and my focus."
4. Open messages, email, or social media.

Start with him and let the rest of your day follow your focus.

If you're ready for more practical steps like this, check out the Everyday Adventure Challenge—a simple weekly challenge designed to help you practice intentionality and embrace the adventure in your everyday life. You can learn more at **everydayadventurebook.com**.

TEN
Refuse to Quit

"Too legit, too legit to quit."[1]
MC Hammer

The final key to developing resilience might sound painfully obvious: **Refuse to quit.**

I know. Not exactly groundbreaking. You turned the page hoping for a hidden secret to perseverance and instead got hit with, "Don't give up." *Thanks, Captain Obvious.*

But here's the thing—what's obvious is obviously pretty hard to live out. Perseverance requires persistence, and persistence means we keep showing up, especially when we don't feel like it. The greatest threat for many of us is not that we'll abandon our faith or throw in the towel on life altogether; it's that we'll quietly settle for something less. In the words of Pastor John Ortberg, "The great danger is not that we will renounce our faith. It is that we will become so distracted and rushed and preoccupied that we will settle for a mediocre version of it."[2]

In our quest for a life of everyday adventure, we will quietly give up, settling for a life of everyday mediocrity.

It doesn't usually look like a dramatic exit. It looks like scrolling instead of praying because prayer feels too quiet and too slow. It looks like avoiding hard conversations in your marriage, convincing yourself it's just not worth the fight. It's hitting snooze again, skipping the workout you promised to start. It's letting resentment simmer because forgiving feels harder than holding a grudge. It's shutting down a dream before it ever takes shape, convincing yourself it was probably unrealistic anyway. It's choosing comfort over calling, distraction over discipline, and busyness over being fully present.

> MOST OF US DON'T CONSCIOUSLY QUIT. WE JUST QUIETLY DRIFT FROM THE FULLNESS OF LIFE, ONE SMALL COMPROMISE AT A TIME.

Most of us don't consciously quit. We just quietly drift from the fullness of life, one small compromise at a time.

But here's what is true of every great adventurer: There were moments they wanted to turn back. Before Edmund Hillary and Tenzing Norgay became the first to summit Mount Everest, at least fourteen expeditions had tried and failed[3]. Ferdinand Magellan, who led the first voyage across the Pacific in 1521, had multiple opportunities to abandon ship, but he didn't.[4]

Every meaningful journey has a moment where quitting feels easier than continuing. That's where resilience is forged. You will always have the option to quit. You just have to make that option irrelevant by keeping your eyes on something greater.

If you want to live a rich and satisfying life, you need to grow your grit, cling to hope, and *refuse to quit.*

QUIET QUITTING

We all had that friend growing up—the certified quitter. The one who tapped out as soon as things didn't go their way. Every childhood friend group had one. And if you can't think of who it was, there's a decent chance it was you.

I'm picturing one of my neighborhood friends right now. If we were playing basketball and his team started to lose, he would literally grab his ball and walk home; leaving us without a ball in the middle of the game. If he got frustrated during hide-and-seek because he couldn't find anyone, he would just leave. No warning, no goodbye. Just gone.

Sure, those are childish expressions of quitting; but the truth is, many of us carry the same tendency into adulthood. We may not storm off the court anymore, but we shut down in the middle of hard conversations. We may not leave our jobs outright, but we disengage, doing the bare minimum while silently checking out. We may not walk out on our spouse, but we quietly withhold love, effort, or honesty.

This posture has a name now. In 2022, career coach Bryan Creely gave voice to what many were feeling in a viral social media post; calling it "quiet quitting."[5] He wasn't the only one paying attention. That same year, Gallup reported that over half the U.S. workforce was quietly quitting: doing just enough to keep their job without investing anything extra.[6] And Arianna Huffington put it bluntly in a LinkedIn article: "Quiet quitting isn't just about quitting on a job—it's a step toward quitting on life."[7]

Quiet quitting may start in the workplace, but it rarely stays there. It creeps into relationships, dreams, and spiritual pursuits. It becomes a slow fade, a disengagement from the life we truly long to live.

We quietly quit in our marriages when we stop pursuing connection. We quietly quit as parents when we shift into autopilot and stop engaging intentionally. We give up on our dreams before we even give them a shot. We quit on community when people let us down. We even quietly quit in our faith when we stop showing up with expectation. It goes by different names—complacency, coasting, settling, silent resignation—but underneath it all, it's the same thing: *disengaging from the life we were made for.*

Another name for quiet quitting is *acedia*, a term that comes from the Greek *a-* (not) and *kedos* (to care). It literally means "a lack of care." In *An Unhurried Life*, Alan Fadling defines acedia as "a place of apathy toward life and a kind of spiritual boredom; it's that umpteenth lap somewhere between enthusiasm of the starting line and the celebration of the finish line."[8] He goes on to describe it as the temptation to "give in, give up, or distract ourselves."[9] Acedia whispers that the life you're living isn't enough and lures you into imagining a better option *anywhere but here.*

Complacency is not just a symptom of spiritual decline; it's evidence that something vital has already died. Faith does not die the moment we stop attending church. It dies when our trust, our obedience, and our love no longer shape our everyday decisions. When faith becomes a category instead of a calling.

To my friends who feel like quiet quitters; don't give up. You were made for more than this. If you're just surviving, going through the motions, keeping things afloat with as little energy as possible; God has more for you. You don't have to live numb. You don't have to stay stuck. Jesus didn't die just to punch your ticket to heaven. He died to bring you life, and life to the full, right here and now.

That doesn't mean every day will feel thrilling. Real adventure is not about chasing a new feeling. It's about showing up fully in the ordinary. It's about waking up to the life God has already placed in front of you and deciding to engage, not just survive. Real life is found in the fight to keep showing up when your spouse feels distant. In the courage to pray again when you feel like your last dozen prayers went unanswered. In the decision to forgive. To stay. To try again. To lead with love even when it costs you something.

> COMPLACENCY IS NOT JUST A SYMPTOM OF SPIRITUAL DECLINE; IT'S EVIDENCE THAT SOMETHING VITAL HAS ALREADY DIED.

In a world that is quietly quitting, we need to be people who loudly stay. Not loud with noise, but loud with love. Loud with presence. Loud with persistence. There are futures hanging in the balance. There are friendships and families that desperately need someone to show up—fully present, fully alive.

WHEN A MARRIAGE GETS QUIET

We're going to talk about marriage for a minute. But before we dive in, let me say this: even if you are not married, don't skip ahead. This section is about more than just marriage; it is about commitment, connection, and perseverance. The principles here can speak to any meaningful relationship or long-term pursuit.

After a decade of marriage, we are starting to enter a stage where some of our peers are considering or actively pursuing divorce. I hate calling it a stage, but that's what it feels like. It is not that something magically breaks at year seven or ten; it's slower than that. Life happens: job changes, babies, loss, stress. Habits form. Distance grows. Intimacy fades. And without meaning to, many couples begin to quietly quit.

Quiet quitting in marriage doesn't always look like conflict or crisis. It often looks like routine. Like coming home and burying ourselves in tasks instead of connecting. Like putting the kids to bed, cleaning up, and retreating to opposite ends of the couch to scroll in silence. Like neglecting additional effort to make your spouse feel seen, valued, and special. It's passive. It's disengaged. It's subtle. And over time, it erodes the very thing we vowed to protect. We keep the rings and the marriage certificate, but lose the intimacy and joy we once had.

One of the most common times a couple divorces is after their last child leaves home. It's not that something suddenly snapped; it's that the drift had been happening for years. The child simply delayed the decision. The marriage had been coasting long before the paperwork was filed. Somewhere along the line, one or both partners quietly quit.

If you are married, hear me clearly: *quit quiet quitting*. If any of this feels familiar, it's time to speak up. Start a conversation. Seek healing. Choose to fight for connection before it's too late. Marriage can be one of life's greatest adventures—but only if you keep choosing it.

10 WAYS TO QUIT QUIET QUITTING ON YOUR MARRIAGE

1. Surprise your spouse with their favorite coffee.
2. Greet them at the door with a kiss and a hug—like you mean it.
3. Leave a handwritten note on the seat of their car (or in their lunchbox, if they pack one).
4. Use lipstick to write a love note on the bathroom mirror.
5. Pray over your spouse before bed—even a short, simple prayer.
6. Text them a specific reason you're thankful for them in the middle of the day.
7. Rewatch your wedding video or look through old photos together.
8. Plan a date night and then follow through.
9. Ask, "How can I serve you this week?" and listen with an open heart and intent to follow through.
10. Pick a time this week to sit down, unplug, and really talk—no phones, no distractions, just connection.[10]

If quiet quitting is doing the bare minimum to keep things afloat, then it is time to go above and beyond to spark something new. God has more for your marriage—more joy, more connection, more life. It doesn't have to stay this way.

HOLDING ONTO HOPE

When I was in college, I went on a backpacking trip with friends in the mountains of Montana. After a long day on the trail, we set up camp, shared a meal around the fire, and turned in for the night. A little while later, I stepped out of my tent to grab something and was hit with a darkness I had not expected. The fire had died down, and thick clouds had swallowed up the stars and the moon. It was *dark dark,* and I scurried back into my tent like a boy scout ready to quit before his eighth birthday. I lay there in the quiet, wrapped in the weight of that darkness, repeating a simple phrase to myself: *Day is coming.*

To hope is to believe that although it is night, day is coming. Biblical hope is more than making a wish; it is a confident expectation or assurance based upon a sure foundation for which we wait with joy and full confidence.[11] Biblical hope rests on a belief that God will always be true to his promises. To hold onto hope is to hold on to God and to his Word. To hope is to believe that God will come through. Hope keeps us looking ahead, even when we cannot see through the darkness.

> "Rejoice in our confident hope. Be patient in trouble, and keep on praying."[12]

Paul's letter to the church in Rome reminds us to cling to hope in the midst of darkness. Just as hope is a reality we can cling to, trouble is a reality we can expect in our lives. Paul's encouragement is to "Be patient in trouble and keep on praying." Sometimes trouble blows through quickly, and other times it sticks around for a while. Trouble is like a teenager coming home from college; sometimes they just pop in for a weekend, and other times, they drop out, move all their stuff in, and settle in without any intention of paying rent. Be patient and keep on praying…

Don't miss the importance of prayer. Prayer and hope are besties.

Prayer amplifies hope. The more we pray, the more hope we have. Even when our trials and troubles don't have resolution, we can have hope. Prayer invites God into our situation and wherever God is present, so is hope. Theologian Richard Rohr put it this way: "The theological virtue of hope is the patient and trustful willingness to live without closure, without resolution, and still be content and even happy because our satisfaction is now at another level, and our source is beyond ourselves."[13] Even without closure, we can be content—trusting God. Even amid darkness, we can cling to a quiet conviction: *Day is coming.*

That's not just wishful thinking; it is anchored in God's promises.

The people of Israel found themselves in a season of waiting, exiled in a land that felt nothing like home. It was in that tension that God spoke this word through the prophet Jeremiah:

> "'For I know the plans I have for you,' says the Lord. 'They are plans for good and not for disaster, to give you a future and a hope.'"[14]

That's not just a verse to hang in your hallway; it is a promise worth clinging to. Maybe right now, a future feels far off. Maybe hope feels like something you lost along the way. But I want to remind you that God has not given up on you.

And that famous promise does not stand alone. Just a few verses later, it says:

> "In those days when you pray, I will listen. If you look for me wholeheartedly, you will find me."[15]

God isn't just offering you a better future. He is offering you himself. He is near. He hears you. And he promises to be found by those who seek him. In the darkest night, in the longest wait, in the deepest ache; *he is still the light that breaks through.*

There are times the outcome we are hoping for may not be the outcome we experience. Biblical hope stretches beyond a basic desire to win the game or even a more complex desire for a loved one to experience healing. Our hope is an eternal outcome that stretches beyond our earthly wishes and temporary desires.

Our hope is fixed on the belief that God is who he says he is, and his kingdom will prevail forever. That is why we never give up. We fix our eyes on what we cannot yet see, on what will last forever. We keep holding on to hope. Russian novelist Fyodor Dostoevsky said, "To live without hope is to cease to live."[16] My prayer is that you continue holding on to hope and keep holding on to life that is truly life.

GIVING UP CONTROL

I could never be a pilot. If you are one, kudos to you. Pilots have so many important things to remember, so many levers and dials, and so many protocols. It really is quite impressive. Even if I were to study all the manuals and understand all the protocols and call signals, there is one major thing that would hold me back from being a pilot—navigating an airplane in zero visibility.

Life is a lot like being a pilot. There are times that feel like clear skies in which you can clearly see everything ahead of you and other times you can't see six feet ahead and you have no idea what to do next. That is where we can continue to learn from our pilot friends. When visibility diminishes, they trust

> GOD ISN'T JUST OFFERING YOU A BETTER FUTURE. HE IS OFFERING YOU HIMSELF. HE IS NEAR. HE HEARS YOU. AND HE PROMISES TO BE FOUND BY THOSE WHO SEEK HIM.

their training, instruments, and the air traffic controller. The air traffic controller's job is to communicate with the pilot by offering direction, course correction, and warnings to help them navigate safely through uncertainty.

That is how God often leads us. By giving him control of our lives, we don't strap ourselves in the cargo compartment of the airplane waiting to arrive at our destination. We turn the volume up so we can hear the voice of the controller, and we abide by his direction, even when we lack visibility. We trust our training, aiming to remember everything we have learned so far. We trust our instruments, leaning into God's Word as the ultimate truth in our lives. And we trust the voice of our controller, embracing the role of the Holy Spirit in our lives as our guide and counselor.

In a chapter about refusing to quit, I am going to say something that might shock you. Ready? It's time to give up. It's time to give up… control.

The tighter we cling to control in our lives, the more likely we are to give up when things don't go as planned. When we believe everything depends on us, we carry the crushing weight of outcomes we were never meant to manage. It's easy to lose hope when progress stalls or things feel uncertain. If we have a death grip on our careers and start to sense instability or boredom, we might react by resigning—either from the position or from putting in real effort.

The same is true in other areas: When our kids start making choices we can't control, we're tempted to disengage instead of staying present. When our marriage doesn't look like the highlight reels we see online, we default to survival mode instead of fighting for connection. When spiritual growth feels slow or dry, we pull back instead of pressing in.

When we try to control everything, we eventually burn out. But when we release control and trust God, hope has room to grow.

I am not suggesting you abandon your will to your employer, your partner, your government, or anyone else. I am talking about surrendering control of your life to God. I am inviting you to let go and ultimately give God the most important vote in your life. Jesus doesn't only offer himself as our Savior but also our Lord. Lordship suggests someone having power or authority over others.[17] To view Jesus as Lord of your life is to give him ultimate control and authority over your life.

> **WHEN WE BELIEVE EVERYTHING DEPENDS ON US, WE CARRY THE CRUSHING WEIGHT OF OUTCOMES WE WERE NEVER MEANT TO MANAGE.**

In high school, I deeply loved Jesus, but I struggled to share my faith with my friends and my classmates. I remember often feeling an urge to tell someone about Jesus or invite them to youth group; but time and time again I would push it away, unwilling to compromise my social status. I wasn't rejecting Jesus—not as my Savior at least—I just wasn't willing to give him his rightful place as Lord in my life.

What changed?

During the summer following my senior year of high school, I went on my first mission trip. Students from our youth group went to Atlanta, Georgia to work with the Atlanta Dream Center. On that trip, I prayed out loud for the first time in a large group setting. I approached strangers to tell them about Jesus and to pray with them. I walked into a home and sat with recovering addicts and men infected with HIV to tell them that Jesus still loved them.

I came back from that trip a different person. I was still a work in progress (and I still am), but I had truly experienced what it was like to surrender my life, my decisions, and my actions to Jesus. I have taken back control of my life countless times since, but I have started to believe that my life is significantly more fulfilling when I submit to God.

Think of something you are holding on to tightly right now; maybe it's a relationship, a career, a financial goal, or a dream. Chances are, you're gripping it so tightly because it matters to you. You don't want to see it fall apart or be mishandled. But this is where we often go wrong: we believe we are the best person to manage what we care about most.

The truth? We are not. God, who created the universe, is far more qualified to handle our lives; including the parts we treasure most.

His ways aren't always our ways, but I have learned to trust that they are better. Life might not go according to my plan, but I've never once regretted surrendering to his plan. I still make plans, but I trust in what Proverbs reminds us: "You can make many plans, but the Lord's purpose will prevail."[18] That's the life I want—a purpose-prevailing life.

What is something you need to release today? What are you clinging to out of fear or pride? I challenge you: Quit trying to control everything. Surrender it to God because he's more dependable than you or I will ever be.

A RESOLUTION TO PERSIST

One of my favorite Pixar movies of all time is *Finding Nemo*. It's hard to believe, but it came out in 2003, when I was just twelve years old. If you've never seen the movie, I am shocked. I am also sorry because I am about to spoil it for you (but that's on you).

A clownfish named Marlin is on a mission to find his son, Nemo, when he bumps into Dory, a blue reef fish who can't seem to remember much of anything. Marlin reluctantly lets her join him on his mission. Dory, who herself is lost, can't remember what she is looking for; so she keeps happily swimming along, singing, "Just keep swimming. Just keep swimming…"

It is through Marlin's persistence and refusal to give up that he and Dory follow clue after clue, eventually leading them to Nemo. Dory's melodic motto is more than just a song; it is the undertone of the whole movie. *Just keep swimming.*[19] It's like a reminder to keep going no matter what. *Just keep swimming.* Even when you get knocked off course and lose your way. *Just keep swimming.*

"Just keep swimming" is more than a song; it's a soundtrack of persistence. It's a resolution to persist and an invitation to never give in. We all need a motto of persistence in our lives. We all need a song that keeps us moving forward. *Just keep swimming. Just keep going. Just keep working. Just keep leading. Just keep loving.*

Every one of us will be tempted to quit. We will experience obstacles that make us want to shut it down altogether, pack it in and head home. We will walk through trials that will attempt to drain us of our love and our life. We will be tempted to quietly quit, resigning to a lesser life, just doing what it takes to get by. Working for another paycheck. Staying together with our spouse to provide stability for the kids. Showing up at church to check the box.

Let this be your encouragement to keep going, to just keep swimming. Let my words be life to you as you step into another day and another opportunity to live life to the fullest. Let this book be the spark it takes to keep climbing toward the summit. Let it be the motivation you need to dig your heels in, to fight another day.

In some of the deadliest battles, it's been said that soldiers aren't driven by a desire to win, but by a determination not to lose. In the most desperate moments, their mindset shifts. It's no longer about gaining ground or defeating the enemy; it becomes about survival. And in that shift, a deeper level of persistence and grit emerges—one fueled not by strategy, but by sheer resolve to keep going no matter what.

One of the greatest qualities in a marriage that lasts is a resolution to persist. While communication, love, and humility are essential, it's the determination to keep going that sustains a relationship through life's storms. Thriving marriages aren't just marked by commitment; they are marked by persistence. This kind of perseverance doesn't just help a marriage survive; it helps marriage to flourish. It guards against complacency, acedia, and boredom by creating an atmosphere of ongoing pursuit, where love deepens, and life continues to grow.

We can have the same resolution to persist in every area of our lives. There are many times in which quitting a job is the right thing for a person to do. We outgrow certain work environments. We develop new passions and desires. God leads us in the direction of new opportunities and ambitions. A resolution to persist doesn't mean we stay at the same job for the rest of our lives. It means we remain determined to persevere in kindness, integrity, humility, honor, and respect. It means we refuse to give anything less than our best, because we recognize our work as an opportunity for worship. Quiet quitting is no longer an option for the everyday adventurer because passivity and complacency are not compatible with the rich and satisfying life we are called to live.

Develop your own declaration of determination. Write your own passage of persistence. Create your own resolution of resilience. Make it the screensaver on your phone. Put it on your bathroom mirror. Hang it next to your desk at work. Keep it in front of you and repeat it as often as you need to.

Love first, love often, and love even when it doesn't return.
Never give in.
Don't quit until the final bell rings.
It's not over until the fat lady sings.
Just keep swimming.

NEVER GIVE UP

One of our household rules growing up was that we couldn't quit a sport once we started it. I had teammates who quit midseason because they weren't getting enough playing time or their parents disagreed with the coach; but quitting was not an option in our house. Well, except for that one time I quit track in seventh grade after two days of practice. That doesn't count. That wasn't quitting. That was just smart.

But I found a loophole. My sophomore year, I decided not to try out for the basketball team. I told everyone it was because I wanted to focus on baseball and work a little bit more.

The truth? I didn't try out because I was afraid. I was one of the smaller kids. I didn't think I was fast enough, tall enough, or good enough to make the team. I compared myself to everyone else and felt like I didn't measure up. So instead of showing up and possibly getting cut, I quietly stepped back and avoided the risk. I quit before I had the chance to fail.

> LIFE TO THE FULLEST IS FULL OF SETBACKS, BUT IT IS ALSO FULL OF GRACE, JOY, AND REDEMPTION.

By doing that, I stayed in control of the narrative. "I didn't get cut, I just didn't try out." But I also eliminated the possibility of making the team. I skipped out on a moment God could have used to stretch me, build my character, and draw me closer to him. Avoiding failure also meant avoiding growth.

This form of *pre-quitting* leads to the same result as outright quitting—missed opportunities, unfulfilled potential, and stunted spiritual formation. Whether you quit before the starting line or halfway through the race, the consequences are the same.

That's why, for the everyday adventurer, quitting is not an option and perseverance is a prerequisite. At the end of the day, the most important key to refusing to quit is simply... refusing to quit.

So don't get tired of doing what is good. As Paul writes: "At just the right time we will reap a harvest of blessing *if we don't give up.*"[20]

Those who persevere will be rewarded. When we stay the course, refusing to give up, we can be assured that it will be worth it. Life to the fullest is full of setbacks, but it is also full of grace, joy, and redemption.

Refuse to give in to the temptation of mediocrity—the kind that convinces you to do the bare minimum just to stay afloat. Don't let acedia rob you of a life that is meaningful and full. As Alan Fadling says, "Counter acedia's enticement to seek some unknown better that lies anywhere but here with an intentional and positive focus on the present."[21] That's where purpose is found—not in someday, but today.

Stay grounded. Stay engaged. Keep holding on to hope. Like my grandma always said: "If I'm not dead, God's not done." Better days are ahead and the best stories are often born in the darkest chapters.

And if you need one more reason to keep going, here it is:

> "God, who got you started in this spiritual adventure, shares with us the life of his Son and our Master Jesus. He will never give up on you. Never forget that."[22]

You may feel like quitting, but Jesus never will. And if he hasn't given up on you, maybe today is the day you decide not to give up either.

Refuse to quit.

I hate running. People that enjoy running have issues. I wanted to say this earlier, but I was afraid my running friends would stop reading, so I held off as long as I could.

After giving up on running in the seventh grade, I decided to give it another go when I was 23. I was peer pressured into signing up for the Fargo Half-Marathon. A few months before the big race, I started "training." In an effort to build up to the 13.1 miles I would be suffering, I was beginning to stretch myself and set out on a four-mile run. At the two-mile mark, my shins were burning. At the three-mile mark, I decided (again) that running wasn't for me. When I got back to my apartment, I pulled the plug on the whole half-marathon thing. I made an emotional decision. I didn't run the half-marathon, but I did get the drawstring bag.

I did show up with some friends to cheer on our more trouble-minded friends. We drove to different spots along the route and we had encouraging signs. As all the runners passed us, I was reminded of why I was standing on the side of the road with a hot coffee and a handmade sign. They looked miserable and angry. I was relieved.

We went to the end of the race route to wait for our friends to finish. We saw several of them limp across the finish line and witnessed the life come back into their faces, knowing they were done torturing themselves. As we waited for our friends, I couldn't remember if I was at the end of a race or in the middle of a war. There were people on stretchers and in wheelchairs and medics running around attending to all the victims.

The next day at church, one of my friends, Colin, who decided to run the full marathon with zero training, hobbled into church on crutches. I resisted the urge to laugh at his pain and walked up to him to ask how he was feeling. He told me about the race and how there were numerous times in which the pain was so bad he wanted to quit. I asked him why he didn't quit and he plainly said, "I told myself I was going to finish, so I finished." He fought past the pain and the urge to give up and he just kept running. He also told me how much encouragement he drew from everyone cheering along the pathway and thanked me for supporting him.

Despite the physical pain he was in, he was happy. I walked away feeling convicted. He got to experience something that I had forfeited. He grew his grit in a way that I never could from the sideline. He limped away stronger, and I walked away the same—Starbucks in hand. He experienced a fullness of life that he had not prior to finishing that race.

If we want to experience all God has for us, we must develop perseverance. Perseverance is what it takes to finish the race. Resilience is what is required for us to endure and ultimately embrace a life of everyday adventure.

Perseverance is built one step at a time, and each step gets lighter when we lighten our load. Release the weight of guilt, fear, shame, distraction, and comparison—the things that keep tripping you up. Then fix your focus on Jesus and the path he has marked out for you. Don't let discouragement derail you or the enticement of comfort convince you to coast. The greatest adventure is found when you refuse to quit. When you fall, get up. And above all, keep going!

You will never experience all God has for you if you quit before you get there. Keep moving forward.

TRAIL MARKERS

TRUE NORTH TAKEAWAY
Resilience isn't flashy; it's showing up when you would rather check out. Everyday adventure grows where you refuse to quietly quit, surrender control to God, and keep moving with hope, love, and integrity—one small, stubborn step at a time.

REFLECTION STOPS
1. In what ways have you been tempted to "quiet quit"? (marriage, parenting, work, friendships, church, your own soul) How is acedia showing up as "just doing the minimum" or checking out instead of engaging?
2. Think about a place in your life that feels dark or stuck. Where do you most need to whisper, "Day is coming" and cling to hope instead of giving in to discouragement?
3. What are you gripping with white-knuckled control right now (a relationship, career, financial future, dream)? What might it look like to treat Jesus as Lord there—not just Savior—and actually surrender your next steps to him?

EVERYDAY ADVENTURE CHALLENGE: JUST KEEP SWIMMING
Persistence does not happen by accident. It is chosen, named, and practiced. Today, write your own Resolution to Persist: a short, personal declaration of how you will keep going when life gets heavy, distracting, or discouraging. Let it become your version of "Just keep swimming."

1. **Name the areas you are tempted to quietly quit**—(faith, marriage, habits, health, calling, dreams, relationships)
2. **Write a 3–6 sentence declaration** that describes who you want to be when things get hard. Focus on persistence, presence, and refusing to settle for less than the life God is calling you to.
3. **Choose your phrase or motto**—a simple line you can return to when you need it. (Examples: "Just keep swimming." "Show up and stay." "I won't drift." "Persist with joy.")
4. **Put it where you will see it.** Set it as your phone wallpaper, tape it to your mirror, or keep it in your Bible or journal.
5. **Speak it aloud once a day for the next week.** Let your resolution become a rhythm—a reminder of the story you refuse to quit.

This is your declaration of determination. Your passage of persistence. Your personal reminder to keep going, keep loving, keep trusting, and keep showing up no matter what.

CONCLUSION
Let the Adventure Begin

"Life is either a daring adventure or nothing at all."[1]
Helen Keller

The idea behind *Everyday Adventure* started when I was a sophomore in college. I remember looking around and realizing how many people were treating life like a holding pattern—just trying to survive college, survive their job, survive their season until something better finally came along. It was like we were all waiting for life to begin... *someday.*

But what if someday is today?

That question changed everything for me. I started to believe that the real adventure wasn't "out there," it was right here in the daily rhythms, the relationships, the diapers, the calendars, and the checkout lines. That belief led me to start a blog[2] in 2010 I called *Everyday Adventure,* and eventually, it led to this book.

I've been living, collecting, and writing my "field notes" for this project for nearly a decade. At one point I even found a rugged faux-leather journal that made me feel like an explorer from the 1800s and scribbled across the first page: "Adventure is an attitude worth pursuing, not a destination." That has stayed true every step of the way. Many of the ideas and thoughts jotted on the pages of that journal have found their way into this book.

There were moments I doubted whether the message was even worth sharing. Like the time I discovered a book by Mark Batterson and Dick Foth called *A Trip Around the Sun: Turning Your Everyday Life into the Adventure of a Lifetime*. I literally thought, *"THEY RIPPED ME OFF!"* (Spoiler: they didn't. But I still took six years to read the book.) What I eventually realized is this: I wasn't called to write their book. I was called to write *this* one.

Because this is *my adventure*.

And that's the point I want to land here: God's not asking you to live anyone else's adventure. He's inviting you into your own.

So if you've made it this far, let this be your reminder:

You don't need a plane ticket to find adventure. You don't need a new job or a new life or a new plan.

You just need to say yes to the greatest adventure of all time: *following Jesus*.

GREATEST ADVENTURE

Three words changed the world forever: "Come, follow me."[3]

That was the simple invitation Jesus extended to his first disciples. He didn't offer a detailed plan, a timeline, or even a guarantee of safety. He didn't feel the need to prove his plan like he was entering *Shark Tank* trying to get investors. He simply stepped into the disciples' everyday lives and invited them into something deeper, something greater. It wasn't flashy or strategic by the world's standards, but it was powerful. And when ordinary people said yes to that invitation, everything changed.

When Peter and his brother, Andrew, dropped their fishing nets and followed Jesus away from the Sea of Galilee, they didn't know what to expect. They didn't know where they were going or when they'd return. At many points along the way, they likely thought, *"Wait, this isn't what we signed up for…"* They discovered that following Jesus wasn't always easy, but it was always worth it.

That same invitation is still being extended to each one of us today.

If you read the Gospels, you will find that the adventure of following Jesus took people places they never would have expected. Peter walked on water.[4] Paul worshiped in chains and was freed from prison by an earthquake.[5] Philip left a city-wide revival in Samaria and obeyed God's leading to a deserted road, where he encountered a single man riding in a chariot. Only after that moment of obedience was Philip supernaturally carried away.[6] That's the kind of story God writes when we say yes.

For much of my early life, I misunderstood what it meant to follow Jesus. I thought it meant giving up fun and playing it safe in a religious bubble. I mistakenly thought it was all about following a long list of stuffy rules. I thought it meant trading adventure for discipline. It seemed as if I would be missing out on *life to the fullest* if I chose to follow Jesus. I was tempted to believe the enemy's lies.

The enemy has had the same tactic since the beginning of time. He offers counterfeits and cheap counter-invitations—*"Did God really say?"*[7] Instead of finding an abundant life in Jesus, he aims to convince us that it is found in pursuing our own interests, satisfaction, and happiness. Like the snake he is, the Devil tries to convince us that instead of following Jesus, we ought to follow our cravings, desires, and lusts. He entices us with wealth, recognition, and attention.

> "You're addicted to thrills? What an empty life! The pursuit of pleasure never satisfies."[8]

In *Thrill Sequence,* Pastor Rob Kettering says, "Real life is found in investing your life rather than milking it for every ounce of self-gratification."[9] Yet, here we are like a farmer, up early milking away; only to realize the *full life* the enemy claims to offer is a mirage, leaving us emptier than before.

The very things we use to fill the void only make it grow. Promotions come and go and we still have our eyes set on the next one. Our 401(k) balloons, but so does our loneliness. The relationship that we hoped would heal us leads to even more heartbreak. That's where we get it all wrong. Following Jesus is not the absence of adventure—it is the very heartbeat of it. Follow Jesus, not your dreams.

Several years ago, a missionary serving in a nation where Christianity is illegal visited our college ministry. As he shared stories of faith and courage, he said something that has stuck with me ever since:

> "If you want an adventure, don't put on a parachute and jump out of a plane or travel to climb a mountain. Live for Jesus and reach the lost. You will never be bored."[10]

He's right. Life with Jesus is anything but boring. It might not always be easy or predictable, but it is always worth it. I've seen it firsthand.

When we said yes to stepping out of our comfort zone and moving across the country, we had no idea what it would require—or what it would make possible. That step of obedience came with its share of challenges, but it also opened the door to moments we never could have planned or predicted.

One of the unexpected highlights of my role during that season was getting to host families at NFL games; creating moments of joy, connection, and surprise that became sacred memories. One of those moments came in 2021 with my friend Giovanni Hamilton, someone I introduced you to earlier in the book. His family came to Indianapolis for a Colts game, and we had the honor of hosting them for a weekend filled with surprises: loading up on team gear, playing our hearts out at Dave & Buster's, and sending his parents out for a well-deserved date night at one of the city's finest restaurants. That alone would have made for an unforgettable weekend. But then I got a call the night before the game from an unknown number. I picked up and the voice on the other end said, "Hey, I'm Trey. I'm the Colts mascot…"

He invited us to the stadium. That night. We drove in under the stadium through the player entrance and parked in the player lot. We met Trey and walked out onto the field under the lights. It was just us. We ran routes, kicked field goals, and threw footballs from the upper deck.

The next day, we spent time on the sidelines before the game. Gio met players, coaches, and members of the Colts organization, soaking in every moment. Watching him take it all in was surreal.

After the game, Trey came back to get us one more time, this time fully suited up as Blue, the famed Colts mascot. Gio ran a few more routes on the field, the same turf his heroes had just stepped off of moments earlier. Then he laid down side by side with Blue, staring up as the massive roof slowly closed overhead. For a quiet moment, everything slowed. It felt like the perfect ending.

But believe it or not, that still wasn't the end of our adventure.

Before Gio and his family flew home, I received one more DM, this time from Pat McAfee, inviting Gio to be a guest on his show. As I watched Gio live out his dream on one of the biggest sports shows in the world, I found myself reflecting on the entire weekend and thinking, *What if I had said no? What if I had let fear win? What if I had chosen comfort instead?*

That moment, like so many others, reminded me: adventure begins with a yes. It's not always stadium lights or supernatural miracles. Sometimes it's the quiet yes of a conversation with a neighbor. It's the simple decision to pray, "God, what do you have for me today? Help me see what you want me to see. I am available. Use me."

Remember Philip. His yes didn't lead to a bigger crowd or a louder platform. It led him to a deserted road and one searching soul. Saying yes to Jesus doesn't always lead to bigger—but it will always lead to better.

Rob Ketterling said, "You will never be more satisfied in life than when you are doing what you were created to do."[11]

I believe that is true. That is the heart of everyday adventure—living on mission, saying yes to God's invitations, trusting that he sees what we can't. A life of pursuing God is truly the best quest.

In *Love Does*, Bob Goff writes, "I used to think knowing God was like going on a business trip with Him, but now I know He's inviting me on an adventure instead."[12]

The same is true for you. Jesus isn't just offering you an eternal destination. He's offering himself. And with him comes the greatest adventure of all: walking in step with the One who created you, loves you, and still invites you.

Maybe you've never said yes to Jesus. Maybe you've heard about him, but you've never opened the door to a relationship with him. Revelation 3:20 says, "Look! I stand at the door and knock. If you hear my voice and open the door, I will come in."[13]

He's knocking. Not with pressure or manipulation, but with an invitation: *Come, follow me.*

If you have never responded to that invitation, now is your moment. And if you have, but you've been living on autopilot, perhaps it's time to say yes again.

Because the best adventures don't begin with plane tickets or gear checklists. They begin with surrender. They begin with Jesus.

CLOSER THAN YOU THINK

On a recent Friday night, our family curled up on the couch for movie night and decided to watch *Up*. If you've seen it, you know it's not just a kids' movie; it's a masterpiece of emotion, imagination, and perspective. And it just might hold one of the most powerful illustrations of what adventure really looks like.

As children, Carl and Ellie are wide-eyed dreamers. They idolize the great explorer Charles Muntz, who famously declared, "Adventure is out there!" Together, Carl and Ellie make plans to chase that adventure, setting their sights on Paradise Falls. But they also dream of a quieter kind of adventure: building a life together, raising a family, and making a home.

As the years go on, their dreams take shape: they fall in love, get married, and begin preparing for a child. Then heartbreak. In a brief, devastating scene, we see them experience a miscarriage. That moment, wordless and tender, changes the course of their story. Unable to have children, they turn their hopes toward their shared dream of traveling to Paradise Falls. They start saving—tucking away coins and dollars in a big glass jar labeled "Adventure Fund"—only to crack it open again and again for car repairs, hospital visits, and leaky roofs. Life happens.

Still, they age together; laughing, loving, living out the ordinary days. Until one day, Ellie is gone. And Carl, left alone in their now-silent house, is full of regret. He never gave her the adventure they dreamed of. So, in a grand, almost desperate gesture, he ties thousands of balloons to the roof of their home and lifts off, headed for Paradise Falls.

What happens next is whimsical and wild. He meets a boy named Russell, a talking dog, and a rare bird named Kevin. But it's what happens in a quiet moment that undoes you. Carl finally arrives at Paradise Falls, pulls out Ellie's old scrapbook—her "Adventure Book"—and flips through the pages. He expects them to be blank, but instead, he finds them filled with photos of their life together: picnics, house projects, birthdays, small smiles, and mundane moments. And at the end, in Ellie's handwriting, he reads:

> "Thanks for the adventure. Now go have a new one."[14]

That's when it hits you—and Carl—Paradise Falls wasn't the adventure. Ellie was. Their ordinary life together—filled with both beauty and disappointment—was the real adventure. Not the trip they never took, but the moments they shared: folding laundry, watching clouds, sitting side by side in the quiet. That's what so many of us miss.

That moment in *Up* is the heartbeat of *Everyday Adventure*. Like Carl, many of us go through life thinking that the real adventure is "out there." If we could just take that trip, land that promotion, make that move, finally reach that milestone, then we would really be living. But what if the greatest parts of life aren't on some mountaintop or exotic beach?

> **THEIR ORDINARY LIFE TOGETHER—FILLED WITH BOTH BEAUTY AND DISAPPOINTMENT—WAS THE REAL ADVENTURE.**

What if they are in your living room on a Friday night?

What if they are in the car ride home from practice or in the 6:30 a.m. wake-up call from your toddler?

What if the adventure you've been searching for is hidden in the exact life you're already living?

Adventure isn't just out there. *It's closer than you think*. George Eliot, an English novelist and poet, wrote, "Adventure is not outside man; it is within."[15] Adventure isn't a destination; it's a mindset. Adventure isn't an experience; it's a way of living that makes the mundane meaningful and gives the ordinary a little extra.

Adventure isn't something we chase; it's something we choose.

And maybe... just maybe... we don't need to look across the ocean to find adventure. Maybe we need to look across the table.

Maybe the real adventure is being home to tuck your kids in at night, to speak blessing over them, or to sing one more silly song. Maybe it's staying awake just a few more minutes to listen to your spouse talk about their day. Maybe it's saying yes to a conversation when you'd rather scroll. Maybe it's changing diapers and cleaning floors and doing it all again tomorrow.

Or maybe, if you're not in a season with a spouse or kids, the adventure looks different; but it's just as real. Maybe it's making a bucket list of every restaurant in your city and trying them all with friends. Maybe it's starting a Tuesday night dinner club, organizing a weekly run group, or volunteering somewhere you've always cared about. Maybe it's deciding to become the kind of neighbor who actually knows their neighbors. Maybe it's choosing to stay in your current city—even if it feels "boring"—and learning to love it deeply.

> ADVENTURE ISN'T SOMETHING WE CHASE; IT'S SOMETHING WE CHOOSE.

I'll be honest: I've struggled with this. We live in Fargo—yes, that Fargo. A place best known for no one knowing about it. A place people either confuse with Canada or associate with the Coen brothers' film. It's not exactly known for being an adventurous hotspot. And I've had moments where I've thought, *"I wish I was anywhere but here."* But I've come to realize, everyday adventure isn't about a new place; it is a new perspective.

Perhaps adventure is becoming the mayor of Mundaneville. Learning the ins and outs of your town. Finding the hidden gems. Knowing people by name. Smiling at strangers and choosing to see beauty where most people only see routine.

Psalm 92:4 says, "You thrill me, Lord, with all you have done for me! I sing for joy because of what you have done."[16] That's it. That's the key. Adventure is found right where you are because God is with you. That's the source of the thrill. That's what brings joy. Not a trip. Not a raise. Not a viral moment. But the presence of God.

That means you don't have to wait for something big to happen to live fully. You can begin right now—in the laundry piles, the car rides, the ten-minute conversations, and the mundane Mondays.

You get to choose how you live. You can continue drifting through life on autopilot or you can move forward with intention; placing your pins, embracing the ordinary, and slowing down enough to see what God is doing right in front of you. You can seek a life of comfort and ease like our culture promises or you can resist complacency in order to step out of your comfort zone and into life to the fullest. You can settle and retreat into a "normal" life at the first sign of challenge, or you can develop the perseverance that is required to live a life of adventure.

The choice is yours.

We often miss out on everyday adventure not because we are too busy, but because we have bought into the lie that real life is somewhere else—sometime later. But it's not. It's now. And it's here.

That's what I want for you.

Whether you're a parent in the thick of it, a young adult wondering what's next, or a retiree reimagining what's possible; there is more adventure in your current life than you think. Because the real thrill of life is not what you do, but how present you are when you do it. God is inviting you to wake up to the wonder of your everyday life.

"Adventure is out there," they said. And sure, it is.

But more than that, adventure is right here.

It's closer than you think.

ADVENTURE AWAITS

You've made it this far. You've heard the stories, wrestled with the questions, and hopefully found something stirring deep in your soul.

Here is the truth:

Life is the greatest adventure—so go live it.

This is your invitation. The abundant life Jesus promised in John 10:10 isn't safe or predictable. It is full of purpose, risk, presence, and beauty. It calls us to reject complacency, resist autopilot, and lean into the unexpected; not because we know what's coming, but because we trust the One who is calling us forward.

A life of everyday adventure doesn't happen by accident. It's a decision. A posture. A mindset. It's not about drifting through life or chasing success in things that don't ultimately matter. As Dr. Dan Erickson put it, "I don't fear failure—I fear succeeding at what doesn't really matter."[17] And that's it, isn't it?

Because far too many of us are exhausting ourselves for things that leave us empty. Promotions, likes, possessions, attention. We climb ladders that lead nowhere, pour ourselves into busyness that bears no fruit, and wonder why we still feel unfulfilled.

Adventure—true, God-given adventure—is found in pursuing what really matters.

But here's the good news: you don't have to figure it out alone.

Every great adventure has a crew. Frodo had Sam. Buzz had Woody. Lewis had Clark. Even Jesus sent his followers out two by two.

So who's your Samwise?

Who can you bring along?

Who are your adventure buddies?

Who can you link arms with and say, "Let's not settle. Let's live like this matters"?

Invite others into your everyday adventure. You'll need their support, their encouragement, and their presence when the trail gets hard or the map gets blurry. And they will need yours too.

But even with a crew by your side, adventure still requires courage. Sooner or later, you'll come to the edge of your comfort zone. The question is: Will you stay tethered to what's familiar, or will you step into what's possible?

> "You can never cross the ocean until you have the courage to lose sight of the shore."[18]
> André Gide

It's time to lose sight of the shore and start your adventure.

Now, don't just close this book and move on. Take a step.

- Sign up for the *Everyday Adventure Challenge:*[19] A weekly adventure to help you live more intentionally, joyfully, and relationally right where you are. Not more pressure—just more presence.
- Want to take this further? Flip to the appendix for practical tools, exercises, and resources that can help you make this lifestyle stick, one small step at a time.

Because this is how it happens.

This is how the life of everyday adventure takes root; not with one big moment, but a hundred little ones strung together by presence, purpose, and courage.

As Annie Dillard once wrote, "How we spend our days is, of course, how we spend our lives."[20]

The life you want isn't far off. Adventure is closer than you think.

It's around your dinner table. In your neighborhood. At your workplace. In your church. In your friendships. In your laundry pile. In your prayer life. In your calendar.

It's in the way you look at your spouse. The way you laugh with your kids. The way you show up for a friend. The way you notice God in the ordinary.

A life to the fullest is not someday. It starts today.

Adventure awaits.

Are you ready?

ADDITIONAL RESOURCES
Continue the Adventure

Everyday Adventure was never meant to be simply read—it was meant to be lived. I've prepared a few key resources to help you put what you've discovered into practice in everyday life. Think of these as simple tools to help you keep moving forward, right where you are.

EVERYDAY ADVENTURE DISCUSSION & REFLECTION GUIDE
A practical companion designed to help you live Everyday Adventure—especially in community. This guide creates space for reflection, explores key ideas and Scripture, and invites meaningful conversation and shared practice together—making it perfect for a small group study.

EVERYDAY ADVENTURE CHALLENGE
A weekly challenge delivered to your inbox to help you take one intentional step toward Everyday Adventure. You'll practice the message with others, share stories, and build momentum together. First challenge: sign up—we believe in you.

WRITE YOUR EULOGY
A reflective exercise rooted in the chapter **Embrace Today**, designed to help you live with the end in mind. This guided activity clarifies what truly matters so you can prioritize it today.

EVERYDAY BLESSINGS
A simple guide inspired by Maximize the Mundane, helping you invite God into ordinary moments through intentional prayer. Drawing from examples in Celtic Blessings: Prayers for Everyday Life by Ray Simpson, this PDF offers everyday blessings that reveal the sacred in the simple.

These resources (and more) can be found at **everydayadventurebook.com**, or by scanning the QR code next to each one.

ACKNOWLEDGMENTS

Gratitude is a key to *Everyday Adventure* and I can't help but thank God and the many people who helped bring this book to life. None of this would have been possible without the community that surrounded me every step of the way, so I feel no desire to apologize for making this section longer than normal. There's just too much gratitude to fit into a single page.

To my wife, Taylor: This book simply wouldn't exist without you. You've stood by me through every early morning at my computer, every day off turned into a writing retreat, and every weekend you generously gave me to focus and dream. You've been my biggest supporter and my favorite adventure buddy. So much of what fills these pages is what we've lived and learned together—in our home, our marriage, our parenting, and the everyday moments in between. You are my greatest adventure, and life with you is the greatest adventure of all time.

To my kids: You've filled our lives with joy, laughter, and more adventure than I ever could've imagined. So much of this book was written with you in mind and because of the ways you've each taught me to slow down, pay attention, and find wonder in the everyday. Kinsley—becoming your dad opened my eyes to a new kind of adventure and joy I didn't know was possible and it was so much fun to include many of them here. Summit—you live with such genuine passion and presence. You remind me so much of myself as a kid—fully caught up in every moment, giving your all, and making life fun for everyone around you. Rowan—you are my loyal sidekick and office companion, and in honor of your love for Cars, thank you for helping me find the beauty in quiet old Radiator Springs. Showing me that slowing down isn't losing speed; it's learning to enjoy the ride.

To my parents, Larry and Carmen: My greatest supporters for as long as I can remember. From riding a bus all the way to Arkansas just to watch me sit on the bench at the Babe Ruth World Series, to cheering me on in every ministry opportunity, to saving my early writings and giving me journals with encouragement to "fill the pages" with my next book. Thank you for believing in me, for helping me believe in myself, and for teaching me that there's no greater adventure than following Jesus.

To my in-laws, David and Joyce: Thank you for welcoming me into your family and cheering me on in all my crazy dreams, even when it meant moving your daughter and first grandchild across the country. Your generosity has given us the freedom to live a life of adventure, and that means more than you know. I'm so grateful for your love, support, and joy along the journey.

To my brother, David: My first adventure buddy. We're opposites in so many ways, but your consistency and steadiness have always inspired me. While I'm often chasing five new ideas, you've mastered the art of faithfulness to one. You, Shari, and Andrew have shown me that a full life isn't about what's next, but about embracing where you are—even if that means cultivating a giant garden right in your own backyard.

To Cordel and Diane: My official editors and unofficial encouragers. You helped make this thing sound like... well, a real book. Thank you for helping me be a better writer while still being me.

To Megan: You read every word of this book (multiple times!), helped write reflection questions, teased out ideas on the podcast, and championed me every step of the way. You made this project sharper, deeper, and better in every way. Grateful to keep building together.

To Ryan: Your designs are incredible and gave this book a heartbeat. A picture that's been rolling around in my brain for ten years finally became a reality because of you. I'm beyond grateful I got to create this with one of my best friends. We are so grateful for you and Ashley's forever friendship.

To Jason: You helped me believe I could be an author. You opened your life, answered my billion questions, and showed me what it means to be both generous and excellent. You're an amazing example and a true friend. And thanks for coming to speak at our conference for pennies compared to what you're worth—I'll never forget your generosity.

To Mrs. Mund-Johnson, Mrs. McKenzie, and Dr. Burns: Thank you for putting up with some pretty sloppy writing and still encouraging me to keep going. Each of you helped spark my love for words in your own way—by making space to create with words, making writing fun, showing me that storytelling could become a calling, and inspiring me to become a true communication ninja.

To Brad: Thanks for being an incredible friend and mentor. You've taught me that adventure is about being faithful, not flashy. Helping you with your book gave me a taste of this whole process and the belief that I could do it myself. I am forever grateful for you and Kay.

To the LOL Crew: Back in 2019 on a retreat with student leaders, we read *If* by Mark Batterson and dreamed big dreams together. I told you all about this book before anyone else, and you've been in my mind through every step of this journey.

To everyone who's been there for me along the way—the pastors who offered support, the family and friends who've journeyed with me, those who prayed, our podcast community, and every person who's read these words—thank you. You've reminded me that no adventure is meant to be lived alone. Here's to the greatest adventure of all—following Jesus, together.

NOTES

Introduction
1. John 10:10.
2. Aquinas, Thomas. *Summa Theologica*. Translated by the Fathers of the English Dominican Province, 2nd rev. ed., Christian Classics, 1981, II–II, Q.35, Art.4.
3. Proverbs 21:17, MSG.
4. See John 10:10, NLT.
5. John 10:10, MSG.

Ch. 1 - Embrace Today
1. Groeschel, Craig. *Divine Direction: 7 Decisions That Will Change Your Life*. Zondervan, 2017.
2. Dillard, Annie. *The Writing Life*. Harper & Row, 1989.
3. Psalm 118:24, ESV.
4. Anxiety & Depression Association of America. "Facts & Statistics." *ADAA*, 2025, https://adaa.org/about-adaa/press-room/facts-statistics. Accessed 13 Jan. 2023.
5. Anxiety & Depression Association of America. "Understanding Anxiety." *ADAA*, 2025, https://adaa.org/understanding-anxiety. Accessed 13 Jan. 2023.
6. Matthew 6:34, MSG.
7. Psalm 118:24, ESV.
8. James 4:13-14, ESV.
9. James 4:14b, MSG.
10. "Sermons about George Bernard Shaw." *Sermon Central*, https://www.sermoncentral.com/sermons/sermons-about-george-bernard-shaw. Accessed 26 Sept. 2025.
11. Graham, Billy. "In His Own Words: Billy Graham to the Graduate." *Billy Graham Library*, 13 May 2021, https://billygrahamlibrary.org/in-his-own-words-billy-graham-to-the-graduate/. Accessed 23 Jan. 2023.
12. Warren, Tish Harrison. *Liturgy of the Ordinary: Sacred Practices in Everyday Life*. InterVarsity Press, 2016.
13. Proverbs 19:21.
14. See Matthew 6:19-21.
15. Winton, Richard, et al. "Kobe Bryant, Daughter Gianna among 9 Killed in Helicopter Crash in Calabasas." *Los Angeles Times*, 27 Jan. 2020, https://www.latimes.com/california/story/2020-01-27/kobe-bryant-helicopter-crash-victims#:~:text=John%20Altobelli%2C%2056%3B%20Keri%20Altobelli,in%20Orange%20Coast%20College%20history. Accessed 19 Feb. 2020.
16. Karimi, Faith. "NBA Legends Remember Kobe Bryant after His Death." *CNN*, 28 Jan. 2020, https://www.cnn.com/2020/01/28/us/nba-legends-kobe-bryant-death-tuesday/index.html. Accessed 19 Feb. 2020.
17. Comer, John Mark. *Practicing the Way: Be with Jesus. Become Like Him. Do as He Did*. WaterBrook, 2024.
18. Learn more about AO1 and Camp Conquerors at *ao1foundation.org*.
19. To hear more of Landon's story, watch the video at: facebook.com/prairieheights/videos/494559921340847
20. Ephesians 5:16a, NLT.

Part 1 - Pursue Intentionality

1. Goff, Bob. *Everybody, Always: Becoming Love in a World Full of Setbacks and Difficult People*. Thomas Nelson, 2018.
2. Ortberg, John. *The Life You've Always Wanted: Spiritual Disciplines for Ordinary People*. Zondervan, 1997.

Ch. 2 - Place Your Pins

1. Psalm 119:105, NLT.
2. "5 Ways to Find North without a Compass." *HERE360*, HERE Technologies, 9 May 2018, https://www.here.com/learn/blog/5-ways-to-find-north-without-a-compass. Accessed 2 Mar. 2020.
3. "Tips for Finding North If You're Lost in a Forest." *ArborCare*, 18 Sept. 2017, https://www.arborcare.com/blog/tips-for-finding-north-if-youre-lost-in-a-forest. Accessed 2 Mar. 2020.
4. Matthew 16:25-26, NLT.
5. Romans 1:25, NLT.
6. 2 Peter 1:3, NLT (emphasis added).
7. Matthew 6:33, NLT.
8. John 14:6.

Ch. 3 - Maximize the Mundane

1. Rolheiser, Ronald. *The Shattered Lantern: Rediscovering a Felt Presence of God*. Crossroad, 1994.
2. "Mundane." *Merriam-Webster.com Dictionary*, Merriam-Webster, https://www.merriam-webster.com/dictionary/mundane. Accessed 22 July 2025.
3. "Life Expectancy." *Centers for Disease Control and Prevention*, National Center for Health Statistics, 3 Jan. 2025, https://www.cdc.gov/nchs/fastats/life-expectancy.htm. Accessed 4 Aug. 2025.
4. "Your Life in Numbers [Infographic]." *Sleep Matters Club*, Dreams, 28 Jan. 2016, https://www.dreams.co.uk/sleep-matters-club/your-life-in-numbers-infographic. Accessed 2 Mar. 2023.
5. "One Third of Your Life Is Spent at Work – Gettysburg College." *Gettysburg College News*, Gettysburg College, 28 Jan. 2019, https://www.gettysburg.edu/news/stories?id=7 9db7b34-630c-4f49-ad32-4ab9ea48e72b#:~:text=work%20%2D%20Gettysburg%20 College-,One%20third%20of%20your%20life%20is%20spent%20at%20work,research%20to%20make%20it%20better. Accessed 2 Mar. 2023.
6. "How Do People Spend Their Time?" *Tempo.io Blog*, Tempo Software, 15 Jan. 2021, https://www.tempo.io/blog/how-do-people-spend-their-time. Accessed 2 Mar. 2023.
7. "100 Interesting Facts You Will Learn for the First Time in Your Life." *Factsd*, 2 Apr. 2014, https://factsd.com/things-in-your-lifetime/. Accessed 2 Mar. 2023.
8. Baumgartner, Meredith. "How Many Diapers Will My Baby Use in the First Year?" *Babylist*, 15 Mar. 2021, https://www.babylist.com/hello-baby/how-many-diapers-babys-first-year. Accessed 2 Mar. 2023.
9. See 1 Samuel 17:34-35.
10. Psalm 8:3-4.
11. 1 Samuel 16:7 (emphasis added).
12. Lawrence, Brother. *The Practice of the Presence of God*. Translated by John J. Delaney, Image Books, 1977.
13. Fun fact: Our middle son's name is Summit. We often call him Mitty — an ode to our good friend, Walter.
14. Colossians 3:23-24, NLT.
15. Warren, Tish Harrison. *Liturgy of the Ordinary: Sacred Practices in Everyday Life*. InterVarsity Press, 2016.
16. The Secret Life of Walter Mitty. Directed by Ben Stiller, Twentieth Century Fox, 2013.

17. Romans 12:1, MSG.
18. 1 Corinthians 10:31, NLT.
19. "Howard Behar." *Starbucks Stories & News*, Starbucks, https://archive.starbucks.com/record/howard-behar. Accessed 26 Sept. 2025.
20. Carver, George Washington. "When you do the common things in life in an uncommon way, you will command the attention of the world." *Goodreads*, Goodreads, https://www.goodreads.com/quotes/33787-when-you-do-the-common-things-in-life-in-an. Accessed 26 Sept. 2025.
21. If you want to dig deeper, I highly recommend *The Celtic Way of Evangelism* — it's an excellent read on this subject.
22. Simpson, Ray. *Exploring Celtic Spirituality: Historic Roots for Our Future*. Hodder & Stoughton, 1995.
23. Nadeau, Joshua. *Room for Good Things to Run Wild*. Resource Publications, 2019.
24. "Anticipation." *Merriam-Webster.com Dictionary*, Merriam-Webster, https://www.merriam-webster.com/dictionary/anticipation. Accessed 26 Sept. 2025.
25. Van Boven, Leaf, and Laurence Ashworth. "Looking Forward, Looking Back: Anticipation Is More Evocative than Retrospection." *Journal of Experimental Psychology: General*, vol. 136, no. 2, 2007, pp. 289–300.
26. Weinstein, Jennie E. "Anticipation Is Part of Being a Fan—And That's a Good Thing." *Psychology Today*, 18 Jan. 2022, https://www.psychologytoday.com/us/blog/the-science-fandom/202201/anticipation-is-part-being-fan-and-s-good-thing#:~:text=Anticipation%20and%20the%20Brain,that%20can%20also%20feel%20good. Accessed 23 July 2025.
27. Yes, yes, indeed they got swept by the Yankees in the playoffs. That's not the point...
28. Gray, Aimee, and Jill Martin. "Cubs Win World Series for First Time in 108 Years." *CNN*, 2 Nov. 2016, https://www.cnn.com/2016/11/02/sport/world-series-game-7-chicago-cubs-cleveland-indians/index.html. Accessed 3 Apr. 2020.
29. Metz, Mary Schmich. "At 108, Cubs Fan Finally Sees Her Team in a World Series." *Chicago Tribune*, 26 Oct. 2016, https://www.chicagotribune.com/news/ct-cubs-108-year-old-fan-met-20161026-story.html. Accessed 3 Apr. 2020.
30. Batterson, Mark, and Dick Foth. *A Trip around the Sun: Turning Your Everyday Life into the Adventure of a Lifetime*. Baker Books, 2014.
31. Kwapis, Ken, director. "Finale." *The Office*, season 9, episode 24/25. Aired May 16, 2013, on NBC

Ch.4 - Slow Down
1. Ortberg, John. *The Life You've Always Wanted: Spiritual Disciplines for Ordinary People*. Zondervan, 1997.
2. Please check on me to see if I'm still alive after publishing that comment. Thanks! (Also, a close #2 is those darn hospital beds dads have to sleep on...)
3. Ortberg, John. *The Life You've Always Wanted: Spiritual Disciplines for Ordinary People*. Zondervan, 1997.
4. Fadling, Alan. *An Unhurried Life: Following Jesus' Rhythms of Work and Rest*. InterVarsity Press, 2013.
5. Fadling, Alan. *An Unhurried Life: Following Jesus' Rhythms of Work and Rest*. InterVarsity Press, 2013.
6. Learn more and listen at stephenglasser.com/podcast.
7. Miller, Donald. *Scary Close: Dropping the Act and Finding True Intimacy*. Thomas Nelson, 2015.
8. Ecclesiastes 9:9.

Part 2 - Resist Complacency

Ch. 5 - Cultivate Curiosity
1. Montague, Brad. *Becoming Better Grownups: Rediscovering What Matters and Remembering How to Fly.* Avery, 2020.
2. Andrews, Evan. "10 Animals Encountered by Lewis and Clark." *History.com*, A&E Television Networks, 30 Aug. 2018, https://www.history.com/news/lewis-and-clark-animals-american-west. Accessed 21 May 2021.
3. "Tips on Nurturing Your Child's Curiosity." *Zero to Three*, 31 Jan. 2010, https://www.zerotothree.org/resources/224-tips-on-nurturing-your-child-s-curiosity. Accessed 21 May 2021.
4. Montague, Brad. *Becoming Better Grownups: Rediscovering What Matters and Remembering How to Fly.* Avery, 2020 (emphasis added).
5. Matthew 18:3-4, NLT.
6. "Taylor Hughes: The Road to Wonder." *[Podcast Title—The Magic Word Podcast]*, hosted by Scott Wells, episode 581, Apple Podcasts, 27 Aug. 2021, https://podcasts.apple.com/us/podcast/taylor-hughes-the-road-to-wonder/id1458376688?i=1000533066712. Accessed 26 Sept. 2025.
7. Disney, Walt. "When you're curious, you find lots of interesting things to do." *BrainyQuote*, https://www.brainyquote.com/quotes/walt_disney_132637. Accessed 2 May 2025.
8. Andrews, Evan. "Did an Apple Really Fall on Isaac Newton's Head?" *History.com*, A&E Television Networks, 16 Dec. 2016, https://www.history.com/news/did-an-apple-really-fall-on-isaac-newtons-head. Accessed 2 May 2025.
9. Baruch, Bernard M. "Millions Saw the Apple Fall, but Newton Was the Only One Who Asked Why." *QuoteFancy*, https://quotefancy.com/quote/21635/Bernard-M-Baruch-Millions-saw-the-apple-fall-but-Newton-was-the-only-one-who-asked-why. Accessed 2 May 2025.
10. Parr, Ellen. "The Cure for Boredom Is Curiosity." *Reader's Digest*, Dec. 1980, p. 174.
11. Ephesians 3:18-19, NLT.
12. Franck, Thomas. "Nigerian Prince Scams Still Rake in over $700,000 a Year." *CNBC*, 18 Apr. 2019, https://www.cnbc.com/2019/04/18/nigerian-prince-scams-still-rake-in-over-700000-dollars-a-year.html. Accessed 15 Nov. 2023.
13. Piper, Barnabas. *The Curious Christian: How Discovering Wonder Enriches Every Part of Life.* B&H Publishing Group, 2017.
14. Windahl, Zach. *See the Good: Finding Grace, Gratitude, and Your Way to a More Meaningful Life.* Penguin Random House, 2022.
15. You can learn more and find an Alpha course near you at alphausa.org/try.
16. Bennett, Roy T. *The Light in the Heart.* Roy T. Bennett, 2016.

Ch. 6 - Become A Lifelong Learner
1. Andersen, Erika. "21 Quotes from Henry Ford on Business, Leadership and Life." *Forbes*, 31 May 2013, https://www.forbes.com/sites/erikaandersen/2013/05/31/21-quotes-from-henry-ford-on-business-leadership-and-life/. Accessed 28 Aug. 2024.
2. James 4:6.
3. Maxwell, John C. "Pride — A Leader's Greatest Problem." *The Christian Post*, 5 Feb. 2007, https://www.christianpost.com/news/pride-a-leader-s-greatest-problem.html. Accessed May 15 2021.
4. Keller, Matt. *The Key to Everything: Unlocking the Secret to Why Some People Succeed and Others Don't.* Thomas Nelson, 2015.
5. Keller, Matt. *The Key to Everything: Unlocking the Secret to Why Some People Succeed and Others Don't.* Thomas Nelson, 2015.
6. Keller, Matt. *The Key to Everything: Unlocking the Secret to Why Some People Succeed and Others Don't.* Thomas Nelson, 2015.
7. Cordeiro, Wayne. *The Divine Mentor: Growing Your Faith as You Sit at the Feet of the Savior.* Bethany House, 2007.

8. Coleman, Robert E. *The Master Plan of Evangelism*. Revell, 1993.
9. Comer, John Mark. *The Ruthless Elimination of Hurry*. WaterBrook, 2019.
10. "Average Cost of College." *Education Data Initiative*, 30 May 2024, https://educationdata.org/average-cost-of-college. Accessed 26 Jan. 2025.
11. You can download my year-end reflection guide for free at stephenglasser.com/reflection.

Ch. 7 - Ditch Your Comfort Zone

1. Assaraf, John. "A comfort zone is a beautiful place but nothing ever grows there." *X* (formerly Twitter), 16 Apr. 2015, 4:31 p.m.
2. Groeschel, Craig [@craiggroeschel]. "You can never fulfill your calling in your comfort zone." *Instagram*, 21 Mar. 2021, https://www.instagram.com/p/CMzykGzAfag/. Accessed 19 Sept. 2024.
3. Genesis 12:1.
4. See Numbers 13:18-20.
5. Numbers 14:7-9, NLT.
6. Numbers 14:9, NLT.
7. "Negative News Statistics." *Letter.ly*, 8 Feb. 2021, https://letter.ly/negative-news-statistics/. Accessed 15 Feb. 2024.
8. "Your Wednesday Briefing." *The New York Times*, 24 Mar. 2021, https://www.nytimes.com/2021/03/24/briefing/boulder-shooting-george-segal-astrazeneca.html. Accessed 15 Feb. 2024.
9. Batterson, Mark. *All In: You Are One Decision Away from a Totally Different Life*. Zondervan, 2013.
10. 2 Corinthians 3:12.
11. Schmich, Mary. "Advice, like youth, probably just wasted on the young." *Chicago Tribune*, 1 June 1997, https://www.chicagotribune.com/columns/chi-schmich-sunscreen-column-19970601-story.html. Accessed 26 Sept. 2025.
12. Emerson, Ralph Waldo. "He who is not everyday conquering some fear has not learned the secret of life." *Goodreads*, Goodreads, https://www.goodreads.com/quotes/757572-he-who-is-not-everyday-conquering-some-fear-has-not. Accessed 26 Sept. 2025.
13. Santo, Allegra Goodwin. "New Jersey Is the Only State Where You Can't Pump Your Own Gas." *CNN*, 9 Aug. 2023, https://www.cnn.com/2023/08/09/business/new-jersey-gas-station-self-service-ban/index.html#:~:text=By%201968%2C%20putting%20fuel%20in,%2C%E2%80%9D%20New%20Jersey's%20law%20states. Accessed 26 Sept. 2025.
14. James 1:2-4.
15. *Zootopia*. Directed by Byron Howard and Rich Moore, Walt Disney Animation Studios, 2016.
16. 2 Corinthians 1:3-4.
17. "Quit Waiting for a Plan; Just Go Love Everybody." *FaithGateway*, https://www.faithgateway.com/blogs/christian-books/quit-waiting-for-a-plan-just-go-love-everybody. Accessed 10 Sept. 2025.

Part 3: Develop Resilience

1. "Perseverance." *Merriam-Webster.com Dictionary*, Merriam-Webster, https://www.merriam-webster.com/dictionary/perseverance. Accessed 26 Sept. 2025.
2. Hebrews 12:1-2, NLT.
3. King, Martin Luther, Jr. *What Is Your Life's Blueprint?* 26 Oct. 1967, Barratt Junior High School, Philadelphia. Speech.

Ch.8 - Lighten Your Load

1. Pavese, Cesare. "If you wish to travel far and fast, travel light. Take off all your envies, jealousies, unforgiveness, selfishness and fears." *Goodreads*, Goodreads, https://www.

      goodreads.com/quotes/746548-if-you-wish-to-travel-far-and-fast-travel-light. Accessed 26 Sept. 2025.
2. Hebrews 12:1, NLT.
3. Philippians 3:13b-14, NLT.
4. "Forgiveness." *Greater Good Magazine*, Greater Good Science Center, University of California, Berkeley, https://greatergood.berkeley.edu/topic/forgiveness/definition. Accessed 13 Jan. 2025.
5. Luke 23:34, NLT.
6. Ephesians 4:31-32, NLT.
7. Luke 12:25.
8. 1 Peter 5:6-7, NLT.
9. Philippians 4:6-7, NLT.
10. "Parental Expectations and Criticism Linked to Perfectionism in College Students." *American Psychological Association*, 31 Mar. 2022, https://www.apa.org/news/press/releases/2022/03/parental-expectations-perfectionism. Accessed 13 Jan. 2025.
11. Maxwell, John C. *Put Your Dream to the Test: 10 Questions That Will Help You See It and Seize It*. Thomas Nelson, 2011.
12. See Genesis 3
13. Psalm 51:5, NLT.
14. Romans 5:12, NLT.
15. Romans 3:23, NLT.
16. "Shame." *Merriam-Webster.com Dictionary*, Merriam-Webster, https://www.merriam-webster.com/dictionary/shame. Accessed 24 May 2025.
17. Genesis 3:7, NLT.
18. Romans 5:8, NLT.
19. Psalm 55:22, NLT.
20. Matthew 11:30, MSG.
21. Psalm 139:23-24.

Ch.9 - Fix Your Focus
1. Robbins, Tom. *Skinny Legs and All*. Bantam Books, 1990.
2. "Greyhound." *American Kennel Club*, https://www.akc.org/dog-breeds/greyhound/. Accessed 24 May 2025.
3. https://www.britannica.com/sports/dog-racing
4. Hebrews 12:1-2, NLT (emphasis added).
5. Colossians 3:2-3, NLT.
6. Matthew 14:28, NLT.
7. Matthew 14:29, NLT.
8. Matthew 14:29-30, NLT.
9. John 16:33.
10. James 1:2-4.
11. Romans 8:28, NLT.
12. See Exodus 14:11-12
13. Fadling, Alan. *A Year of Slowing Down: Daily Devotions for Unhurried Living*. InterVarsity Press, 2022.
14. James 1:12.
15. Maxwell, John C. *Failing Forward: Turning Mistakes into Stepping Stones for Success*. Thomas Nelson, 2000.
16. "Edison on His Methods." *The Electrician*, vol. 87, 1921, p. 619.
17. "Thomas Edison's Theorem for Success." *Medium*, Cry Mag, 17 Apr. 2020, https://medium.com/cry-mag/thomas-edisons-theorem-for-success-b96591bf7dd1. Accessed 28 May 2025.
18. Mautz, Scott. "11 Famous Failures That Will Inspire You to Success." *Inc.*, 9 July 2019, https://www.inc.com/scott-mautz/11-famous-failures-that-will-inspire-you-to-succes.

19. Ziglar, Zig. *See You at the Top*. Rev. ed., Pelican Publishing, 2000.
20. Amatt, John. *Straight to the Top and Beyond: Nine Keys for Meeting the Challenge of Changing Times*. Wiley, 2004.
21. Goff, Bob. *Live in Grace, Walk in Love: A 365-Day Journey*. Thomas Nelson, 2019.
22. Hebrews 12:1, NLT.
23. Romans 12:2.
24. See John 10:10.
25. John 21:21, NLT.
26. John 21:22, NLT (emphasis added).
27. Batman Begins. Directed by Christopher Nolan, Warner Bros., 2005.
28. Hebrews 12:2, NLT.
29. See Luke 22:42.

Ch.10 - Refuse to Quit

1. MC Hammer. "2 Legit 2 Quit." *Too Legit to Quit*, Capitol Records, 1991.
2. Ortberg, John. *The Life You've Always Wanted: Spiritual Disciplines for Ordinary People*. Zondervan, 1997.
3. Anders, Angela Benavides. "Before the First Ascent: Early Climbs on Everest." *ExplorersWeb*, 13 May 2022, https://explorersweb.com/before-the-first-ascent-early-climbs-on-everest/. Accessed 18 June 2025.
4. Kiger, Patrick J. "Why the Magellan Expedition Was So Treacherous." *History*, A&E Television Networks, 20 July 2023, last updated 27 May 2025, www.history.com/articles/magellan-expedition-facts-dangers. Accessed 18 June 2025.
5. Blake, Eliza. "Before It Became 'Quiet Quitting,' There Was Just Doing Your Job." *Los Angeles Times*, 27 Aug. 2022, https://www.latimes.com/entertainment-arts/story/2022-08-27/la-ent-quiet-quitting-origins. Accessed 26 Feb. 2024.
6. Harter, Jim. "Quiet Quitting Is about a Lot More than Quitting." *Gallup*, 6 Sept. 2022, https://www.gallup.com/workplace/398306/quiet-quitting-real.aspx. Accessed 26 Feb. 2024.
7. Huffington, Arianna. "Let's Quit Quiet Quitting." *LinkedIn*, 3 Sept. 2022, https://www.linkedin.com/pulse/lets-quit-quiet-quitting-arianna-huffington. Accessed 26 Feb. 2024.
8. Fadling, Alan. *An Unhurried Life: Following Jesus' Rhythms of Work and Rest*. InterVarsity Press, 2013.
9. Fadling, Alan. *An Unhurried Life: Following Jesus' Rhythms of Work and Rest*. InterVarsity Press, 2013.
10. Looking for a place to start? Check out our *Monthly Marriage Meeting Guide*. It's been a game-changer for us—helping us connect intentionally, plan our calendar, check in on our relationship, and dream together. Download it free at stephenglasser.com/freebies.
11. "What Does the Bible Say about Hope?" *GotQuestions.org*, https://www.gotquestions.org/Bible-hope.html. Accessed 12 June 2025.
12. Romans 12:12, NLT.
13. Rohr, Richard. *Preparing for Christmas: Daily Meditations for Advent*. Franciscan Media, 2008.
14. Jeremiah 29:11, NLT.
15. Jeremiah 29:13, NLT.
16. Dostoevsky, Fyodor. "To live without Hope is to Cease to live." *BrainyQuote*, BrainyQuote.com, www.brainyquote.com/quotes/fyodor_dostoevsky_154348. Accessed 13 June 2025.
17. "Lord." *Merriam-Webster.com Dictionary*, Merriam-Webster, https://www.merriam-webster.com/dictionary/lord. Accessed 13 June 2025.
18. Proverbs 19:21, NLT.
19. *Finding Nemo*. Directed by Andrew Stanton, performances by Ellen DeGeneres and Albert Brooks, Pixar Animation Studios, 2003.

20. Galatians 6:9, NLT (emphasis added).
21. Fadling, Alan. *An Unhurried Life: Following Jesus' Rhythms of Work and Rest*. InterVarsity Press, 2013.
22. 1 Corinthians 1:8-9, MSG (emphasis added).

Conclusion: Let the Adventure Begin
1. Keller, Helen. *The Open Door*. Doubleday, 1957.
2. I can't believe I am sharing this: https://stephenglasser.blogspot.com/
3. Matthew 4:19.
4. See Matthew 14:22-33.
5. See Acts 16:16-40.
6. See Acts 8:26-40.
7. See Genesis 3.
8. Proverbs 21:17, MSG.
9. Ketterling, Rob. *Thrill Sequence: Finding the Joy of God in Your Everyday Life*. Salubris Resources, 2017.
10. Travis A. Sermon. Fargo Moorhead Chi Alpha, 26 June 2018, Fargo, ND.
11. Ketterling, Rob. *Thrill Sequence: Finding the Joy of God in Your Everyday Life*. Salubris Resources, 2017.
12. Goff, Bob. *Love Does: Discover a Secretly Incredible Life in an Ordinary World*. Thomas Nelson, 2012.
13. Revelation 3:20, NLT.
14. Up. Directed by Pete Docter, co-directed by Bob Peterson, Walt Disney Pictures and Pixar Animation Studios, 2009.
15. Eliot, George. *The Spanish Gypsy: A Poem*. William Blackwood and Sons, 1868.
16. Psalm 92:4, NLT.
17. Erickson, Dan. *Finding Your Greater Yes: Living a Life of Purpose with Passion*. Thomas Nelson, 2009.
18. Gide, André. "You Can Never Cross the Ocean until You Have the Courage to Lose Sight of the Shore." *Goodreads*, Goodreads, https://www.goodreads.com/quotes/192564-you-can-never-cross-the-ocean-until-you-have-the. Accessed 26 Sept. 2025.
19. Visit everydayadventurebook.com.
20. Dillard, Annie. *The Writing Life*. Harper Perennial, 1990.

ABOUT THE AUTHOR

Stephen Glasser is a writer, speaker, and coach who is passionate about Jesus and helping ordinary people live their everyday life to the fullest. For more than a decade, he has served in a variety of ministry and non-profit roles—from pastoring and discipleship work to mentoring young adults, leading teams, and serving as a longtime camp pastor for teens. No matter the setting, Stephen carries a pastor's heart and a steady belief that intentionality, gratitude, and joy can transform how we move through the world.

He is the founder of JourneyWay, where he offers coaching and creates intentional-living resources and workshops that help people pursue clarity, purpose, and spiritual growth. Stephen develops practical tools and reflection guides that invite people to slow down, pay attention, and step into a more meaningful everyday life. He also hosts The Everyday Podcast, exploring faith, growth, and the adventure found in ordinary moments.

When he's not writing, coaching, or speaking, you'll find Stephen enjoying life with his wife, Taylor, their three kids—Kinsley, Summit, and Rowan—and family and friends (who feel like family), laughing their way through the beautiful chaos of real life.

Learn more at stephenglasser.com.

Connect with Stephen on Instagram @stephenglasser.

Everyday Adventure Podcast

Stephen Glasser

Most people move through life on autopilot—busy and distracted. The Everyday Adventure Podcast invites you to slow down and rediscover purpose in ordinary life. Each week, we explore intentional habits, meaningful rhythms, and practical next steps through stories and conversations that help you live with greater presence, courage, and joy

**DOWNLOAD OR LISTEN TODAY
WHEREVER YOU LISTEN TO PODCASTS!**

STEPHENGLASSER.COM/PODCAST

A GUIDE FOR THE JOURNEY YOU'RE ALREADY ON

If this book stirred something in you—clarity, restlessness, hope, or a desire for more—you don't have to figure out what's next alone. JourneyWay exists to help everyday people slow down, get their lives back from autopilot, and take meaningful next steps toward a fuller, more intentional life.

Through coaching, cohorts, courses, workshops, retreats, writing, and speaking, JourneyWay takes the heart of Everyday Adventure and helps you live it out through real rhythms and real relationships. Whether you're navigating faith and spiritual rhythms, marriage and family, friendships, transitions, purpose, leadership, focus, or simply trying to feel present again—this work is designed to meet you where you are.

JourneyWay offers custom experiences for individuals, groups, churches, and teams—because no two journeys look the same, and growth is better when it's personal and relational.

Learn more or schedule a call with Stephen:
journeyway.co

LIVE INTENTIONALLY.

MORE PRAISE FOR
Everyday Adventure

In a world that's constantly chasing what's next, Everyday Adventure invites us to find meaning in what's now. Stephen Glasser challenges us to live on purpose, to notice God in the normal, and to bring fresh energy to our daily lives. Grab a cup of coffee, an inspirational background track in your airpods, and enjoy this read - you can remain confident that your adventure awaits!

Josiah Kennealy, Co-Founder of youngadults.today

Stephen Glasser's perfect mixture of wisdom, humor and down to earth perspective will help you unlock the wonder and fulfillment that is too often hidden or missing as we walk out the seemingly mundane aspects of everyday life. Everyday Adventure will inspire you to see, feel and think differently as you step into each new day and the opportunities that surround you.

Steve Jamison, Global Pastor, Eastridge Church

With heartfelt stories and practical encouragements, Stephen Glasser unveils the adventure in front of every one of us. Everyday Adventure won't change your world but it will give you a new lens to see it through.

Grant Olson, Defensive Coordinator (Football)
North Dakota State University
Amy Olson, Former Professional Golfer

Everyday Adventure reminds us that God created us to live for Him in every moment. This book is a roadmap for embracing a perspective that sees adventure in the ordinary. Take the kids sledding, go on a spontaneous date with your spouse, bake with your family—adventure often looks like choosing joy in the simple things. Through these pages we learn that life doesn't begin on the weekend. God has given us the ability to live a life of adventure right now, in this very moment.

Michael Bloom, Founder of Hip Hope & Hope

Everyday Adventure is a refreshing reminder that life's most meaningful moments often happen in the ordinary. Stephen Glasser invites readers to slow down, pay attention, and rediscover joy and purpose in the places they already stand. It's practical, heartfelt, and full of wisdom for anyone longing to live more intentionally.

Ty Buckingham, Author and Speaker

Made in the USA
Coppell, TX
26 February 2026

72781868R00142